Ready!

99 Must-have Skills for the World-Conquering Teenager (and Almost-Teenager)

Roopa Pai

hachette INDIA

Roopa Pai is one of India's best-known children's authors. She has written more than 20 books, spanning subjects ranging from popular science to fantasy and philosophy to economics. Her books, which include the award-winning national bestseller *The Gita for Children*, and *Taranauts*, India's first complete fantasy-adventure series for children, are enjoyed by readers of all ages.

This computer engineer brings together three other loves – history, working with young people, and her home town Bengaluru – in her day job as a guide with BangaloreWalks, a history and heritage walks and tours company.

She is currently hard at work trying – and often failing – to master the 99 skills she believes every world-conquering teen must possess. (No, she is no longer one.)

To all the cheerful, self-reliant, resourceful, fair-minded, brave, hard-working and generous young people out there – the world is richer for having you in it.

PS: Also, the WoCoTeen Squad is looking for you!

First published in 2017 by Hachette India
(Registered name: Hachette Book Publishing India Pvt. Ltd)
An Hachette UK company
www.hachetteindia.com

SRD

Photograph on page 11 by J.S. Matthews, courtesy Vancouver Archives
Photograph on page 89 by S.K. Desai, courtesy Wikimedia Commons
Photograph on page 319 by Carol & Jesse, courtesy Wikimedia Commons

ISBN: 978-93-5195-131-5

Hachette Book Publishing India Pvt. Ltd
4th & 5th Floors, Corporate Centre
Plot No. 94, Sector 44, Gurugram 122003, India

Typeset in Minion Pro 11/14 by
Manmohan Kumar, New Delhi

Printed and bound in India
by Manipal Technologies Limited, Manipal

MIX
Paper | Supporting responsible forestry
FSC™ C043100

CONTENTS

✷

'Where is there a boy to whom the call of the wild and the open road does not appeal?'
– Lord Robert Baden-Powell, Founder of the Scouting Movement, 1908

'Where is there a young person to whom the call of the electronic device and the open Instagram feed does not appeal? Sighhh.'
– Every parent in the world, 2017

'Ha! Where is there an older person who understands that young people do as their adults do, not as they say?'
–Every teenager in the world, forever

'Where is there a young boy or girl who does NOT want to be a WoCoTeen?'
– Every teenager reading this book, now

✷

OF COURSE YOU WANT TO BE A WOCOTEEN! THE QUESTION IS – DO YOU HAVE WHAT IT TAKES?

Of course you have worked it out already – WoCoTeen is short for **World-Conquering Teenager**. Which could be you, if you are willing to work for it.

Make no mistake, it is hard work. Membership in the elite WoCoTeen Squad is not for the whiny, the slothful, the selfish, the pusillanimous, or the irresponsible; it demands of its aspirants grit, grime, sweat, toil, tears, blood (okay, maybe no blood), and above all, a sunny, can-do attitude to anything that life may throw at them. Including exams.

If that sounds just a bit airy-fairy, it's because it is. Luckily, WoCoTeens are anything but. In fact, there is a proper list of requirements that a regular boy or girl must fulfil before he or she can take a shot at WoCoTeen-ism. Here's a quick run-through.*

**Bear in mind that completion of this set of requirements will grant you only entry-level membership into the Squad, i.e., the right to call yourself a WoCoTeen. Staying a WoCoTeen is the real challenge – as you grow, you will discover tonnes of other skills that you will need to master. Completing the basic requirements well gives you a solid foundation and great practice for this – so go for it!*

1. A WoCoTeen begins each day by taking the WoCoTeen Pledge (page 3).
2. A WoCoTeen follows the WoCoTeen Law (page 4).
3. A WoCoTeen is guided by the WoCoTeen Motto (page 6).
4. A WoCoTeen spends a regular number of hours each week mastering the 99 Essential WoCoTeen Skills and completing the requirements of the 24 possible WoCoTeen Merit Badges to be won at this level (*all relevant info included in this handy manual*). There is no deadline to race against – you can take as long as you like to win your Badges, but the recommended time period for completion is a year.
5. A WoCoTeen understands and acknowledges the inspiration and mentorship provided to him and the Squad by the Scouts and Guides – members of the legendary international youth movement founded by Lord Baden-Powell (B-P) in 1908. B-P was also trying to create a Squad of WoCoTeens, only he didn't refer to them using quite those words. (*More on B-P and his movement on page 6.*)

The requirements look simple, really, when you put them down like that. You probably read through that list in a minute. The trouble is, you've now got to actually *do* everything on that list.

Think you're up to it? Do you believe you can dig deep enough to find the discipline, dedication and fire in the belly that becoming a WoCoTeen demands?

If you are shaking your head 'No', that's too bad, both for you – you've just opted out of a great adventure – and for everyone else, for our crazy, sad world could always use the services, skills and cheer of another WoCoTeen.

If you are still a little unsure, and wondering what to say, we would urge you to dive in. After all, what's the worst that could happen – you discover it is all too overwhelming for you, and drop out after mastering just 67 skills instead of 99 and winning only 18 badges instead of 24. (*But you will still have learnt those 67 skills and won those 18 badges, see?)*

If you are nodding eagerly, and smiling 'Yes! Yes! Yes!', welcome to the best ride of your life! By the end of it, you would have learnt tonnes of new things, challenged yourself and won, and stepped out of your comfort zone, only to find glorious new worlds waiting to be explored. What's more, you will be a far more accomplished, self-reliant and responsible young person than you were when you started out. Best of all, you will be a happier, more fearless boy or girl, for you would have discovered in yourself reserves of strength and intelligence and courage and resourcefulness you did not know you possessed.

Rest assured that, throughout your journey, the Squad* will be by your side, cheering you on, sending you love, waiting to welcome you home.

Let's go!

THE WOCOTEEN PLEDGE

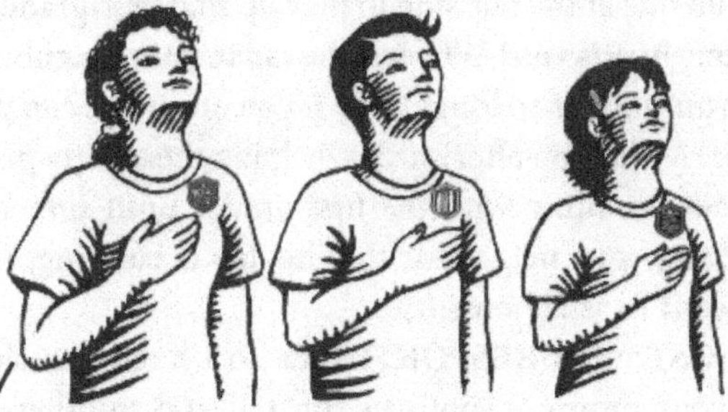

The pledge below is to be recited from memory, with right hand (left hand for left-handers) placed flat on the chest, over the region of the heart.

Today, on my honour, I promise to be
The very best person that I can be
To work at being healthy and fit and strong
To think before I act, to choose right over wrong
To help those around me, in every time and location
To be courteous and kind, whatever their station
To be a friend to every animal, bird and tree
With a mind that is open, and a heart that is free.

**Here's something you should know about the Squad – anyone who has ever been a WoCoTeen continues to be an honorary member, even after he or she is well past teenagerhood. WoCoTeens don't advertise their membership, but they are all around you, and will show up to help and support you when you need them. Maybe one, or more, of them lives in your home! Or next door. Or is part of your family. Or teaches at your school. Or is in your history or science textbook. The possibilities!*

THE WOCOTEEN LAW

1. **A WoCoTeen is CURIOUS:** To be curious means to never lose your sense of wonder about things. How does a refrigerator work? Why is the sky blue? Who is Elon Musk? What makes ISIS so angry with the world? Why are younger siblings so annoying? Curiosity opens doors of discovery and learning in ways that nothing else can.
2. **A WoCoTeen is AWARE:** To be aware means to be sensitive and alert to everything that is going on around you. Is that elderly person finding the pavement too high to step down from? Is there no one at the bus stop to pick up that first-grader who takes the same bus as you? Why has the tap in your neighbour's garden been running for so long? Only if you are aware can you take the appropriate action afterwards – helping the elderly person off the pavement, waiting with the first-grader until someone arrives, informing your neighbour that his tap is running, or closing it yourself if he isn't home.
3. **A WoCoTeen is RESPONSIBLE:** To be responsible means to keep your promises, both to yourself and to others. Have you promised mom that you will tidy up your room by Saturday? Did you tell your teammate you would finish your part of the work on the science project before tomorrow? Did you decide you wouldn't watch more than an hour of TV per day this week because your exams are around the corner? Honour those promises! Being responsible earns you respect.

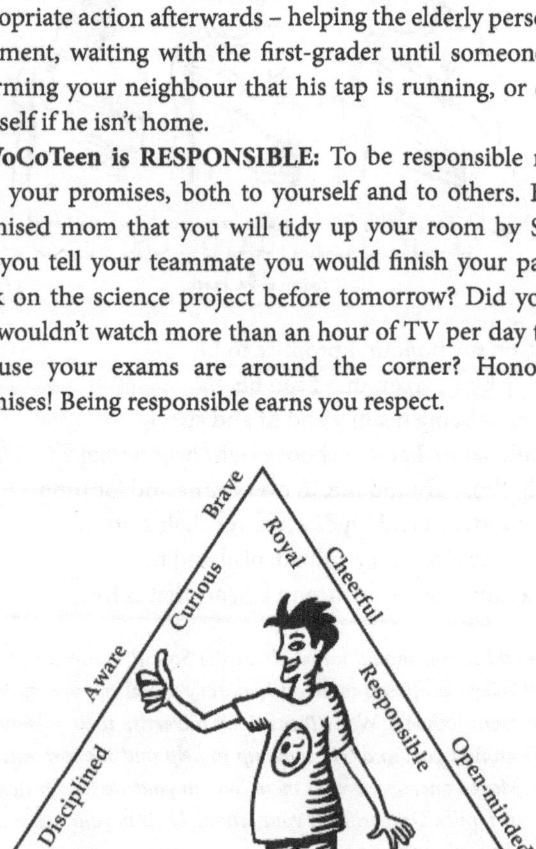

4. **A WoCoTeen is BRAVE:** To be brave doesn't only mean fighting tigers barehanded or taking a bullet for a friend. It also means speaking up against a bully, even if that bully is your best friend; walking away from a stupid, risky dare even when you know your friends are going to think you are a sissy; and taking on a difficult challenge even when you believe you are likely to fail. This kind of bravery may never make the news, but you will walk a little taller each time you practise it.
5. A **WoCoTeen is DISCIPLINED**: To be disciplined means to follow a routine religiously, however boring it may be, simply because you know it is good for you. Finishing your homework before going out to play, waking up early each morning to go swimming with your mom, playing chess with your grandfather once a week, eating healthy... Whatever the routine, sticking with something against all odds makes you feel good about yourself and gives you the confidence to take on new challenges without batting an eyelash.
6. **A WoCoTeen is LOYAL:** To be loyal means to stand up for causes and ideas you believe in, and to always have your friends' backs. It means that as long as you are a member of a community – whether the community is your class, your school, your Squad, or the world, you work from within to make it better – by changing things you don't approve of, by speaking up against bad or unfair practices, by being a good team player, by helping others to see things differently.
7. **A WoCoTeen is OPEN-MINDED:** To be open-minded means being willing to listen, without prejudice, to another point of view, never mind that it is the complete opposite of what you believe. It means being willing to have a discussion, in which both sides benefit from hearing a different opinion, instead of an argument, in which one side has to win. It means having the grace to accept that maybe you were wrong, to agree that some questions – for instance, is a human life more important than an animal's; is nuclear power evil? – will never have easy answers.
8. **A WoCoTeen is KIND:** To be kind means to say and do nice things for other people, whether you like them very much or not. It means giving your mom a hug when she has had a particularly stressful day, even if she has lost her temper with you for no reason. It means inviting a classmate who is not very popular –

because he 'sprays' when he speaks, maybe – to your birthday party so that he doesn't feel left out. It means the ability to put yourself in someone else's shoes, understand why they behave the way they do, and be nice to them regardless of whether they are mean or snobby or belligerent.

9. **A WoCoTeen is RESOURCEFUL:** To be resourceful means to have a backup plan when things go wrong, and if you don't have one, to make it up as you go along. The guy just ahead of you in line got the last ticket to the IPL match? Instead of whining about it, you invite friends over and watch the match together on TV – simple! Everyone looks up to someone who can think on his feet.
10. **A WoCoTeen is CHEERFUL:** To be cheerful means – hey, we all know what being cheerful means. Stuff happens, and not all of it is good, but a bright, upbeat attitude can certainly help smooth things along, both for you and for everyone around you. A permanently hangdog 'what-is-my-life?' expression does not do your personality or your emotional health any favours. Smile!

THE WOCOTEEN MOTTO

READY! WILLING! ABLE!

THE ORIGINAL WOCOTEEN

The Life and Times of the Most Amazing Lord R.S.S. Baden-Powell
I Was A Boy Once.
Say this was the opening line of a book. Say someone asked you to rate it on a scale of 1 to 10. You'd probably give it a, what, 5? As opening lines go, it certainly does not have the intrigue of 'When Mr Bilbo Baggins of Bag End announced that he would shortly be celebrating his eleventy-first birthday...' (*The Lord of the Rings: The Fellowship of the Ring*, by J.R.R. Tolkein) or the what-was-that-again weirdness of 'I write this sitting in the kitchen sink' (*I Capture the Castle* by Dodie Smith).

And yet, believe it or not, the book that opens with this line – *I Was A Boy Once* – went on to become one of the most influential books of the 20th century. The book, which was first published in England in 1908, in six instalments of approximately 70 pages each, was called *Scouting For Boys: A Handbook for Instruction in Good*

Citizenship (yeah, sombre title too) and was written and illustrated by a Lieutenant-General Robert Baden-Powell (see box on page 16 for the correct pronunciation of his surname – or just take the easy way out and call him B-P, which is what he called himself).

IF IT LOOKS LIKE FUN, I'LL TRY IT!

As he himself admits, B-P was a boy once. Born in London in 1857, Robert Stephenson Smyth Powell (he was named after his godfather Robert Stephenson, who built locomotives and railway bridges and is often called 'the greatest engineer of the 19th century') lost his dad when he was just three, and was brought up single-handedly by his strong mother, Henrietta Grace. It was she who changed the family name to Baden-Powell in memory of her late husband, the Rev Baden Powell. B-P was a bright child, and a curious one, always interested in learning new skills – bricklaying, piano-playing, acting.

I'M IN THE ARMY NOW – OH-OO-OH!

Soon enough, B-P had won a scholarship to Charterhouse, one of Britain's most prestigious public schools. In Charterhouse, he had a grand time, not so much at his lessons as at his adventures in the nearby woods, which were strictly out-of-bounds to students. Every so often, he would slink away into the woods, where he silently stalked his Masters or hunted squirrels and rabbits, which he cooked and ate, making sure that telltale smoke didn't give him away. Each time, he covered his tracks so thoroughly that he was never caught. Vacations were no less exciting. With his brothers and half-brothers, he spent his time canoeing – they once traced the River Thames to its source – and yachting – one holiday, they made an expedition around the south coast of England!

In 1876, when he was just nineteen, B-P decided to sit the Army Exams, and stunned everyone by placing second among 700 candidates. Winning the rank of Lieutenant in a regiment called the 13th Hussars, he came out to India to serve (Britain ruled most of the world then, and joining her army was considered a great way to travel the world, live an outdoor life full of adventure, and browbeat the locals).

In India, B-P took several courses in surveying (in which you walk around, examine, measure and record the topography and area of a piece of land to draw a map of it – a very useful skill whether you are planning a military manoeuvre or trying to find your way around a city with a phone that doesn't have a data plan). He also took courses in reconnaissance (in which an army's special forces – the smart, skilled, brave 'scouts' – go ahead of the main army into enemy territory to do things like (1) check if/where enemies are hiding or landmines are concealed; (2) find a strategic spot from which to mount an attack; (3) map the safest route for the army to march along, and so on. If you think about it, these skills can be useful when you are trying to avoid someone or planning a surprise party for a friend in her house too!). In 1884, B-P published his first 'book' – *Reconnaissance and Scouting: A Practical Course of Instruction, in Twenty Plain Lessons, for Officers, Non-commissioned Officers, and Men.*

Through the '80s and '90s, B-P had a spectacular military career, serving also in Afghanistan, South Africa and Malta. He also had 'endless fun big-game hunting in the jungles of India and Africa'. Using the skills he had perfected in Charterhouse, he often travelled behind enemy lines disguised as a butterfly collector, cleverly incorporating the drawings of military installations into his drawings of butterfly wings! In 1895, he returned to Africa, where he led a successful military campaign against the Ashanti people of Ghana. The very next year, he was assigned to Zimbabwe, where he made a friendship that would set the stage for his next big adventure.

BROTHERS-IN-ARMS

Frederick Russell Burnham was the Chief of Scouts (we are still talking military scouts here) for the British Army in Africa. What made Burnham so fascinating to B-P were his advanced 'woodcraft' skills ('woodcraft' is a catch-all name for all the skills required for surviving in the wild: hunting, fishing, camping, making a fire, building shelters, knowledge of wildlife behaviour, knowing how to use maps and compasses, camp cooking, wilderness first aid, and so on), skills that B-P did not have. Burnham's knowledge was drawn from traditional Native American practices, and from the experiences of the early American pioneers who had improvised, innovated and survived as they travelled west across the huge unmapped continent. B-P wanted to learn everything Burnham knew.

With B-P as his eager student and co-scout, Burnham led several reconnaissance missions into enemy territory. During these missions, the two men talked about how the world and the old ways of fighting wars were changing (by this time, the colonies had begun to rebel against the Empire: in India, the Indian National Congress had been formed, in South Africa, Mahatma Gandhi had begun campaigning against racial discrimination). They dreamt about starting a programme that would teach young men essential woodcraft skills to help them survive wherever in the world they found themselves.

WHAT HAPPENED AT MAFEKING

Three years later, in 1899, B-P found himself in Mafeking, a small town in South Africa, with a small group of British officers and troops, trying to hold the town against the attack of a much larger army of Boers, European farmers who had settled several generations ago in South Africa. With the town surrounded by the Boers, and desperate to keep the fighting men he had, B-P created the Mafeking Cadet Corps, a group of boys between 12 and 15 years of age, who were trained to act as couriers, carrying messages to smaller forts outside, riding their bicycles across open ground, fully exposed to enemy gunfire. The boys were also trained to act as lookouts – to check, for instance, what part of the town Boer cannon were pointed at, and then to warn people there to fire back or evacuate. The cadets wore khaki uniforms and hats with one side turned up, and people often commented on how smart they looked.

The *Siege of Mafeking* went on for 217 days, from October 1899 through to May 1900, and was the most famous British military action of what became known as the Second Boer War. Its progress was reported through all the eight months by British newspapers, and followed closely by the British public. Finally, on 12 May 1900, the Boers were cornered and defeated. Britain exploded in joy. People poured into the streets, mafficking. (Mafficking is an actual word, scout's honour! It means 'to celebrate boisterously and publicly', and it entered the dictionary as a tribute to the brave troops at Mafeking.) B-P, who had become a national hero, was promoted, becoming, at age forty-three, the youngest Major-General the army had ever had.

There was another, more unexpected, outcome of Mafeking. B-P came home to find that his new book, *Aids to Scouting*, which had been published in 1899, had become a huge bestseller during the siege. *Aids to Scouting* had been intended for the use of soldiers, but boys in England had become fascinated by it, and youth organizations and schoolteachers had started using it as part of their lessons and activities. In Mafeking, B-P had experienced for himself the usefulness of well-trained boys, and he decided it was time he wrote a boys' version of the book.

THE SPARK THAT BECAME A BLAZE

In 1907, he wrote the draft for a book called *Boy Patrols*, in which he set out his methods for boys to organize themselves into groups, with an elected patrol leader, so that they may practise their scouting skills as a team. To test out his ideas, he organized a camp at Brownsea Island in 1907, with 21 boys from different social and economic backgrounds, selected from various schools across England. His experiences and learnings here went into *Scouting for Boys*, the boys' version of *Aids to Scouting*, which came out in 1908. In it, B-P omitted most of the military aspects of the earlier book, and focused on the woodcraft skills of civilian heroes like explorers, backwoodsmen and sailors. He also introduced the Scout Method, through which he hoped to inspire young boys to be independent, to have a strong moral code and to enjoy learning things by themselves, following the example of their patrol leader.

Scouting for Boys went on to become one of the top-selling books of the 20th century, selling close to 150 million copies. Across the country, with no particular organization leading the effort, boys spontaneously created patrols and began practising the skills and trying out the adventurous games suggested in the book. In 1909, the first Scout Rally was held in Crystal Palace in London, and 11,000 Scouts turned up! Some of them were girls who, not willing to be left out, came dressed in the same uniform, calling themselves Girl Scouts.

Finally, in 1910, at the age of fifty-three, realizing that his little book had spurred a nationwide movement, B-P retired from the army to form the Boy Scouts Association, and soon after, with his sister Agnes Baden-Powell, the Girl Guides Association, for girls. At its very first census, taken in 1910 itself, the Boy Scouts had over 100,000 members! By the end of the year, Scouting had taken root in over 20 countries including India.

Baden-Powell inspecting troops of Boy Scouts at Hastings Park, Vancouver

Soon, there were demands that the Scouts movement should not be restricted to boys and girls between 11 and 17 years of age, as B-P had envisioned, but must include younger children and older young adults as well. B-P complied, creating the Cub Scouts (for younger boys), the Brownies (for younger girls), and the Rover Scouts (for young adults from the age of 18 to their early 20s).

CHIEF SCOUT OF THE WORLD

However, hot on the heels of all that international feeling of brotherhood came the First World War (1914–1918), which tore Europe apart and ensured that Scouts practised most of their skills in the trenches. Fortunately, this did not destroy the movement. In 1920, at the first World Scout Jamboree (a jamboree is an American word meaning 'joyful, noisy gathering' and is the name given to large Scout conventions whose main purpose is to develop a feeling of camaraderie between young people from different places and backgrounds) held in London, B-P was conferred the title of 'Chief Scout of the World.'

In 1937, after the fifth World Scout Jamboree, B-P retired from public scouting life. He died four years later, at the age of eighty-three. As his last message he left a tracking sign on his gravestone – a circle with a dot at its centre, which is the symbol for 'I have gone

The WOSM Logo is a a fleur-de-lis encircled by a reef knot (which you will soon learn to make!).

home'. (When Scouts go exploring or hiking, they leave specific signs along the trail for patrol members who have fallen behind.)

Today, the World Organization of the Scout Movement (WOSM) is the largest international Scouting organization. It has 163 countries as its members (just as a comparison, the United Nations, of which every country in the world, except the Vatican and the State of Palestine, is a member, has 193 member countries), and over 40 million participants. Its counterpart is the World Association of Girl Guides and Girl Scouts (WAGGGS), which has 145 countries as its members, and more than 10 million participants. The Indian arm of the movement is called the Bharat Scouts and Guides, and serves almost three million Scouts and a little over a million Guides.

And all this was achieved because of *one* very special man who loved the beautiful world we live in, and wanted to teach his fellowmen the great joys of observing it, enjoying it and negotiating it. Not as superior, dominant beings, mind, but as one small part of the grand inter-web of life, connected to everything else around them.

Suitably inspired? On to mastering skills and winning those Merit Badges then!

HANG ON A MINUTE – WHY MUST I BE A WOCOTEEN? WHY CAN'T I JUST BE A SCOUT OR GUIDE?

Aaaah. Good question. And the short answer to that is – Sure you can, and must! *If* your school offers scouting and guiding as an extra-curricular activity, that is.

What if it doesn't, though? Why should you miss out on the wonderful opportunity to learn a bunch of cool skills that will help you 'adult' in the best way? Ergo, WoCoTeen.

Of course, WoCoTeens don't do the *exact* same activities and learn the *exact* same skills that B-P expected his Scouts and Guides to do and learn. That's because, for one thing, B-P wrote his book over a hundred years ago, to help young people negotiate and master a very different world. For another, B-P was a British Army officer from a time and place very different to where you are growing up today.

Despite these differences, it must be reiterated – very strongly! – that WoCoTeens are most certainly guided by the spirit of B-P's original Scouting movement. That means the 99 skills WoCoTeens are expected to master and the 24 badges they need to win to be accepted into the Squad are all geared towards giving them the kind of well-rounded, practical education that enables them to become, in the 21st century, just the kind of independent, resourceful, service-minded young men and women that B-P hoped his Scouts and Guides would become in the 20th. What's even cooler, any WoCoTeen can add to this set of recommended skills any others that he or she thinks is vital to WoCoTeenism, and if the Squad votes in favour, it immediately becomes part of the manual. In that sense, WoCoTeenism is like the Wikipedia of world-conquering.

We bet the Chief Scout would be very chuffed with the WoCoTeens, for, by creating their own set of skills to master instead of blindly following those recommended for another time, they only embody B-P's biggest, most important lesson – 'The principle on which Scouting works is that the boy (...) is encouraged to educate himself instead of being instructed.'

Hail, Chief Scout! Go, WoCoTeens!

BEFORE YOU BEGIN – THE CHALLENGE CHECKLIST

You know by now that there are 99 challenges to be completed, and 24 badges to be won, before you are considered eligible for membership in the Squad as a WoCoTeen. But who decides if you are worthy of each badge? And in which order (is there even a right order?) are you supposed to complete the challenges? Here's a quick rundown of everything you want to know about the merit badge process.

1. Get a squad together: Your Squad is a bunch of like-minded comrades who have decided to seek WoCoTeen membership as a group, by completing the challenges together. You need to get a Squad together rather than trying to go it alone, for a couple of reasons.

- There's strength in numbers! When you work on challenges as a group, it's not only more fun, but you will also constantly inspire and motivate each other.
- Some of the challenges, especially those that involve hitting the streets of your city, are more effective, and safer, when done in a group.

How big should your Squad be? Ideally, you should have no more than five or six members – a small group is easier to work with (and to round up for meetings!).

What about the Squad's composition? You could do Squads of just boys or just girls, but mixed groups work too. It's most convenient if all members of the Squad live close to one another, or go to the same school. Whether all members should be the same age is something you have to figure out on your own – both kinds (same-age and multi-age, especially those including siblings) work well.

2. Find a Squad Leader: Let's get this somewhat uncomfortable fact out of the way first – your Squad Leader must be an adult. And not any old adult either – he or she needs to be responsible and committed, and willing to give a few hours of time to the Squad each week or fortnight. Needless to say, it would help immensely if that adult is also fun to be around.

Brainstorm with your Squad to come up with a few potential leaders – a parent, a cool aunt, uncle or grandparent, a lively neighbour, the aunty who organizes fun activities for kids in your building, even a favourite teacher (if you think your school would let you do this as an after-school activity), are all possibilities. Then go around and ask each of them, one by one, if they'd be willing to take on the job. If two of them want to do this together, that's fine too – you could then have two Squads instead of one if you can get enough friends interested.

Typically, a Squad Leader's responsibilities would include:

- *Supervising completion of challenges:* Only the Squad Leader can decide if each member of the Squad has completed a challenge successfully.
- *Facilitating challenges*: Some challenges, especially the Community and Outdoor challenges, may need a Squad Leader's intervention to make them happen.

- *Awarding Merit Badges:* Once all the requirements for winning a particular merit badge have been completed to the Squad Leader's satisfaction, he or she awards the requisite badge to the applicant.

3. Name your Squad: That's simple enough – find an inspirational name, based (if you like) on a hero, male or female, that you all look up to. Legendary explorers are a good place to start – you might call yourself Amundsen's Army, say, or The da Gama Derivatives, or Tenzing's Tigers. Sportsmen – Klub Kohli, maybe, or Sania's (or Saina's) Supernovas, or Dravid's Goliaths – are another great source of names. Pioneers who pushed all sorts of boundaries, even fictional ones, are another treasure-trove – Bapu's Besties, Kalam's Rockets... let your imagination run wild!

4. Decide where and how often the Squad meets: This is vital. Meeting once a week or once a fortnight (more often during school vacations) is ideal. Once you have decided, try and be as disciplined as you can about attending meetings and staying abreast of everything that's going on in your Squad.

5. Complete the challenges: Sure this isn't a race, or a contest, but here's the bottom line – if you want to be a WoCoTeen, you've got to win those badges! There are two ways to go about this.

- The quickest way to win a badge is to complete all the challenges required to win that badge (any badge, you don't have to do this in any particular order) before picking another. It also helps everyone – including the Squad Leader – if the whole Squad decides which badge they are going to work towards in a particular month. In this case, you can all help each other and can be tested together.
- But it may not always be possible to do things that way. In such cases, just try and set yourself a target – for instance, 'I will learn one skill and complete the corresponding challenge each week' (or complete four each month). Let your Squad Leader know beforehand which four you would like to be tested in at the end of each month, so that she can fix a time and date for it.
- In your WoCoTeen notebook (any notebook will do), use the first few pages to draw up a two-column table, titled 'Almost A

WoCoTeen!'. In the first column, list all the 99 challenges you need to crack to win your 24 Badges. Leave the second column blank. As you complete each challenge, make sure you have your Squad Leader sign off against it in the second column.

6. Fill up your Escutcheon: Before you even tackle your first challenge, make a chart with the words 'Proud to Be a WoCoTeen!' emblazoned on it, and put it up where you can see it every day. This is your 'Escutcheon'. Every time you win a badge, cut it out from the end pages of this book and stick it up on your Escutcheon.

As it fills up, feel your heart swell with pride.

Say It Right!

What's the correct way to pronounce Lord Baden-Powell's name? We'll let the Chief Scout of the World tell you himself, via a little verse he wrote to clear all confusion.

Man, Nation, Maiden
Please call it Baden.
Further, for Powell
Rhyme it with Noel.

Get it? Not Bad-en, but Bay-dn, not Pow-well, but Po-el.

THE PERSONAL DEVELOPMENT COVENANT

I BELIEVE IN BEING THE BEST THAT I CAN BE

The Healthy Human

The Communicator

The Master-at-Arms

The Hobbyist

The Handicrafter

The Entrepreneur

THE PERSONAL DEVELOPMENT COVENANT

I BELIEVE IN BEING THE BEST THAT I CAN BE

6

MERIT BADGES TO BE WON

The Healthy Human

The Communicator

The Master-at-Arms

The Hobbyist

The Handicrafter

The Entrepreneur

WHAT A BOY LEARNS FOR HIMSELF, IS WHAT IS GOING TO STICK BY HIM AND GUIDE HIM LATER ON IN LIFE FAR MORE THAN ANYTHING THAT IS IMPOSED ON HIM THROUGH 'INSTRUCTION' BY A TEACHER.

– **B-P, in Camp Fire Yarn No. 22, *Scouting for Boys***

Let's start at the very beginning, i.e., with you. Yup, we're starting with the teen in the mirror. Because only when you've got him/her figured can you go out and conquer the world.

Through this section, you will be getting fit, making cool stuff with your own hands, finding some kind of passion, using your brains, and – hold your breath! – earning your own money by the time you're done with this section! Woohoo! On the way there, though, you're going to have (respectively) aching limbs, dirty hands and several but-what-if-I-don't-have-a-passion/but-this-is-too-hard/but-who-will-pay-good-money-for-*this*? moments of hopelessness. But that's all good.

Just grit your teeth and stick with it, because there's a lot more waiting in that pot of gold at the end of the tunnel (yeah, we mixed our metaphors, but it works in this case) than just membership in the Squad. You see, the skills you are building to win these badges are habit-forming skills that will last you a lifetime – no matter what course of study you choose to pursue, what kind of career you pick, or where in the world you eventually live. They are the best friends you will ever make and they will journey with you constantly (without taking up space in your suitcase!), comforting you when you are feeling low, making sure you are never bored, winning you friends, keeping you safe, and helping you stay fit and healthy in mind, body and spirit.

Why would you whine about working hard if it gets you to that kind of happy place? So square your shoulders, stick your chest out and get started!

WOCOTEEN MERIT BADGE 1

THE HEALTHY HUMAN

> *I told him (...) that the way for a lad to gain endurance was not by trying to perform feats, as these would very probably injure his heart and break him down, but by making himself strong and healthy, by good feeding and moderate exercise.*
>
> **– Camp Fire Yarn No. 17, *Scouting for Boys***

Enough has been said on the importance of staying healthy and fit in every kind of media aimed at humans, so we don't see any reason to do it all over again here.

Simply put, a healthy body sets you free to do the things you really want to do, and chase the dreams you want to chase. What's not to like about that?

SKILL 1
WATCH WHAT YOU EAT

Watching what you eat does not mean starving yourself, cutting fat and/or sugar entirely from your diet, or following whatever faddish diet everyone else is. It just means being aware of what you are putting into your body, and how much of it you are putting in, at every mealtime (and post-mealtime, and snack-time, and in-between time, and just-popping-a-biscuit-in time, and open-the-fridge-and-glug-half-a-bottle-of-cola time), that's all. It just means pressing the pause button on your life in between thinking of eating something and actually putting it into your mouth, to really 'see' it.

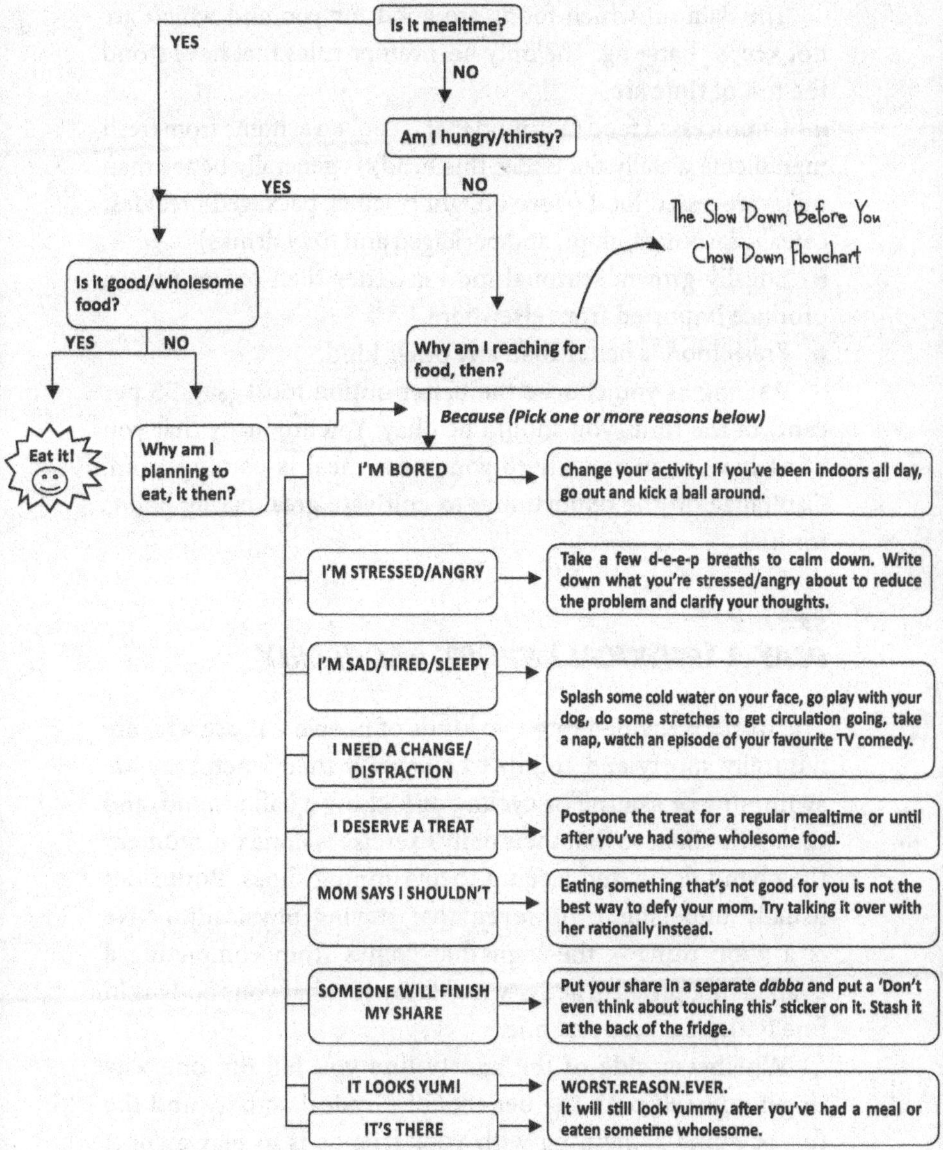

Here's a fun 'slow down before you chow down' flowchart that you could use each time you reach for something to eat or drink. Copy it and tape it up where you can see it. Refer to it until the flowchart becomes part of your everyday food life.

The data on which foods are good for you and which are not keeps changing. The only no-brainer rules that have stood the test of time are –

- Unprocessed food (any food that is cooked at home from fresh ingredients usually fits under this head) is generally better than mass-processed food (store-bought biscuits, packaged breakfast cereals, savouries, chips, and packaged and fizzy drinks).
- Locally-grown, seasonal food is better than out-of-season produce imported from elsewhere.
- Fresh food is better than any other kind.

As long as you choose the better option most (say, 75 per cent) of the time, you should be okay. You are lucky that you don't have to worry where your next meal is coming from. Capitalize on the opportunity to cultivate great eating habits for life!

SKILL 2
PLAY A (PHYSICAL) SPORT REGULARLY

The world is divided into two kinds of people – those who are naturally sporty and couldn't be happier than when they are swimming or skating or cycling or kicking a ball around, and those who believe that their daily exercise is done the moment they bend down and lace up their running shoes. Both sides usually understand, however, that staying physically active is a good thing – the high that comes from completing a challenging physical activity and knowing that your body is in fine fettle, is a very real one.

Whichever side of the sporty line you fall on, one way to get yourself both the benefits of physical activity and the fun of doing something with your friends is to play a sport regularly.

- **Why a sport? Isn't it possible to get your exercise or build your stamina from dancing or working out at the gym as well?** It is, but playing a sport offers you benefits that are way more than purely physical. A sport teaches you to take victory and failure in your stride, it teaches you to pick yourself up each time you fall and begin again, it turns you into a lean, mean fighting machine with great hand-eye / foot-eye / mind-body coordination, and it will stand you in good stead in other, non-sport-related, tough situations in life. If you play a team sport, there are even more lessons you will learn – how to be unselfish, how to put your team's goals above your individual ones, how to work well with other people, how to harness very different individual strengths and combine them into a winning whole.

What sport should you pick? It depends both on the kind of person you are, and the circumstances.

- **If you live close to a playground** or in an apartment complex with a playing area, and have friends and neighbours who get together every evening to play something – cricket, football, badminton – join in.
- **If you'd rather play a sport in school**, stay back and join the group of students playing your favourite sport.
- **If you live close to a sports centre** that offers coaching in sports like tennis, table-tennis or badminton, sign up.
- **If your parents are members of a neighbourhood club** that has a swimming pool and a coach, learn a most essential life skill that is also – hallelujah! – a wonderful sport.
- **If you'd rather play a sport alone** than as part of a team, running and cycling may be good sports for you to get into. Once you feel confident about your abilities and your stamina, check out weekend runs that are happening in your city and join in.

SKILL 3
GET SOME YOGA INTO YOUR DAY

Oh, stop with the groaning and moaning already. You may think of *Hatha Yoga* – the branch of yoga that concerns itself with physical fitness, as slow and b-o-r-i-n-g and pretty pointless, but just listen up for a minute while we give you the lowdown on what's to love about it. You see, Hatha Yoga:

■ Is ours! It was developed right here in India (or whatever this tropical landmass was called then), thousands of years ago, and is probably therefore a more suitable fitness routine for a warm country.

■ Requires no equipment other than a mat.

■ Can be done anywhere – at home, in a hotel room, by the beach, on a mountain, anything goes.

■ Does not require any learnt skills or innate talent and can be practised by people of any body type.

■ Is as much about developing mental strength and a calm spirit as it is about physical fitness (like Judo and Kung-fu).

■ Helps you de-stress by teaching you the right way to breathe (you didn't even know there was a 'right' and a 'wrong' way to breathe, now, did you?).

■ Is so popular across the world that chances are that your future university, wherever in the world it may be, will have a yoga society you can be part of. Or you can start one yourself!

One of the cornerstones of a daily session of yoga is the *surya-namaskar*, or Salutation to the Sun – a series of 12 yoga asanas (or poses) performed in sequence. Apart from being a complete cardiovascular workout (that means it gets both your heart and circulation going), it helps you stretch and smooth out the kinks in your spine and muscles (which is why it is best done early in the morning, before you've had anything to eat), and gets you all limber and alert and fully set to face the day.

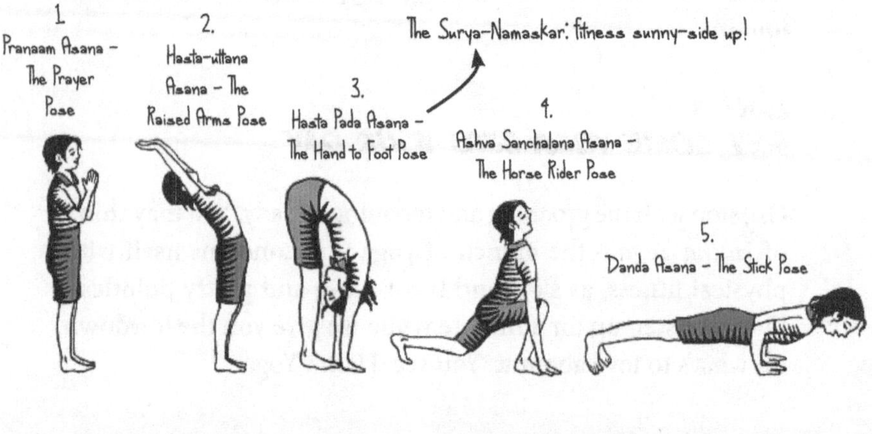

The best thing about the *surya-namaskar* is the spirit behind it – the whole slow dance is also a grateful acknowledgement that we humans – and the trees and the bees and the beasts and the birds – would not exist if it wasn't for Sol Invictus, the invincible sun. Plus, if you do your *surya-namaskar* in the open air, in the gentle light of the rising sun, you will also end up getting some essential Vitamin D into your system.

If you don't know the prayer that is often chanted with the *surya-namaskar*, or don't want to chant it, don't. Just send up your own customized prayer to the universe, giving thanks for all the blessings you have received.

If you absolutely hate the idea of yoga itself for some reason, decide, along with your Squad, what daily fitness routine you guys would rather incorporate into your lives – Zumba, Aerobics, whatever – and substitute it for the yoga. Just make sure it includes lots of bends and stretches, gets your heart pumping, and gives you that heady hit of endorphins – those stress-relieving, happy-making brain chemicals – that all good exercise should.

Note: *Remember, yoga, or any other fitness routine, is best done under the supervision of a trained expert who will make sure you do not overdo the exercises or overexert yourself.*

12. Pranaam Asana – The Prayer Pose

11. Hasta Uttana Asana – The Raised Arms Pose

10. Hasta Pada Asana – The Hand to Foot Pose

9. Ashva Sanchalana Asana – The Horse Rider Pose

8. Parvata Asana – The Mountain Pose

7. Bhujanga Asana – The Cobra Pose

6. Ashtanga Namaskara – The Eight Limb Salute

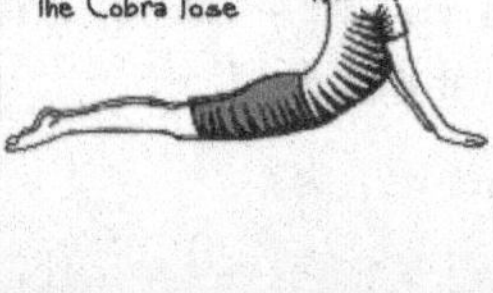

SKILL 4
MAKE DISCIPLINE YOUR FRIEND

Most human beings find being disciplined the hardest thing in the world. We make New Year resolutions, and break them within the first week of January. We promise ourselves that we will be good – eat right, watch less TV, spend less time on social media, study every day (and not just before the exams) – but cannot stick to our own noble aims. Which is a pity, because self-discipline is a superpower – it guarantees success at any task you undertake.

Here's the reassuring thing, though – discipline is learned behaviour, not something you are born with. Start practising 'being disciplined' with one of the most essential skills for any WoCoTeen – staying healthy and fit.

Here are a few general tips to help you make discipline a part of your life.

1. Start with baby steps. Whatever healthy habit you are trying to cultivate – eating right, sleeping at least seven hours a night, exercising each day, waking up early – or whatever awful habit you are trying to break, start with setting yourself small goals. If you're trying to eat right, for instance, and potato chips are your downfall, start with not eating more than 28 chips over a week. You can decide if you want to eat four chips a day (recommended) or eat all 28 at the end of the week (although this may make you crave chips through the week!).

Here's one way to trick your brain into being disciplined – there's a theory that if you stick with something for 21 days, just 21 days, it becomes a habit. Do it!

Achievable goals give you a sense of accomplishment, and the confidence to set yourself progressively tougher goals and see them through.

2. Do things in moderation. Don't overdo anything – the exercise, the food discipline, the sports, the yoga. Eat everything you love, but in moderation. When you exercise, listen to your body, and stop when it tells you to – Exercise is supposed to make you feel rejuvenated, not defeated.

3. Reward yourself when you succeed. When you reach a target that you had set yourself, pause for a moment to savour it. Congratulate yourself on a job well done, and allow yourself a tiny reward of some kind.

4. Forgive yourself when you fail. No one likes thinking of himself as a failure, but you can't win every time. There will be times, many times, that you fail to reach your target – a doorstopper wedge of cheesecake will sing siren songs to you, and you will succumb to its charms before you know it; a late-night Snapchat session with friends will end in you throwing your alarm clock into the laundry hamper and skipping your morning tennis lesson. The thing to remember is not to flay yourself with guilt and shame when this happens. Pick yourself off the floor, and begin again.

5. Stick with it. Perhaps the hardest thing of all to do in your practice of discipline is sticking with it. While it is more common to give up on something after a couple of failures, giving up after a string of successes is not unusual either. You feel so chuffed about having been disciplined about something for a while that you imagine taking a few days off from it will not hurt you. The problem is, it is very, very hard to return to the discipline later. It also usually means starting from scratch all over again.

By simply starting on the path to the discipline, you have already made many gains, not all of them obvious. Why sacrifice all that and have to start over? Stick with a reasonable, moderate 'watch-what-you-eat' and 'play-a-sport-and-do-some-yoga' routine for a couple of months without flagging, and you will see how it becomes a wonderful habit, a part of your life.

THE HEALTHY HUMAN'S CHALLENGES

#1
THE WATCH-WHAT-YOU-EAT CHALLENGE

Individual challenge: For one whole week, keep a written record of what goes into your stomach. Don't stop yourself from eating or drinking anything at any time – just write it all down, along with the time of day that you ate the meal or snack at. You could make a table like this –

	Monday	Tuesday	Wednesday	Thursday	Friday	Saturday	Sunday
6–8 am							
8–10 am							
10–12 noon							
12–2 pm							
2–4 pm							
4–6 pm							
6–8 pm							
8–10 pm							

At the end of the week, analyse your personal eating chart. How much processed food did you eat compared to unprocessed fresh food? How often do you snack, and which times of day do you tend to snack more? Was there a day when you ate much more than you normally do, particularly the snacky, junky stuff? Why? (It could have been something as simple as a friend's birthday party or a festive family dinner, or something that upset you and made you binge).

Doing this exercise will accomplish several things.

1. Whenever you are reaching for something to eat or drink the next week, you will pause a moment to actually notice it and record it, even if subconsciously. That will automatically make you eat more healthy.
2. You will figure out your 'eating triggers', the things that make you want to stuff your face with junk.
3. You will become aware of your 'binge slots' – the times of day you are most likely to reach for a snack. You can then actively choose to do something else at that time so that you don't succumb.

#2
THE PLAY-A-SPORT CHALLENGE

If you have never played a sport regularly, sign up for classes in a sport you think you might like, and don't miss a single class for a month. Or join a group in school or in your neighbourhood that plays something every evening, and play with them at least three times a week for a whole month.

#3
THE DAILY-FITNESS CHALLENGE

Spend 15 minutes each morning before school – and before breakfast! – for two weeks (okay, you can take Sundays off) doing the *surya-namaskar* or whatever fitness routine you have chosen to adopt with your Squad. Drink at least two full glasses of water – and make sure you don't gulp them down too quickly – at least ten minutes before you begin. Start with simple stretches and bends to limber up first so that you don't pull a muscle somewhere. If you have picked the *Surya-namaskar*, do at least 3 full cycles each day (one cycle involves two rounds - the first with your right leg extended back in steps 4 and 9 and the second with your left), ramping up to 5 cycles by the end of 2 weeks. Have a parent sign off on your fitness log each day, and show the completed log to your Squad Leader. (PS: If you miss a day or two in between, you can make it up on the Sundays. If you miss more than two days, too bad, you will simply have to start over.)

#4
THE DISCIPLINE CHALLENGE

There is no separate Discipline Challenge! If you've managed to complete your other three 'Healthy Human' challenges, you've completed this one too – hurrah! It takes a *lot* of discipline to maintain an eating chart for a week, not miss a sports class for a month, and spend 15 minutes each morning before school for two weeks exercising.

Start on all three challenges the same day, and get your Squad Leader to sign off on your Discipline Challenge at the end of a month!

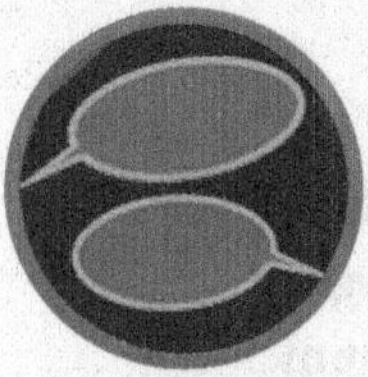

WOCOTEEN MERIT BADGE 2

THE COMMUNICATOR

You have to go by the very smallest signs, and if you talk and think of other things you are very apt to miss them. Old scouts generally are very silent people.
– Camp Fire Yarn No. 5, *Scouting for Boys*

In the animal world, oral communication – whether through squeaks, barks, growls or purrs – is limited but very effective. The sounds animals make convey very clearly to members of their own species and others what the animal is trying to say – I am happy / I am hungry / Hey! This is my space – keep off! The irony is that we humans, despite having so many words and so many ways to communicate, often do not do it as well. Too many problems in the world, whether it is hate between people of different religions or fights between best friends, are caused because people did not – or could not, because they didn't know how to – communicate properly with each other.

There are many reasons why people do not communicate right – they don't want to appear weak (or too dominating) so they say something they don't really mean, they are not really listening to the other person so their response is not what the other person was hoping for, they are mad at the other person so they say things in the heat of the moment that they really wouldn't have had they been calm, and so on. Either way, the right messages are not communicated, civilized conversation breaks down, arguments break out, and anger and bitterness become inevitable.

But every breakdown in communication need not result in such dire consequences. Sometimes, bad or ineffective communication can have other, but equally undesirable, results – solvable problems lie on the table unsolved; people misunderstand what was said to them and go ahead and do things they shouldn't; people simply do not understand what is being said because the language used is so convoluted – yup, bad communication wastes everyone's time and energies.

The Squad believes so strongly that good communication is a key WoCoTeen skill that they decided it needed an entire badge to itself! Here are the four skills you need to master before you can win it.

SKILL 5
LISTEN WITH YOUR BODY

Hearing. Listening. We use these words interchangeably, but there is a whole world of difference between the two. *Hearing* is something that automatically happens when you have functioning ears – sound waves hit your eardrums, setting off vibrations in your head that your brain interprets as words or music or noise. *Listening*, on the other hand, is a learnt skill – when you listen, you are focusing on one particular string of sounds among all the others around you, and absorbing it into your consciousness with intelligence and understanding.

Listening with your ears is hard enough, but what in heck does listening with your body mean?

- **Listen with your eyes.** When someone is talking to you, make the effort to take your eyes off whatever device you are using, and look at the other person – it shows that you care about what he or she is saying. Looking into the other person's eyes several times during the conversation allows her to trust you. Also use your eyes to interpret the speaker's body language – are her shoulders drooping even though she is speaking aggressively? Maybe the aggression is just a front – reassure her in some way. Does he look away when you try and make eye contact? Maybe he is hiding something. You may not know it, but all of us have the ability to read unspoken signals in body language. It is an evolutionary gift we have received from our Neanderthal ancestors.
- **Listen with your mouth.** Don't purse your lips, hum, clear your throat unnecessarily, or make noises when someone is

speaking. Most importantly, don't talk until they have finished. Interrupting someone mid-flow makes them hear 'What you are saying is not as important, accurate or relevant as what I have to say', or 'I don't care for your opinion', or 'I'm more important than you'. Of course you must butt in if you haven't understood something or need a clarification, but wait for a pause to do that.

- **Listen with your hands.** Do not fidget – clicking a ballpoint pen over and over, doodling on the sheet in front of you, fussing with your phone, or glancing at your watch are all big no-nos when you want to show someone that you are completely focused on what he is saying. Keep your hands quiet, in your lap, on the arms of your chair, or on the table, and in sight of the speaker.
- **Listen with your feet.** Do not fidget with your lower limbs – don't tap your feet (indicates impatience), jiggle your knees (indicates inattention) or cross and uncross your legs (indicates you are not comfortable with something, possibly what the speaker is saying). Instead, keep your feet and legs still.
- **Listen with your body.** Lean in slightly when someone is speaking – it indicates that you are interested in what she is saying. Don't overdo it though – lean in too much and you are intruding on her personal space, which could intimidate her, annoy her, or both. Relax your body and keep your body fully turned towards the speaker if possible (notice how hard it is to speak seriously to someone when you are sitting side by side?
- **Listen with your brain.** It sounds a little confusing, but the rule is – Listen to listen, don't listen to respond. In other words, when someone is speaking, don't start thinking of what you will say to her in response. Doing that will distract you from what she is saying. Oh also, listen without bias.
- **Listen with your heart.** Sure the person is saying something using his mouth, but can you look beyond to what he is really saying? Is his I-don't-care-about-this-conversation attitude really hiding his fear that *you* don't care about a conversation that he cares about very deeply indeed? A lot of problems are solved when you listen with your heart.

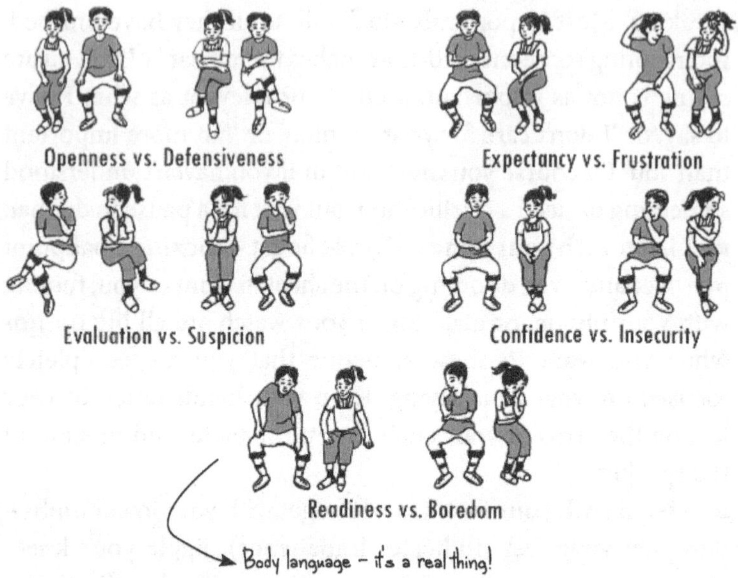

SKILL 6
RESPOND WITH BOTH HEAD AND HEART

How you respond to someone is just as important as how you listen to him. Think about these few pointers the next time you are doing it.

- **Pause before you respond.** What someone has just told you might have made you mad or sad, but don't respond in haste. Words can hurt and damage, so think about what you want to say and how you want to say it instead of/before lashing out.
- **Don't dump your opinions.** If a friend has just shared a problem with you that she is grappling with, don't respond instantly with a 'solution', even if it's clear as daylight to you. It is always easier for the unaffected outsider (you) to see a solution that someone who is deeply involved in the problem (your friend) cannot. Also, very often, when people tell you their problems, they don't even want your opinions – they just want someone to listen.

Instead, turn the question back to her – ask her what *she* thinks is the best of the several bad options (clearly she thinks they are bad options, or she wouldn't be opening her heart to you) available to her. The thing is, most people know quite well what the solution to their own problem is – they just need someone to help them arrive at it.

- **Empathize.** As you listen to the speaker – he could be accusing you of something, yelling in anger, or sharing a problem – try, for one moment, to hold back your own reaction while you put yourself in his shoes. Do this with a genuine desire to see the problem from his point of view. You may discover, after this exercise, that he has a valid point (at which point you apologize, and say something like, 'I hadn't thought of it like that before. How can I make it up to you?'). Or you may feel that he is simply being unfair or not seeing the issue the right way, at which point, you respond by explaining to him that you understand where he is coming from, because of x, y and z reasons, but, 'This is what I feel about it, and I can explain why if you let me.'
- **Be patient.** Don't be a sentence-grabber, finishing the speaker's sentences for her. She may be getting to some entirely different point from what you think she is getting to. Finishing her sentences makes you look like a know-it-all (and a know-it-all who is wrong, to boot!), humiliates or annoys her, and derails the conversation.
- **Use language that your listener can understand.** Don't browbeat the speaker or use big words to show off or confuse him and make him feel small, or use a language he doesn't know well. That ensures that no effective communication can happen between the two of you. And that's not cool, is it?

SKILL 7
LEARN TO DISAGREE AGREEABLY

Clearly, it is only when the two sides disagree about something that a conversation has the potential to break down and lead to arguments, yelling, anger, bitterness and feelings of betrayal. But there are techniques you can use to disagree agreeably. No, seriously. Take a look.

■ **Pick your battles.** In other words, don't argue about every little thing. Understand that it is a waste of time and energy to challenge and counter every rule your parents lay down – no staying out past 9 p.m., no sleepovers, no Facebook, no fancy mobile phone, no hanging out with a set of friends. Instead, accept some of the rules gracefully, and save your ammo for fighting for the stuff that really matters to you. If you are generally seen as a reasonable person who is good about keeping his part of the bargain, the person on the other side will be more willing to listen to your point of view on anything.

This is especially true of disagreements with your parents or teachers, people in authority who are in a position to make decisions in your life.

■ **Think about what is at stake.** If you push your arguments down a friend's throat, will it destroy your friendship? On the other hand, if you agree with your friend simply because you don't want to lose her friendship, will it be against your own values? Once you understand what is at stake, ask yourself if it is still worth doing what you are planning to do. Pause. If the answer is yes, go ahead. If not, let it go.

■ **Find out what the other person's real concern is.** You may think your parents have banned sleepovers because they just want to ruin your life, but it is likely that it is your safety that is their concern. Maybe they don't know the parents of the friend you want to visit well enough, maybe they don't trust the friend you are visiting to be responsible about your needs. That's why, in any argument that seems unreasonable to you, ask the other person, respectfully, 'What is your real concern here?' That not only helps you to understand where they are coming from, it helps them clarify what their real issue is.

■ **Keep calm.** You cannot argue or present your point of view in any reasonable manner if you are angry or close to tears. Also, you could lose sight of the argument and attack the person instead of her argument, and that never ends well. Wait until you are calm before you speak.

■ **Be respectful.** Dissing the other person's opinion is never a good idea. Instead, say 'I hear what you are saying, but I think xyz is a valid point too. What do you feel?' That always goes much better. In general, state your argument in a non-aggressive, non-threatening manner, and say what *you* think instead of pulling down what the other person is saying.

- **Agree to disagree.** An argument isn't a contest where someone wins. In fact, if the argument gets bitter, both sides lose. Understand that the other person has a right to her opinions just as much as you believe you have a right to yours. Present your arguments respectfully, calmly and logically, using facts instead of emotions, understanding what is at stake, and letting the other person see that both his friendship and his opinion are important to you. If the other person isn't convinced at the end of it, that's fine. Just shrug and say, 'I guess we have to agree to disagree on this issue, and that's okay. Let's argue about other things now – haha!'
- **Try and reach a compromise.** If both sides give a little, both sides go away feeling they've won. It's something like what happens when you bargain with the *sabziwallah*. He quotes a price that he knows is on the higher side, you quote a ridiculously low price back at him, and you both agree on a price that's somewhere in the middle. You feel triumphant that you got him to back down, he is congratulating himself on still making a decent profit. Win-win all around!

SKILL 8
BE A CONFLICT DE-ESCALATOR

Conflict De-escalator is just a fancy title for a peacemaker, someone who is not actually involved in the argument but can see that it is not going to end well for either party, and takes steps to prevent conflict. A peacemaker makes a great addition to any team, is a respected member of any community, and is a leader that everyone wants to get behind. Learn to be one!

- **Take yourself out of the equation.** Forget about your loyalties for a moment, and about the fact that one of the parties in the argument is a friend or family member. Think about

the issue, and about which of the two parties is being more provocative, or angry, or causing the argument to escalate. Then focus your attention on calming that person down.

■ **Bring the focus back to the subject of the argument.** If things are getting personal, instead of sticking to the subject under debate, say something like, 'Hey, back it up for a second. What exactly were you both arguing about again?'

Ask both sides to say what they feel about the issue, making sure that the other side does not interrupt. Listen very carefully. When they're done, state both sides' position again, in a clear, objective, non-emotional manner, with, 'Correct me if I'm wrong, but this is what I understand you both are saying...' Both sides are likely to listen less emotionally when a third person states the argument, but only if they believe your biases are not getting in the way.

■ **Do not offer your opinion.** This is not a contest, and you are not the judge. You are just the moderator, making sure that the argument stays civilized – no name-calling, no blaming, no yelling. This is a vital skill that every moderator should have – to understand that he is merely an objective witness who cannot and should not take sides.

THE COMMUNICATOR'S CHALLENGES

#5 AND #6
THE COMMUNICATION CHALLENGE

How well do you communicate? And how well do you listen? What are the real-life challenges that come up during everyday communication? Here are some games you can play to find out.

Activity 1

This one is done in pairs. Each pair comes up to the front and sits back to back. The Squad Leader gives one of the pair (A) a paper and pen and the other (B) an abstract drawing of 8-10 different-sized, interlinked geometrical shapes. B shows the picture to the rest of the Squad but not to A. Now B has 3 (or 5) minutes to describe the drawing to A using only words, so that he can recreate the same drawing on his paper. At the end of three minutes, compare the two drawings. Then repeat the exercise with A describing a different drawing and B trying to recreate it.

Play the same game with the other pairs in the Squad. After everyone has had a turn, sit in a circle and discuss your observations and learnings with the Squad Leader. Which pair had the drawing that most resembled the original? Was that because the speaker described the drawing better or because the listener listened and understood better? What specific words helped describe the drawing better? What words caused the listener to get confused? What did the exercise teach you about effective communication?

Activity 2

If you have a Squad member (or a Squad member's parent) who is a trained classical dancer (Bharatanatyam, Odissi, Kuchipudi, Kathak...), have him or her tell you a short story using the vocabulary and grammar of the dance form. Maybe he or she can show you a few *mudras* (hand gestures) to be used in the story before she begins, and explain what they mean.

Watch the language of the dancer's hands, body and face carefully, and then share with the Squad what you think the story was about. Then let her reveal the actual story and perform the same piece again. How much did you understand of the story the first time, knowing what certain *mudras* meant? How much did you understand the second time, when you had understood how the *mudras* linked up to form the story plot? Even if you didn't understand the whole story the first time around, were you able to decipher the emotion – joy, sadness, disgust, wonder, peace, valour, affection, romantic love – that the dancer was trying to depict? What does that tell you about how we communicate through our bodies?

Activity 3

The Squad Leader picks one pair from the Squad to come up to the front of the room. The idea is for one of the pair (A) to talk for 3–5 minutes continuously about something – his favourite gaming app, an incident in his life that affected him deeply, or a movie he just saw. The other partner (B) is only allowed to say three things in the entire time A is talking, but it is B's duty to make sure that A continues talking.

Once A is done, have a discussion about the activity. Questions you may want to ask A and B may include: How did it feel talking to someone who did not contribute to the conversation, how did it feel being allowed to say whatever one wanted without being interrupted, how did B's body language make A feel (Was B looking bored, amused, dismissive, or attentive and interested? How did that affect A's conversation?), how did B feel about not having the freedom to

It takes all pieces to complete the puzzle!

butt in and challenge or agree with the things A said, how did the fact that there was no pressure for B to contribute to the conversation make him feel, what did B choose to say when he spoke (remember he was allowed to speak three times), how uncomfortable were the silences that happened because B could not fill them with conversation?

#7 & #8
THE CIVIL-DEBATE AND CONFLICT-DEFUSION CHALLENGES

Together with your Squad, watch a 30-minute primetime television debate on a topic that you all understand well. Be pure observers; don't take sides yourself. You may make notes on the debating styles of different panelists and how specific points were debated. At the end, sit in a circle with your Squad and share your thoughts about these and other questions. Did the discussion proceed in a civil manner, with everyone getting a chance to voice their thoughts? Were people listening when someone was speaking, or thinking of what they were going to say in rebuttal? Did people of one side respond sensitively to the concerns of the other side, or simply continue to state their points of view? Did the moderator, who is supposed to be a conflict de-escalator, play his part well or badly?

Now have your own debate about the same topic or any other one of your choice, after having appointed one of the Squad members as moderator. Try and make this the ideal kind of debate, with people listening when others speak and addressing the other person's specific concerns when they respond, and within a given time limit. Then discuss these questions: How difficult is it to have a civil conversation about something two people do not agree on? How often was the speaker interrupted or voices raised? What steps did the conflict-defuser (moderator) have to take to bring the debate back on track? Did those steps work? How could each of you have conducted yourself better?

WOCOTEEN MERIT BADGE 3

THE MASTER-AT-ARMS

To be able to defend oneself is even more important than being able to injure an antagonist.
*– **Scout Tests and How to Pass Them***

If you had been a scout in Baden-Powell's day, the Master-at-Arms badge would have been an important one to win. Remember that this was a time when Britain was often called 'the land of the never-setting sun' because the British Empire was so vast and covered so many time zones that the sun was always shining in some part of the Empire! That Empire was won and run by people and soldiers – essentially, British politicians, administrators, businessmen and officers, supported massively by native administrators and soldiers – who knew (well, most of them at any rate) how to use 'arms' in the military sense. This was also the time when the world was devastated by two World Wars, so knowing how to use weapons was considered a key skill.

Today, the Master-at-Arms badge sounds like a dated, even politically-incorrect, idea. In fact, in the USA, the badge has been discontinued (in the UK, it still survives, modified for today's world).

But if you think about it, there are several ways to interpret the term 'Master-at-Arms', the most basic one being the ability to protect and defend yourself and if possible, others, in a conflict situation. 'Arms' doesn't have to mean weapons, or something exclusively physical or violent; it could simply mean being constantly mindful of the possible dangers in your environment, so that you can avoid them; or knowing whom to call or what to do before a potentially violent situation gets out of hand; or learning what to say to defuse a school-playground situation that threatens to blow up into something more dangerous. It is about being prepared, and being able to rely on yourself not only for your own safety but also the safety of others in a hostile situation.

And that's why the WoCoTeen Squad has retained the Master-at-Arms badge. Master the skills in this section and crack the challenges that follow to discover for yourself why they are so important.

SKILL 9
BE RESPONSIBLE FOR YOUR OWN SAFETY

Make no mistake about it – all kinds of dangers lurk around every street corner. One way to avoid, overcome or escape these dangers when you might be on your own is to be mindful when you are on the street.

What exactly does that mean? Here are some pointers:

- **Look, listen, smell, feel.** When you are walking down the street – whether to school or to a friend's house or the supermarket or the park, and no matter what time of day or night it is – be aware of what is going on around you. Is a stranger walking too close to you for your comfort? Is someone leaning into another person, looking angry? Is a child being bullied by an adult? Has an unusually-large knot of people gathered, and are they speaking in raised voices? Is there a growling pack of strays at the corner of the street? Is there a missing paving stone on the pavement, or a bunch of exposed wires hanging off an electricity pole? Can you smell smoke? Heed all warnings from your senses.
- **Shut down the devices.** Needless to say, you are far less likely even to notice any of these dangers in the first place if you are: (a) peering into your device; (b) texting or talking to someone on your phone; (c) talking super-animatedly to the friend you are with; (d) listening to music on your headphones; (e) daydreaming. Make sure your senses are all on

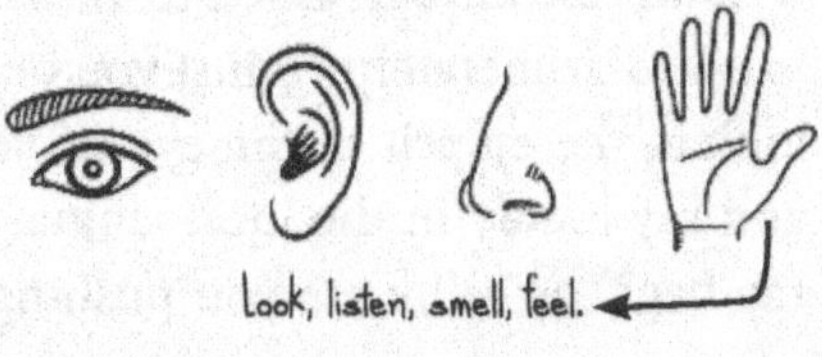

high alert when you're out in public on your own – it may save your life, or someone else's.

- **Walk away.** If you notice something that seems dangerous, the best thing to do is to avoid getting in the way. Change your route, step away from the broken pavement or the electric wires, cross the street to the other side, duck into a store until the danger passes, whatever it takes. However wussy it may seem, walking away from a potentially dangerous situation is often the most sensible thing to do. Even if there is someone who genuinely needs help – either medical help or protection from a more powerful or angry person – do not try to handle it alone. Call in adult reinforcements – passersby, a policeman (whom you have already noticed since you have had your wits around you!) or a security guard nearby. If there has been an accident, call an ambulance. (And what was the number again?)
- **Stick to busy streets after dark.** Try not to walk in the streets after dark, especially alone. If you have to, make sure you stick to familiar, well-lit, busy streets. And stay on high alert.
- **Always walk in the direction of oncoming traffic.** That way, no one in a vehicle can surprise you from behind. You will also notice a speeding or out-of-control vehicle if it starts getting too close to the pavement, and you can safely get out of the way.
- **Make eye contact with people around you.** Statistics show that potential attackers, pickpockets, device-snatchers and other criminals often abandon their plans if they realize someone has noticed them, since most of them are counting on the element of surprise when they assault their victim. So actually look at people around you – when you're walking, standing at a bus-stop, waiting for someone on the side of the road. Make the eye-contact casual, brief and non-aggressive.
- **Don't be embarrassed to make a lot of noise.** If someone brushes deliberately against you or tugs at your bag in a crowd, look at the culprit in the eye (if you can identify him or her) and say loudly in the local language, 'Why are you tugging at my bag?' or 'Why are you pushing me?' (Calling it out aloud

identifies the issue and the perpetrator for everyone around and forces them to get involved.)

If you feel intimidated by a stranger on the street, yell, 'I don't know who you are!' That immediately lets people around you know that there is a 'situation' here – most people are reluctant to interfere in a situation if they think it is a private or family matter.

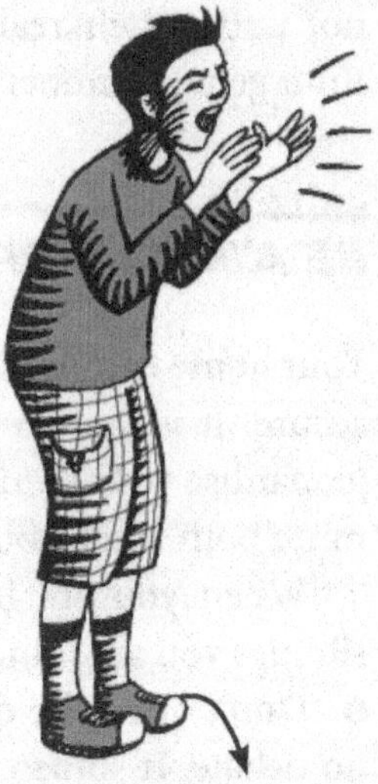

Yup! Make some noise, boys and girls!

- **Before getting into an autorickshaw or cab,** take a picture of its licence plate and WhatsApp it to a friend or family member. If you are taking a taxi service, forward the details about the vehicle and driver to someone. Pretend to talk to someone on the phone while you are in the vehicle, or *actually* call someone – a parent, the friend you are visiting – telling them where you are headed and how long it will take you to get there. Once you reach, message someone to let them know.

Seriously, being extra-careful does not hurt. Plus, once you make this checklist a habit, it will stop feeling like a chore.

- **Always let someone know when your plans change.** Say you've stepped out of the house for lunch with your friends. The restaurant is closed for some reason, so you decide to go to another one a little further away instead. You know you are not expected back home for another hour and a half at least, so you decide to go along with the new plan. Which is fine, but do make sure you let your mom or dad know. It's just a safety thing.
- **Always carry ID.** If you carry a wallet, make sure there is a card in there with your photograph, home address, phone number to call in an emergency, your family doctor's contact number, your blood group, a list of medications you are allergic to and information on whether you wear contact lenses. On your phone, store your parents' numbers under Mom and Dad,

not under their real names. Also store their numbers under Emergency Number 1 and Emergency Number 2.

SKILL 10
BE MINDFUL OF YOUR HOME'S SAFETY

Your home is your family's fortress, the place where you all feel secure. It is your responsibility not to compromise that and jeopardise your family's safety. Here are a few things to keep in mind both when you are inside and outside the house.

When you are inside the house alone, or with younger siblings you are minding:

- **Don't open the door to strangers.** That's a cardinal rule – no debate. If someone is delivering something, call and ask if they can deliver it the next day. If you live in an apartment, ask the security guard to let you know when the delivery guy arrives so that you can go to the lobby of your building and sign/pay for it. The most sophisticated home security system is completely useless if you throw open your door yourself and let an intruder in.
- **Know where the main power switch to the house is and how to turn it off.** In case of an electrical emergency – you smell burning insulation, you notice electrical sparking, the power goes off and you smell burning, switches or plugs become blackened and hot – turn off the main electric supply. In case there is a fire or you smell a gas leak or discover a major water leak, turn off the mains. Do not turn it back on until a professional has had a look at it.
- **Know where the gas cylinder/pipeline is in the kitchen and how to turn the gas valve off.** If you smell a gas leak – teach yourself what cooking gas smells like first, so you can identify the leak – turn the valve off immediately. Go out of the house for half an hour or more while the gas dissipates and inform your parents and your apartment complex authorities. Do *not* turn on any electrical switch or light a match anywhere in the area for at least 30 minutes.

• **Know where the main water supply inlet valve to your house is, and how to turn it off.** If a pipe bursts somewhere in the house or a tap gets stuck and cannot be turned off when you are home alone, turn the main water valve off. If you live in an apartment and don't have access to the water valve, call building security over your intercom immediately.

• **When there is no one in the house and you are heading out yourself,** pause to tick off your home security checklist.

? Have you locked *all* the access doors to the house?

? Have you turned off all the lights (unless your family's strategy is to always have a couple of lights on to dissuade potential burglars)?

? Have you turned off the gas valve?

? Do you have your house key (and your ID) in your pocket?

Leave home only when you are satisfied with your answers and have completed any tasks that were entrusted to you. And make sure the front door is securely shut behind you!

? Were there any specific safety instructions your parents had given you before they left the house today – hand the front door key over to the neighbour, message me when you leave?

SKILL 11
LEARN SOME BASIC SELF-DEFENCE MOVES

Why? For one, being trained in a martial art can certainly help you feel more confident when you are in a dangerous situation. Equally, though, a grounding in martial arts helps you focus and centre your mind as well as your body, and trains you to 'think' about how you would defend yourself if you had to. Often, just having thought through the steps is enough to give you a huge advantage. Here's a list to help you start off:

• **Run!** Sometimes the best move is to run away from the situation as fast as you can. Do a lightning-quick SWOT (Strengths, Weaknesses, Opportunities, Threats) analysis of the situation and your opponent. If you feel at the end of it that running is your best bet, well then, run! Ask yourself:

? Am I alone?

? Does he have a weapon? (Sexist as this may be, we are going with 'he' for the potential assailant. Sadly, assailants are more often 'he's' than 'she's'.)

? Is he way bigger than I am?

? Does he have a vehicle into which he can bundle me?

? Is he spoiling for a fight? (That means he is either angry or determined to hurt you and will not listen to reason.)

? Is there an escape route around that I can use to get into a more populated, better-lit area quickly?

If the answer to all (or most) of these questions is 'Yes', don't hesitate – run! If you are on a pavement, run into the road – *after* checking that it is safe to cross! – people are more likely to notice someone running in the middle of the road than on a pavement. It also means that the assailant is more likely to be seen if he follows you. If you are on a playground, run towards an adult.

● **Give in.** Sometimes, the wise strategy – if the attacker is a mugger who wants your gold chain or your wallet, for instance – is to give it to him and run. Your wallet is not more important than your limbs or your life.

● **React quickly**. Understand that the first 30 seconds will establish which way the situation is going to go. This is all the time you have to analyze, yell, call attention to yourself, push back and move. This is also the time you have to inflict maximum damage on your attacker, while conserving your own energy (which you will need for running away).

♦ **Yell and push back.** One way of causing an attacker to 'brain blink', and for you to seize that moment is to do something he isn't expecting. If he's too close, push back hard on his chest, yelling 'Back Off!', very loudly and aggressively straight into his face. Your aggression not only surprises him, but it also signals clearly that you are not an easy target, apart from the added bonus (for you) of getting the attention of people around. Use that moment of surprise, when his focus is off, to run away.

♦ **Move.** If you are cornered – move, move, move. Weave from side to side if he attempts to chase or punch you; duck or wriggle wildly if he grabs you. A stationary target is far easier to hit or transport than a moving one.

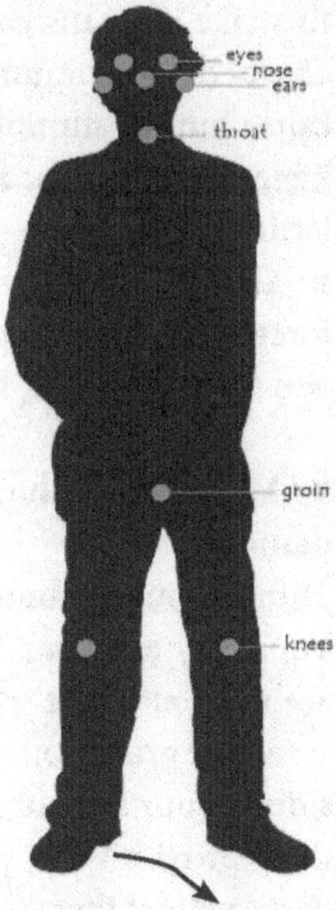

The 'Ouch!' map – remember it!

● **Attack the most sensitive body parts**

What are the most sensitive body parts, then? Here are the main ones, based on suggestions from self-defence experts:

■ **Eyes** – Go straight and strong for the eyes with the index and middle fingers of your dominant hand. Scratching and gouging also helps. Just seeing someone coming for his eyes is often enough to distract the attacker. But don't get closer simply to attack the eyes – try something from a little distance away first.

■ **Nose** – You know how painful it is when someone or something slams into your nose? Use that knowledge to handicap the attacker temporarily. Use the heel of your palm to strike upwards from under his nose, putting the entire weight of your body behind that strike. Remember you can do this even if you are shorter than the attacker!

■ **Ears** – Clap your open, tight palms strongly against the attacker's ears.

■ **Neck** – Make a strong, open, 'knife hand' – fingers held straight and tightly together, thumb tucked in and bent slightly at the knuckle – and strike with the outer edge (thumb towards you) at the side of the neck or straight and hard at the windpipe. Ouch!

■ **Knee** – The knee is the ideal target, because it is accessible from all sides and you don't have to get too close to the attacker to strike at it. Instead of kicking straight at the kneecap (that causes the maximum damage if your kick is strong, but it won't cause him to stumble or lose balance), aim for the side of the knee – it will cause it to buckle, and may result in the attacker letting go of you.

■ **Groin** – If he has grabbed you from behind, use the full force of your open palm to strike hard at the groin. If he has you from the front, knee him in the groin – hard!

• Attack with the body parts that can inflict maximum damage

Think about the boniest, sharpest, hardest parts of your body. Yup, they are your skull, your knees and your elbows. They are most effective when the attacker is very close to you, so if someone grabs you – from the front by the shoulders, from the side by your arm, or from the back by your neck – you can turn their proximity to your advantage by using your bony body parts against them.

■ **Head** – Butt him hard in the chin or face.

■ **Knee** – Knee him in the groin or in the small of his back.

■ **Elbows** – Instead of punching him with your fists, bend your arm at the elbow and thrust it into his windpipe or upwards into the underside of his chin.

• Use everyday objects to injure

■ When you are walking home after dark, walk with a pen with its cap off, or a key, between your middle and ring fingers. You can jam it into someone who gets too close.

■ Carry a canister of deo or hairspray in your bag – you can spray it into an attacker's eyes and temporarily blind him. If you are pushed onto the ground, grab some sand or dust and throw it into his eyes.

REMEMBER! These tips are to help you protect yourself against an ATTACKER. Do NOT use these moves against a sibling or a friend, even in jest.

■ Umbrellas, handbags, high-heeled shoes (very useful for stamping on your attacker's foot, hard), a nail file, a fork from your lunch bag – they are all effective weapons. It just helps to have thought about them as weapons before, so do a quick inventory of your bag now and make a mental list of potential weapons that you carry in there, everyday.

SKILL 12
EDUCATE YOURSELF ON CYBER SAFETY

This is something you probably hear *ad nauseam* (an ancient Latin phrase that means 'until you want to throw up') from hand-wringing, super-stressed parents, teachers, and all kinds of well-meaning adults, but cyberspace is a slippery slope, and there are very real dangers lurking out there. So bear with us as we list out some basic rules here, yet again.

You never know who's hiding behind that screen!

Please, puh-leese do NOT:

- **Give out personal information on the Internet.** Your mobile phone number, your home address, your parents' credit card number, and other such sensitive information is private. However discreet you think you have been, there are ways for people to hack into your conversations and find that information.

- **Agree to meet someone in real life whom you have only met on the Internet before.** Unless you are with a bunch of your own friends. Unless you know for a fact that he is a real person who looks like his DP, is the age he claims to be, and goes to the school he claims to go to. And do tell your parents that you are going to meet him when you do.
- **Advertise your family's travel plans on social media.** Nobody needs to know – via a Facebook announcement, at that – that your home is going to be empty for the next few days. It's no different from you opening the front door and inviting burglars in. Think about *Home Alone*, and be scared, be very scared.
- **Bully or troll people you know – and don't – on social media.** Here's a simple rule of thumb – don't say anything to anyone on the Internet that you would not say to their faces. Also, it is just good manners to keep your disagreements and fights private, so only share your anger or your opinions directly with the person who you are upset with, not the whole world.
- **Post messages to people – or pictures of yourself – that you may be embarrassed about later.** Here's the bottom line – think about what you are posting before you post it. You may think you're a privacy settings champ, but Internet privacy is a murky area. Anything you send into cyberspace remains there forever and can be found by people interested in finding it, including law enforcement agencies and future employers. You don't want to jeopardise your future – even slightly – by being impulsive about what you share on the Internet.

THE MASTER-AT-ARMS' CHALLENGES

#9
THE PERSONAL-SAFETY CHALLENGE

With your Squad, identify five or six (as many as there are Squad members) short (around 500 m) stretches of road in your neighbourhood or around your school. Decide in which order each Squad member will take the six routes – the first will go in the order Route 1, Route 2, Route 3, and so on, the second will start with Route 2 and follow it up with Route 3, Route 4, Route 5, and so on, the third will begin with Route 3 and then do the other routes in sequence – basically, no two Squad members will do the same route at the same time.

Each day, for six days, walk along your designated stretch for the day, (according to your sequence of routes), observing that stretch very carefully for things that could be dangerous – hanging electrical wires, a badly paved stretch of footpath, a tree branch too low to the ground, an aggressive pack of stray dogs, very fast traffic, broken or no street lights. Also look for exit points and safety measures available – shops to duck into, low gates that you can climb and jump over, a security guard you can call upon, an exit that takes you into a busier area. Make sure you are always carrying your ID on you.

Record your observations in a notebook, and compare them with other Squad members at the end of the week. Not only will you know your own neighbourhood better at the end of the challenge, you will hopefully make it a habit to observe things while you're walking henceforth.

#10
THE HOME-SAFETY CHALLENGE

Ask your parents to show you how to turn off the gas valve, the power supply and the water supply to your home, and how to turn them back on again. Also ask them what the general safety rules of your household are, and repeat the list back to them when they've finished. Have your parents sign off on a note saying that you are now a bona fide Home Safety Soldier, and submit the note to your Squad Leader.

#11
THE SELF-DEFENCE CHALLENGE

Have a self-defence expert – it could be someone from among your neighbours or older friends or cousins too – come and do a half-day workshop or an hour-long demo for your Squad on basic self-defence moves and techniques. If possible, sign up for a martial arts class – Tae Kwon Do, Judo, Kick-boxing, Kalaripayattu – for at least three months.

Important: Do not try any moves on your siblings or Squad members unless there is a trained adult present!

#12
THE CYBER-SAFETY CHALLENGE

With your Squad and Squad Leader, read up about an anti-cyberbullying software called ReThink (www.rethinkwords.com), which was picked as one of the Top 15 Google Science Fair 2014 Global Finalists. ReThink was created in 2013 by 13-year-old Indian-origin American Trisha Prabhu as a reaction to a shocking story she read about an 11-year-old Florida schoolgirl, who had committed suicide because of cyberbullying. by her classmates. The software helps people pause and think about the mean comment they are about to post online before they actually do it, and studies show that teenagers who use ReThink change their mind about their post a staggering 93 per cent of the time. Think about how you can implement ReThink, or something like it, at your own school.

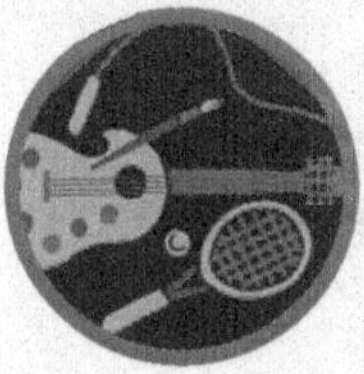

WOCOTEEN MERIT BADGE 4

THE HOBBYIST

From hobbies, introduced by way of the Proficiency Badge system, many a boy has found his life interest and life work.
– **Camp Fire Yarn No. 22, *Scouting for Boys***

Here we are – at Badge No. 4 in the Personal Development Section. The three badges so far focused on gaining skills that were somewhat non-creative, but the next three – The Hobbyist, The Handicrafter, and The Entrepreneur – will focus on – ta-daaa! – igniting your latent – or not-so-latent – creativity.

If you've always thought of yourself as someone who isn't creative, perish the thought. Maybe you just haven't found the right occasion or passion to help your creativity burst forth. One of the easiest and most fun ways to find your creative side is to take up a hobby. Of course not all hobbies need to be ones generally classified as 'creative', but we bet that just finding yourself the right hobby will end up engaging your mind in dozens of creative ways.

What *is* a hobby, though? Well, a hobby is an interest, activity, pastime or passion that you pursue in your spare time. Your mainstream occupation is being a student, which means 'studying' cannot be your hobby (although some people are so passionate about learning that it might well classify as one!), but playing a sport can be. However, if you play competitively, taking part in inter-school and intra-city tournaments, the sport stops being a hobby, it becomes one of your more mainstream occupations.

This checklist will help you decide if what you think of as your hobby is truly one.

1. Is the activity something you do in your spare time?
2. Does doing the activity give you pleasure and joy?
3. Does the activity make you feel relaxed and calm after a tough day at school?

4. Do you get so immersed in the activity that you forget even to check your phone (no, 'chatting with a friend on Skype, on my mom's laptop' does not qualify as a hobby)?
5. Does the activity help you build some kind of skill or knowledge base?
6. Do you do it because you want to, not because someone tells you that you should?
7. Do you wish you had more time to devote to that activity?
8. Do you make sure you find time for this activity at least a couple of times a week?
9. Do you feel it helps you to get in touch with a side of yourself – a playful side, maybe, or a nerdy side, or a funny one – that your mainstream occupation does not?
10. Do you make any money out of this activity?

If you answered 'Yes' to the first nine questions, and 'No' to the tenth, yes, you have a hobby! Congratulations! If you said no to even one of the first nine questions, though, you need to take some steps to correct that if you hope to win yourself the Hobbyist badge.

Before we go on to the specific skills you need to build to qualify for the badge, here's a quick dekko at why the Squad thinks having a hobby so important that they instituted a badge for it.

WHY SHOULD YOU HAVE A HOBBY?

- **A hobby reduces stress.** In today's world, it seems as if we are all constantly being judged and graded on everything we do. An activity that is done entirely for pleasure, where no one (except yourself) is demanding effort and perfection from you, can be wonderfully relaxing.
- **A hobby straddles fun and learning.** It is easy to tire of something that is just fun, but anything that combines both fun and learning, like a good hobby, is a sure-fire winner.
- **A hobby helps you to discover yourself.** Who would have thought that you had a talent for fashioning Harry Potter likenesses from rubberbands on a Rainbow Loom? Did you

Spend as much time choosing your hobby as you want - good research pays off in the long run!

ever, in your wildest dreams, think you had the patience or stick-with-it-ness to complete a 1,000-piece jigsaw puzzle? Yup, a hobby helps you find qualities in yourself you never suspected you had.

- **A hobby helps you focus.** Most hobbies require plenty of your attention (which you are delighted to give them, because you enjoy them so much). That kind of dedicated attention to something does two important things - it clears your mind of all the other stuff that's crowding it, and lets you focus on just one thing, thus stilling your mind and allowing you to access your quiet core - yup, it's a kind of meditation, really.
- **A hobby boosts your confidence.** When you do something you enjoy, with full focus and attention, chances are that you will get pretty good at it. The usual route after that is to set yourself a challenge - say, you have postcards from five States in the country, so you decide to start a postcard collection that will be complete when you have one from every State; or you love football stats, so you want to be able to rattle off from memory who scored the winning goal in the finals of every FIFA World Cup since the inaugural one in 1930 - whatever it is, when you finish the challenge to your satisfaction, you feel a sense of quiet accomplishment, and a confidence that will help you face and overcome challenges in other areas of your life.

■ **The joy you get from a hobby is yours, and yours alone.** It is something you can hug to yourself every night and enjoy.

Convinced? Go get yourself a hobby then!

SKILL 13
TRY SOMETHING NEW

If you don't already have what qualifies as a hobby, it's time to get one. You could pick up a hobby that one of your parents or siblings is already into, but there is no need at all to limit yourself to the familiar. In fact, choosing something that your family knows nothing about will get you out of your comfort zone, which in itself is a brilliant thing. Overcome your fear of the unknown in the hobby department, and soon you will have the courage to do it in other life departments as well.

Here is a list of hobbies to get your brain firing. Or pick something else entirely. Just enjoy exploring different things, spending a few weeks immersed in each – you will need at least that much time to know if it can become a hobby that engages you over a long period. Just making it a mission to try out things you've never done before – hula-hooping, calligraphy, juggling, leaf collecting, papermaking – can introduce you to so many activities that give you pleasure while turning you into an entertainer or making you an expert on something,

You may even be able to keep two or more hobbies going at the same time, especially if one of them is a collection kind of hobby and another is a outdoorsy hobby, like, say, gardening.

- **Hobbies that involve producing something:** Soap and candle making, film-making (using your phone camera and free downloadable film-editing software), cooking, *rangoli*-making, knitting, embroidery, photography, paper-flower-making, tie-and-dye, origami, jigsaw puzzles, scrapbooking, journaling (similar to scrapbooking but more of a diary with your own drawings and illustrations accompanying it), model-building (with matchsticks, lego blocks, from model-building kits, whatever), jewellery-making, quilling, pottery, woodworking, blogging.

- **Hobbies that involve collecting:** Seashells (if you live in a city by the sea or your family holidays by the seaside often), postcards, fridge magnets, leaves and flowers (which you then press and preserve), movie memorabilia, books, action figures, recipes (which you have tried and have produced spectacular dishes with), key-chains, ticket stubs from your favourite movies.
- **Hobbies that involve developing a knowledge base or a skill:** Solving the Rubik's cube, or solving crossword puzzles, bird-watching, gardening, amateur astronomy, board games, fish-keeping, tree-identifying, hip-hop dancing, visiting all the historical monuments in your city and learning their stories, specialized movie-watching (pick a film studio/actor/genre), understanding how a car works and comparing different cars on various parameters, mastering one particular software (Microsoft Excel, say), computer coding, gaming. Also, any sport at all – skating, swimming, golf, wall-climbing...
- **Hobbies that involve DIY:** DIY is short for do-it-yourself, and it usually involves building, repairing or repurposing. The main rule is that no expert is involved in the activity and it is a purely amateur thing. Making working models of clocks or a solar-powered robot from a science kit are also examples of DIY.

SKILL 14
FIND A HOBBY YOU CAN STICK TO

As long as you have to go to school and finish homework and write exams, you are never going to have too much time or energy to devote to your hobby. So pick wisely.

Here are some pointers.

1. **Is the hobby likely to be an expensive one?** Like collecting action figures, say, where you have to actually buy each one? Or magic, where you may need to buy specialized equipment for each trick? Even if you are not thinking of making your

parents spend on it (good for you!), and planning to use your own birthday money to expand your collection, it is not the kind of hobby that will engage you on a daily or even weekly basis. Keep this as your secondary hobby, and pick another, more engaging hobby as your primary one.

2. **Does the hobby involve travel?** Like seashell-collecting, which can only happen when you travel on vacation, say? Or stargazing, which you can only do properly when you are away from urban light pollution? If yes, bring in another element into the hobby. If you are a seashell-collector, in between seaside vacations, research the different kinds of seashells already in your collection, find out their names and the kinds of creatures that might have lived in them, label them, make a drawing of each in your sketchbook and add all the info you have found out about each. Go deep into it – it's a sure-fire way to ensure that the hobby endures.

3. **Is the hobby very time-consuming?** A hobby that requires too little engagement is just as unlikely to sustain as one that requires much of your attention. Pick something in between.

4. **Does the hobby involve plenty of device-time?** Then you might want to clear it with your parents first, especially if they don't approve of that kind of thing. Explain what you are trying to do – maintain a blog, become an expert at an online game – why you love it, and what benefits you think it has for you. Allow them to lay the ground rules for you, and stick to those mutually agreed-on rules.

SKILL 15
GET DEEP INTO YOUR HOBBY

Anything you do becomes far more enjoyable, and enriching, when you engage with it at a deeper level. That's really when all the benefits of having a hobby begin to really kick in. What does 'getting deep into a hobby' mean, though? It could include:

- **Scheduling dedicated time for it every week.** If your weekdays are full of after-school activities and music or sport or dance lessons, work on your hobby on weekends, especially if your hobby is something like baking. If it is something like rollerblading, which you can do every evening as part of your outdoor play time after school, that's great – except make sure you do it at least twice a week, even if you want to play cricket on the other days.
- **Exploring every aspect of it.** If your hobby is a sport, find out all you can about it, apart from just playing it. Watch national- and international-level tournaments on TV, or in a stadium (if they happen to be played in your city). Read about the heroes of your sport, past and present, arm yourself with stats from various matches, find out India's position in the world standings in that sport. If specialized movie-watching is your hobby, educate yourself on all the trivia around those movies. Learn about each director's style, who composed the soundtrack, the film's budget, and so on.
- **Sticking with it until you become a minor expert on it.** Some hobbies come with an expiry date. Hobbies like collecting postcards from every State in India, say, which ends when you have the entire collection; or learning to solve the Rubik's cube. That's fine. You can then move happily to another hobby, but when you are still with the hobby try to become an ace at it. If you're collecting postcards, don't just complete your collection – instead, become an expert on the monument or beach or festival or handicraft depicted in the postcard you have. So many possibilities to know more!

SKILL 16
SHARE YOUR HOBBY WITH OTHERS

If you thought your hobby – collecting every disposable pen you have ever used – is weird, you're so wrong, There are people whose hobby is 'playing dead' – they create elaborate death scenes for themselves and have someone take their pictures! – or collecting tea-bag covers, or appearing in the background of important events on TV. So whatever your hobby is, share it with others – you will be astounded to see how many fellow-weirdos are out there. Jokes apart, though, here are some seriously good reasons for sharing your hobby with the world.

- **It helps you become part of a community of people who also love the same thing.** You can pick up all kinds of interesting tips and ideas about your interest from them, find a mentor, and make friends of all ages and all nationalities who are bound by nothing but a common passion. Sometimes, you may even create the community yourself.
- **It helps you become more committed than you already are.** Knowing that there are other people with the same interest who are far ahead of you on the 'hobby curve' – maybe their DIY projects are way more complex and intricate than any you have attempted – urges you to lose your fear and challenge yourself with tougher projects.
- **It helps you sustain your hobby.** Just like it's easier to keep to an exercise or study regimen when you do it with a couple of friends, a fellow-collector or running enthusiast will make sure you keep up with your hobby.
- **It helps you get appreciation and acknowledgement.** Someone who has never attempted to make a perfect origami tulip will never understand how difficult it is to do, but those who have – like others who share your hobby – will. That kind of peer appreciation is excellent for building your self-esteem. In fact, you will earn the appreciation of even those who haven't ever tried it for themselves. Either way, you win!

THE HOBBYIST'S CHALLENGES

#13
THE EXIT-YOUR-COMFORT-ZONE CHALLENGE

Pick a pretend-hobby for yourself. It should be as weird or unfamiliar a hobby as possible, like 'Fighter Planes that Participated in World War II' or 'Small Mammal Taxidermy'. Do some online research on your hobby, as if you were a true hobbyist. Make a 10-minute presentation about your pretend-hobby to the Squad, using charts you've made or a presentation you've created on a laptop. By the time everyone has finished their presentations, you will have discovered that seemingly weird hobbies can be wonderful too.

#14, #15 AND #16
THE HOBBY CHALLENGE

Pick a real hobby for yourself, using the tips under Skill 14 to help you. Spend three months building a collection or making things or building a knowledge base (depending on the nature of your hobby), and basically, becoming a minor expert in that field. Three months later, along with the rest of your Squad, host a little 'Hobby Fair' to which you invite your family and friends. After the guests have seen all the hobby displays, make one-minute 'sales pitches' to the audience about your particular hobby, telling them why you love it so much and why you think they should take it up too. Have them vote on the most convincing, the funniest, and the most expert hobbyist.

WOCOTEEN MERIT BADGE 5

THE HANDICRAFTER

Much distress and unemployment results when boys have been allowed to come to manhood without any trade at their command. They have little with which to earn a living or make their spare time interesting.

– **Camp Fire Yarn No. 22, *Scouting for Boys***

What exactly is a handicraft? A handicraft is anything that is useful, or decorative, or both, that is made chiefly by hand. Tools may be used in the making of it, of course, but there are often no machines involved in producing it. Even if there are machines, they always have a much smaller role than the human's. Because the machine's involvement is so minor, any handicraft – and this includes handspun yarn and handloom textiles – takes time and effort to produce, which is why it is usually more expensive – and often more beautiful – than a similar machine-made one. Handicrafts are, therefore, necessarily produced in smaller numbers.

Handicrafts have their roots in rural societies – originally, most handicrafts used local materials and were meant to serve the needs of only the local community. They are closely linked to the traditions, culture and often, even religion, of the place of their origin, and have usually been practised for hundreds, even thousands, of years, the skills having been transmitted within families or communities in an unbroken line, from one generation to the next. In that sense, they are part of our heritage – they contain within them the story of the land from which they come, and of the people who have inhabited it.

This is just one of the reasons why it is so important to preserve them, though. The other is that handicrafts and handlooms provide livelihoods to millions of Indian families. It is vital that we ensure that traditional artisans and handicrafters can make a decent living doing what they do, because if they don't, they will abandon it altogether in favour of a higher-paying job in the nearest city, and a whole way of life, and a wonderful art-form, will disappear forever.

Why is it important for every WoCoTeen to educate himself or herself about handicrafts, and learn how to make a handicraft or two himself? There are several good reasons, but here's Gandhiji's take on it – in an article on education in 1937, in *Harijan*, a weekly journal he published himself, he wrote: 'By education I mean an all-round drawing out of the best in child and man – body, mind and spirit. (...) Literacy in itself is no education. I would therefore begin the child's education by teaching it a useful handicraft and enabling it to produce from the moment it begins its training.'

Gandhiji practised what he preached too – each day, for years and years, he hand-spun cotton into yarn on his charkha. He also proposed a new and entirely different system of education for India. He called it 'Nai Talim'.

According to Nai Talim, just theoretical knowledge – knowing how to read, write and count, and knowing a bit of history, geography and science, was not a complete education. Only when a person knew how to work with his hands to produce something useful, beautiful and saleable, only when a person was not only a generous and hard-working and self-respecting member of the community but also a self-reliant one, only when he not only taught others what he knew but also learnt equally from them, could India become an equal society where the 'educated elite' did not consider the 'illiterate craftsman' as someone beneath him or someone to be despised, but as someone he could teach and learn from.

Old B-P believed in his Scouts being good at Handicraft too, although his definition of Handicraft was somewhat different (the idea was still self-reliance and self-sufficiency though, just like Gandhiji's). Check out the requirements for a Handicraft Merit Badge from the original 1911 edition of the *Boy Scouts Handbook*.

To obtain a merit badge for Handicraft, a Scout must be able to:

1. *Paint a door*
2. *Whitewash a ceiling*
3. *Repair gas fittings, sash lines, window and door fastenings*
4. *Replace gas mantles, washers, and electric light bulbs*
5. *Solder*
6. *Hang pictures and curtains*
7. *Repair blinds*
8. *Fix curtains, portière rods, blind fixtures*
9. *Lay carpets and mend clothing and upholstery*
10. *Repair furniture and china*
11. *Sharpen knives*
12. *Repair gates*
13. *Fix screens on windows and doors*

Aren't you glad the WoCoTeen Squad has much lower expectations of you? Go finish your set of challenges and win that badge, then!

SKILL 17
LEARN ABOUT INDIAN HANDICRAFTS

This is where being an Indian* WoCoTeen can become a bit of a drag – to master this particular skill, you have to do tonnes more swotting than those in most other countries. Almost every district of every State in India has groups of artisans turning out some unique kind of handicraft in every traditional

**You do realize that these skills are country-specific, don't you – Peruvian and Senegalese WoCoTeens, for instance, will be required to educate themselves about the handicrafts of their own countries, not India's. The logic is that the process of getting to know about your own will build a lifelong interest in handicrafts in general, and you will then want to know about every other country's as well, and how they are similar or different to yours, and why.*

material you can think of – wood, leather, cloth, metal, stone, bone, earth, plant fibre, wool, animal horn, ivory...

The good part is that you don't have to visit a museum to see them – in India, handicrafts are still vibrantly alive and part of our daily lives. They are in craft fairs that come to your city, among your mom's sarees and your dad's kurtas, in the wooden toys that your little cousin plays with, in the silver jewellery that your teachers wear, in the khadi jackets that our politicians love to be seen in, in the woven baskets of vegetable-sellers at the local market...

How do you educate yourself about Indian handicrafts, when there are so many of them around? You can achieve a lot simply by taking an inventory of all the handcrafted items in your own home, and digging a little deeper – what kind of handicraft is it, does the technique or skill have a name, which part of India is it from, how long does it take to produce (a small 6 x 4 ft Kashmiri silk rug could take two skilled craftsmen two and a half years to finish!). The more you train your eye to notice handicrafts, the more you will begin to appreciate them. Buying hand-made over machine-made (whenever it makes financial and practical sense) will become a habit.

Follow that up with attending craft fairs in your city, watching craftsmen at work (they are usually around at craft fairs and occasionally in State government emporia that showcase and sell the main handicrafts of your State), visiting an artisans' village or a handicraft 'factory' in places that you visit on vacation, suggesting to your school to take you out on excursions around your city or town where you can see local artisans in action. Soon, willy-nilly, you will find that you are something of an expert, that you begin to speak about handicrafts with passion and intelligence, thus convincing more and more people to jump on the save-the-crafts bandwagon.

On the next page is a fun exercise for you to kick-start your education. An old-fashioned game of Match the Following, where Column 1 has the names of States, and Column 2 a major handicraft associated with those States.

STATES	TRADITIONAL HANDICRAFTS
Andhra Pradesh	Black stone pottery
Bihar	Coir mats
Chhatisgarh	Leather shadow puppets
Gujarat	Juttis (decorated Indian shoes)
Jammu and Kashmir	Dhokra metal art (the Dancing Girl of Mohenjodaro was made using this technique!)
Karnataka	Marble craft
Kerala	Bronze sculptures (a technique first developed 1,000 years ago by the Cholas)
Manipur	Chikan embroidery
Punjab	Madhubani paintings
Rajasthan	Bandhni (fabric tie-and-dye technique)
Tamil Nadu	Walnut wood carving
Uttar Pradesh	Lacquered wooden toys

Answers on page 320

SKILL 18
DISCOVER THE WONDER OF INDIAN TEXTILES

Textiles is another area where India has always been a world leader. Cotton was first spun in India some 7,000 years ago (archaeological finds from the Neolithic era include copper beads strung through with cotton thread), and began to be cultivated in a large-scale manner by the fine folks of the Harappan Civilization some 2,000 years later. The same folks were also rearing silkworms for silk, spinning it into yarn and weaving it into cloth.

Today, India is not only the second-largest cotton-producing country in the world (close behind China), but also the world's second-largest exporter (which says plenty about the quality of Indian cotton – everyone seems to want it!), behind the USA. It is also the second-largest producer of silk in the world after China, and – no surprises there – the largest consumer of silk in the world (just look into your mom's and grandmoms' wardrobes for proof!). Yup, we can't seem to get enough of these two fabrics in this country.

But what makes Indian textiles truly special is our bright and happy colour combinations, the fine quality of our weaves and the number of wonderful ways in which we have learnt to weave them, treat them, dye them and block-print them. You can spend a lifetime learning about and enjoying Indian textiles, and now is as good a time as any to begin!

Here's another Match-the-Following activity to start you off.

STATES	TRADITIONAL WEAVES
Andhra Pradesh	Tussar
Assam	Kanchipuram
Bihar	Jamavar
Gujarat	Pochampalli
Jammu and Kashmir	Paithani
Madhya Pradesh	Baluchery
Maharashtra	Patola
Odisha	Muga
Tamil Nadu	Chanderi
West Bengal	Sambalpuri

Answers on page 320

SKILL 19
TEACH YOURSELF BASIC 3-D DRAWING

Well, you are saying, that's a sudden shift of gears! What in heck does learning to draw 3-D figures have to do with being a handicrafter? Isn't that more art than craft? Umm, not really. Whether you are making a drawing of a box or a table or a room or a designing a suspension bridge, 3-D drawing is a life skill that everyone should have, a natural consequence of living in a 3-D world.

How to 'see' a 3-D object while looking at its 2-D views.
What do you think the 3-D version of these views look like?

(1) (a) Top view

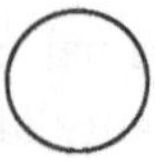

(b) Front view

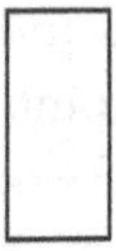

(c) Side view

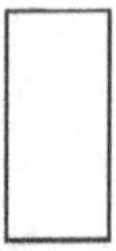

(2) (a) Top view

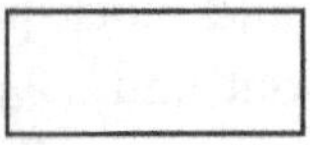

(b) Front view

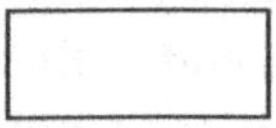

(c) Side view

(3) (a) Top view

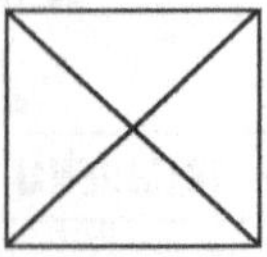

(b) Front view

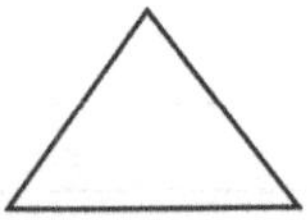

(c) Side view

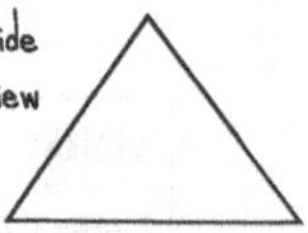

(4) (a) Top view

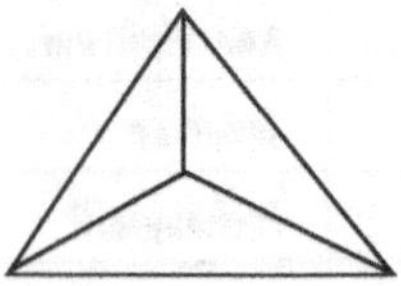

(b) Front view

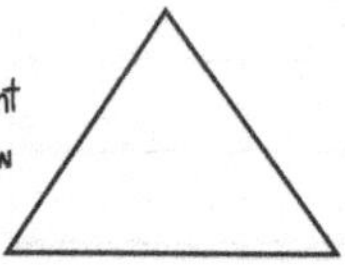

(c) Side view

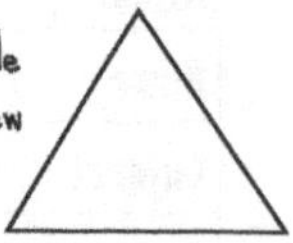

(5) (a) Top view

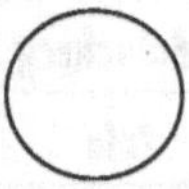

(b) Front view

(c) Side view

(6) (a) Top view

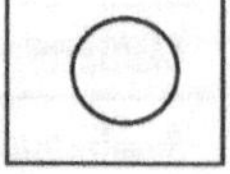

(b) Front view

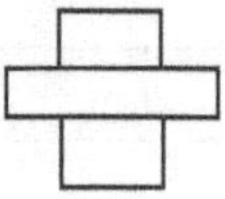

(7) (a) Top view

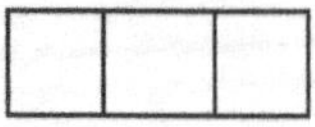

(b) Front view

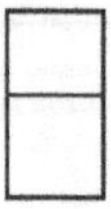

(c) Side view

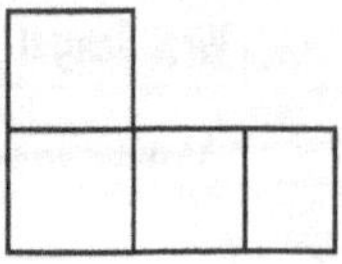

(8) What do you think these everyday objects may be?

(a) Front views

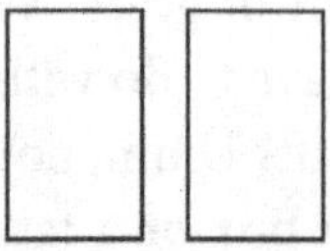

(b) Top views

Answers on page 320

If you ever hope to be an engineer, or an architect, or a designer (of anything, including computer games), or a chef (notice how the contestants in *Masterchef Australia* always make a drawing of the final plating before they begin to cook?), you need working knowledge of perspective drawing (another name for 3-D drawing). Even if you never want to be any of these things, you need these skills simply to help someone else 'see' something that *you* can see perfectly well in your head – topographical maps of fantasy worlds, a cool solar-powered vehicle, an enclosure for your pet rat/snake (you have to be able to sketch it out for the carpenter who is going to build it, duh!). More immediately, it will even help you understand the 'vertical/horizontal/diagonal cross-section of stem' diagrams in your bio textbook better!

How do you learn to draw in 3-D? The best way is to ask someone who is good at it to teach you. Or look for books that teach perspective drawing, or online videos that do the same thing. Once you know some basic rules, begin practising – first copy other people's drawings or photographs to understand some techniques, and then progress to drawing objects from life.

There's another useful trick you can learn – showing a 3-D object as two separate 2-D images, including front views and top views (this is what architects do when they design houses – they show clients two drawings – one of the *elevation* of the building (aka a front view, sometimes in 3-D) and one of the *plan* of the house (a top view, always 2-D). This technique helps the viewer imagine the entire object from all angles.

SKILL 20
MAKE SOMETHING THAT SOMEONE WILL WANT TO BUY

If you go by a very technical definition, making something, anything, with your hands, that is either useful, decorative, or both, qualifies as a handicraft. But what qualifies as decorative? And what qualifies as useful?

Imagine that you were someone looking for exactly the thing you've crafted – a fired clay pot to hold knick-knacks, a greeting card for any occasion, a jasmine-scented candle, painted diyas around Diwali time, whatever. Now ask yourself what you would look for in something that you are looking to buy. The Squad thinks any saleable handicraft should satisfy all, or at least two (No. 1 is mandatory) of the following conditions.

1. **It should look professional** – that means, no hanging threads, no sequins and other bits coming unglued, no patchy painting, no jagged edges, no oily finger-marks, and so on.
2. **It should be genuinely attractive** – Individual tastes vary, of course, and even if it doesn't appeal to the particular taste of a customer, he or she should go away feeling it is nicely crafted.
3. **It should be genuinely useful** – If what you have crafted is meant to be something useful, then it must fulfil that purpose. For instance, gift bags that are too flimsy, shallow or wide are going to be of no use to anyone.

Here's the kicker though – *you don't actually have to sell your piece at all!* Keeping a buyer – and the Squad's conditions – in mind whenever you make something is a kind of mental trick – doing it will simply ensure that whatever you build or craft will be done with great attention to detail, workmanship and finish, be attractive and useful, and give you a deep sense of accomplishment when you're done.

THE HANDICRAFTER'S CHALLENGES

#17
THE INDIAN-HANDICRAFT CHALLENGE

Along with your Squad Leader, make a visit to a village or factory where a handicraft originating from your state is made. If that isn't possible, visit a crafts fair in your city where artisans are doing displays and demonstrations of their craft. Wherever you visit, talk to the artisans and find out about their lives and their craft – Can they make a living from it? Have they taught their children or other young people the craft? How long does it take them to make one complete product? What are the raw materials they use? Take pictures and videos and post them along with your interview on a Squad blog. Share with friends and family.

#18
THE INDIAN-TEXTILE CHALLENGE

If your city has a hand-weaving centre or is located close to a weavers' village, take a trip there to see how rugs and sarees and dhotis are actually woven. If not, ask your parents and grandparents to show you sarees and shawls of different weaves, from different regions of India, that they have in their cupboards. Pick your favourite one and find out as much as you can about the uniqueness and special attributes of that particular weave. Have an Indian textile show-and-tell day where you (and everyone else) introduce the intricacies of the weave to the rest of the Squad.

#19
THE PERSPECTIVE-DRAWING CHALLENGE

Make a perspective drawing of your study desk, your bed or any other object in your room. If you are not able to do it from real life, take a picture of it and then copy it. Also make the two 2-D drawings – front view and top view – of the same object. Share it with your Squad and your Squad Leader.

#20
THE MAKE-TO-SELL CHALLENGE

Make or build something decorative and/or useful with your hands. Take the trouble to ensure that it is well-finished, clean and as close to professional-quality as possible. Show it to five different people and ask them to tell you, honestly, if they think it is of that kind of quality. If at least three people say yes, chances are that you have won this challenge. But your Squad Leader has the final, deciding vote!

WOCOTEEN MERIT BADGE 6

THE ENTREPRENEUR

The fellow who begins making money as a boy will go on making it as a man... If you begin and if you go on, remember, you are pretty certain to succeed in the end – especially if you get your money by hard work.

– **Camp Fire Yarn No. 22, *Scouting for Boys***

Rule set in stone: Every World Conquering Teenager needs to know how to earn his or her own livelihood and not just through working for someone else. And that's why this WoCoTeen Merit Badge is so important – if you spend some time acquiring the skills and smarts to be an entrepreneur – someone who can think up an idea for a business*, find the money to get it started, execute the business idea, and eventually earn a profit from it – you will always land on your feet! What a wonderful place to be, right?

There is a reason so many people choose *not* to become entrepreneurs, though. They may be terrified that their business idea will fail, that they will not be able to find the money they need to begin, or that the risk is too high. One great way of overcoming these stumbling blocks is to have experimented with being an entrepreneur when you still live with your parents (like now). By the time you are all grown up, you will have gained yourself tonnes of learning about entrepreneurship in general, which will give you the confidence to try it again. Those seem like pretty good reasons to go all out to win this badge, don't you think?

SKILL 21
FIND A BUSINESS IDEA

This is probably the toughest part – finding the right idea for your business. Primarily, is it a *product* – self-tying shoelaces,

** Of course, you will not be entering into any formal business contract until you are legally an adult, or find an adult partner to go into business with.*

Sometimes, an idea is really all it takes!

a voice-activated recipe reader an automatic garbage-segregator – you want to sell? Or is it a *service* – performing magic shows at children's birthday parties, overnight dog-sitting for pets whose owners want to go away for a weekend, being a social media consultant to older people who run businesses from their homes and don't know how to spread the word about their products online – that you are offering?

Here are a few tips for coming up with the right business idea.

1. Who needs What because Why. Never mind that it sounds ungrammatical, this is what entrepreneurs call a problem statement – if you can fill in the who, what and why after you've thought of your idea, chances are that it is a good business idea. For instance, in our recipe reader idea, the problem statement would read – Everyone who is cooking a dish according to a recipe (who) needs a voice-activated recipe reader (what) because it is too much of a hassle to constantly switch between cooking and reading a recipe, and it could end up with the dish being ruined, or the recipe book/device on which the recipe is displayed being ruined, or both (why).

2. Don't start with an idea, start with a problem. The classic entrepreneur mistake is to start with, 'Hey! I have this great idea for a product!' The thing is, you may love your idea, but the point of a business is to create something that *other* people love. The correct way to do it, therefore, is to find an existing problem – 'when people who own pets want to get away for even a weekend, they have to drive for an hour across town simply to drop off their pets because there is no pet-sitting service in my neighbourhood' – and then create a business around a service – 'Weekend pet-sitting in your own home!' – that solves that problem. If it is a problem that bugs you personally – perhaps you are a pet owner too – you are likely to find a better solution to it than anyone else, because you understand what's needed.

3. Talk to people. You may think you have found a problem to solve, but other people may not think of the problem as a problem at all. For instance, pet owners in your neighbourhood may have figured out other convenient arrangements for pet-care when they are out of town – maybe the household help doubles as a pet-sitter, or maybe a relative comes over to stay when they are not around, combining both dog-sitting and house-sitting in one. In that case, the service you are offering will have no takers at all. Talking to people – what is officially called 'Doing a market survey' – can help avoid such basic goof-ups. You can even create a written questionnaire that you can hand out or e-mail to friends and relatives.

A good place to catch people for surveys is at supermarkets. If you are thinking of starting a cookie business, for example, hang out outside your local supermarket, and ask people what kind of cookie they wish was available in stores.

4. **SCAMPER!** Your business idea need not be for an entirely new product or service. Instead, look at the gaps in existing products (the gap in our recipe-reader example was 'ease of cooking to a written recipe') or services (the gap in our pet-sitting example was 'lack of pet-sitting services in my neighbourhood') and fill them. SCAMPER is an innovative idea-generation technique, which believes that everything new is some kind of modification of something already in existence. The acronym SCAMPER stands for:

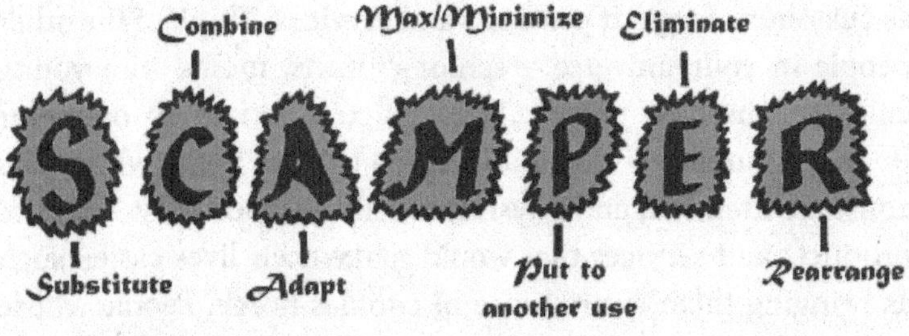

- **S - Substitute** – If you were thinking of running a cookie business, you could differentiate your cookies by substituting flour with healthier atta or millets.
- **C – Combine** – Since you are good at baking, sell brookies (a combination of a brownie and a cookie) instead of plain cookies. That's an innovation that's bound to be popular!
- **A – Adapt** – Since people like to dip cookies in their milk or their tea, and cookies are often the wrong size to fit into a narrow-mouthed glass, make your cookies narrow and long. The unique shape will help differentiate your cookies, as well as win you some serious chai-dipper fans.
- **M – Maximize or minimize** – Maximize what is most popular with your market and minimize what isn't. If you know that chocolate is a popular flavour among cookie-buyers, make more chocolate flavoured ones – choco-chip, choco-cream, choco-dipped.
- **P – Put to another use** – Why not shape your cookies into spoons, so they can do double-duty as stirrers and cookies?
- **E – Eliminate** – If your market survey shows that most young children don't like nuts in their cookies, or shows that many children are allergic to nuts, eliminate nuts from your cookies.
- **R – Rearrange** – McDonald's, when it was founded, 'rearranged the restaurant' by getting customers to pay first and eat later (even today, most other restaurants have it the other way round). You can rearrange the cookie business by maybe taking samples of your different flavours around the neighbourhood, and having customers taste the samples before they decide what to order, instead of selling cookies in sealed packages.

5. Cater to the margins. Don't think only of people like yourself as customers for your products and services. Think of the other people in your universe – senior citizens, moms with young children, disabled people. What is common to all of them? Reduced mobility – due to old age, a baby at home who needs constant attention, and physical inability respectively. Think of products and services that would make their lives easier, such as bringing them their choice of cookies home. People whose needs are routinely ignored by most businesses are more likely to respond eagerly to any business that addresses those needs.

SKILL 22
MANAGE YOUR RISK – BEGIN WITH A SMALL FINANCIAL INVESTMENT

A business idea built around a *product* usually requires some initial financial investment – you need to put in some money for raw materials (flour, eggs, and butter if it is a cookie business, beads and string and clasps if it is a jewellery-making business, paints and brushes and T-shirts if it is a custom T-shirt painting business) before you can make the product.

Business ideas built around *services* (running errands, pet-sitting, computer tutoring, conducting holiday camps for younger kids using your skills – music, dance, theatre, sport), on the other hand, will need little or no money to begin, because all you will need to spend on is getting the word about your service out (if you advertise only via Whatsapp or other social media, you will need zero money, but if you want to distribute flyers door to door or put up posters on apartment and community centre bulletin boards, you will need a small amount).

Whichever business you pick, though, make sure it doesn't require a major investment, at least to begin with. Keep your risks low until you've been through the whole business cycle at least once. (A 'business cycle' starts with ideation [coming up with the idea], goes through production [making the product], and marketing [letting people know about your product], and ends with sales [actually getting someone other than your parents or grandparents or best friend to pay for your product or service]). Remember that unanticipated problems in any of these stages – maybe it takes very long to make your product and you simply cannot spare that kind of time, maybe nobody wants to use your service, maybe you just don't know how to sell your product – could stymie your business temporarily, or worse.

Finishing the business cycle will establish what entrepreneurs call 'proof of concept' – validation that your business idea works on every level and has a reason to exist. It will also help you learn a lot of valuable lessons from first-time mistakes that you will (definitely) make.

The thing is, it isn't big money that makes a successful business – it is thought, time, effort, skills and commitment. Until you know that you can commit to the business, don't throw (too much) money at it.

SKILL 23
UNDERSTAND HOW TO PRICE YOUR PRODUCT

What are the different elements you should you take into consideration when you are trying to decide the price of a product? Is it the producer (you) who decides what is the 'right' price of a product, or the consumer? These are difficult questions, and there is no real formula to crack them. But here are some pointers to help you with the process, anyway.

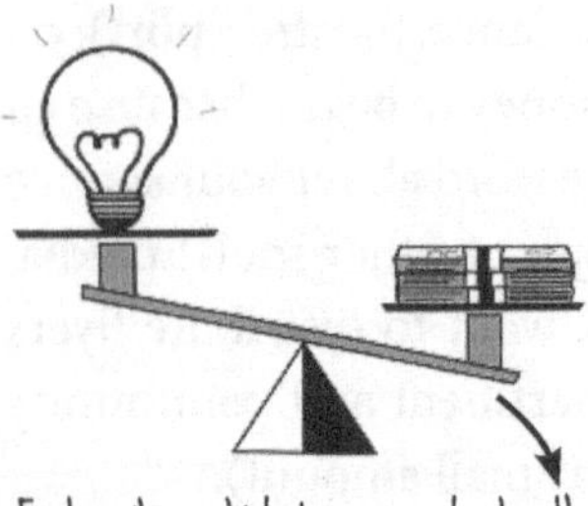

Finding the right balance can be hard!

First question first. What are the things you should consider while pricing your product? Here are the four main ones.

1. **The cost of the materials that went into producing it** – this includes not just flour, butter and sugar if we're talking cookies, but also the electricity you used up while baking them and the cost of the oven you used (in a cookie factory, you would use ovens over and over again for several years and maybe bake 1,00,000 cookies in them before you change them, so you would divide the cost of the ovens by 1,00,000 and add that small amount to the price of each cookie). It would also include the rent for the space in which you baked them (sure, in your case, your parents gave you their kitchen to bake in, but technically, that cost also has to be included).

The skill charge is what makes some artists' work more expensive than other artists'.

2. **The labour that went into producing it** – That essentially includes your time and effort, and the salaries of anyone who helps you produce it. Obviously, the labour cost of something that took you 10 minutes to produce will be lower than the labour cost of something that took you half an hour to produce. It also includes your skills – for instance, very few people can do good caricature portraits of people, but most people can fetch groceries. That's why the former is called a skilled job, while the latter is an unskilled one. If you have employed unusual skills in producing your product, tack an additional 'skill charge' on to the price.
3. **How rare or common your product is** – If there are three stalls selling lemonade at your community's Diwali mela and yours is one of them, you can't really price your product very high. But if you are the only one selling water in a desert, you can charge a high price and people will still line up to buy it.
4. **The cost of the marketing and distribution of your product** – This includes whatever you spend on advertising your product, and transporting it to its point-of-sale (the place people can actually buy it from – a store, a kiosk at a mela).

On to the second question: who decides what is the 'right' price for a product?

If you think about it, costs 1 and 4 above are fixed costs that everyone understands. If your raw materials and your marketing and distribution cost you ₹100 in all, no one can argue with that – that's what it cost. The point of contention is really point no. 2 – you and your customer can have very different opinions on what your skills and time and labour are worth in terms of money, and much of that opinion (on your customer's part) will depend on point no. 3. You may think your cupcakes are brilliant and add a big 'skill charge' towards your superior baking skills, but your customer may plump for the cupcakes at the little bakery at the end of the street instead because she thinks they taste just as good at half the price. When that happens, you realize that you have overpriced your product, and drop its price without changing its quality. If more people start buying your product now, you know you have reached the 'right' price.

The other situation is when you sell out your product without even trying too much. That kind of customer behaviour sends you a strong message – your product is popular, for one of two reasons – because it is very good and people are willing to pay its price, or because it is 'not bad' but priced cheaper than similar products in the market. To figure out which reason it is, you raise your price a little. If people continue to buy your product, great – you are getting closer to the 'right' price.

This is what economists are talking about when they say that 'the *market* decides the right price of a product'. The market makes this decision, based on a famous law in economics called 'The Law of Supply and Demand'. In short, according to this law, there are four players involved in deciding the price of something.

- **The supply of a product:** how many cupcakes you can make.
- **The demand for a product:** how many cupcakes people want to buy.
- **The quantity of the product in the market:** how many cupcakes are available – *in all* – for people in your neighbourhood to buy – yours, your neighbour aunty's, at the bakery at the end of the street. In other words, how much competition you have; and

- **The 'perceived value' of the product:** how much a customer is willing to pay for a cupcake. Customers have to decide on what things they want to spend their limited money, and if cupcakes are priced more than what they think cupcakes are worth, they will buy biscuits instead.

SKILL 24
LEARN TO SELL YOUR PRODUCT

Don't make the mistake of assuming that just because you have a great product, people will buy it without any more effort from your side. Unfortunately, customers have limited money and limitless options on where and how to spend it. If you want your product to be one of the things they spend their money on, you must make very sure that you know how to sell it.

1. **Know your product.** You must know every aspect of your product – what it is, why it is better than others like it, what specific needs of the customer it can fulfil. That way, you will be able to answer any questions customers ask about it.
2. **Broadcast your advantage loud and clear.** Make sure your customers know the benefits they will get from choosing your product over other similar ones. Don't be shy!
3. **Know your customer.** You have already figured out who your customers are when you were doing your market surveys and coming up with a business idea. Now do your homework to understand their needs and concerns really, really well, and then address those concerns when you are trying to sell them your product. Let's say your business idea is fetching groceries and medicines for senior citizens. Your offer to fetch their groceries may offend them, because they want to feel they are perfectly capable of doing it themselves. How would you sell them your service in a sensitive way? → *You can only come up with good ideas for this if you have taken the trouble to understand your customer first.*
4. **Fit into your customer's routine.** Make sure the customer has to do very little work to buy your product. Take cupcake samples door to door and note down orders right away, so that they don't have to leave their homes at all and even get a treat in the bargain (everyone loves free samples!). Deliver the product to their doorstep after checking with them what time of day suits them best. Offer them the option of payment

on delivery (most people like to have the product in hand before they pay for it). Remember, the customer is king and queen!

SKILL 25
DON'T BE AFRAID TO GO BACK TO 'START'

Successful entrepreneurs did not get there by magic, although there are so many 'invisible' things in their success story that you could be forgiven for thinking that. The visible things are, of course, the money, the fame, the glamour and the great business idea; the invisible things are the blood, sweat, toil and – the most important one – the tears that came with the many failures along their long and winding road to ultimate success.

What made these entrepreneurs successful was their ability to see when an idea was not worth pursuing any more (and this only after they had spent hundreds of hours toiling over it), drop it without too much regret (because they were sure they had given it their very best shot), pick themselves off the floor, and go back to the drawing board, to come up with the next 'Big (or Improved) Idea'.

Do all the work it takes to make your product successful, but don't get too attached to it. The good part about failure is that you can learn a lot from it. So embrace it, and head for your next entrepreneurial adventure with a song in your heart and a spring in your stride. All the best!

THE ENTREPRENEUR'S CHALLENGES

This is basically going to be one mega-challenge, where you come up with a business idea and take it through the entire business cycle, but there are mini-challenges under each head.

#21
THE BUSINESS-IDEA CHALLENGE

Individually or in pairs or threes, come up with a business idea that you think can work. Remember that the best entrepreneurial ideas are ones that solve an existing problem, so find a real-world problem to solve. You will have to take this idea through to completion, so pick something that you can execute and test out. Make sure you do a proper market survey before you begin. Once your Squad Leader approves the idea, you can get on to the next stage.

#22
THE STAY-THRIFTY CHALLENGE

One condition that your business idea must take into consideration is this: No one on the team is allowed to put in more than ₹250 as an initial investment for raw materials. You may need an investment if you are making a product, but remember that if you are offering a service, you may not need an investment at all. To raise the money, pitch your business idea to your investors (parents and grandparents, most

likely) like real entrepreneurs do on the TV show 'Shark Tank' (haven't seen it? It is a good show to watch with your Squad before you plunge into the Entrepreneur Challenge). Tell them why they should back your business, and what percentage of the profits they will get as a 'return on investment' once your business starts making money. Make sure you keep very detailed accounts of how you spend your money – your investors can demand to see the 'books' whenever they wish.

#23
THE PRICE-IS-RIGHT CHALLENGE

With your team, using all the tips and pointers under Skill 23, come up with what you think is the right price for your product. On market day, if you find that people are reluctant to pay what you are charging, you can announce a 'price-drop' and see what happens.

#24
THE SALESMAN CHALLENGE

Start selling your product or service! If you have invested money, the challenge is to double the investment. If you have invested ₹250, say, on raw materials and advertising and whatnot, you should make ₹500 by selling your product, to win this challenge.

If you have invested no money, you should still make ₹500 in sales to win this challenge.

#25
THE BEGIN-AGAIN CHALLENGE

If you failed the Entrepreneur challenge, i.e., your business plan faltered at some stage of the cycle – go back and start again from scratch, until you come up with a business idea that earns your team at least ₹500 in sales. Go for it!

THE FAMILY AND HOME COVENANT

I BELIEVE IN BEING SELF-RELIANT

The Housekeeper

The Cook

The Farmer

The Handyman

The Caregiver

The Money Manager

THE FAMILY AND HOME COVENANT

I BELIEVE IN BEING SELF-RELIANT

6

MERIT BADGES TO BE WON

The Housekeeper

The Cook

The Farmer

The Handyman

The Caregiver

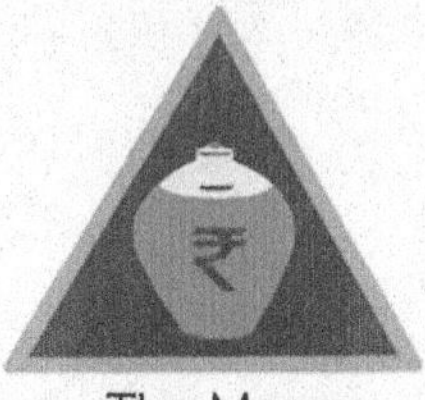

The Money Manager

THE TRUTH IS THAT MEN BROUGHT UP IN A CIVILIZED COUNTRY HAVE NO TRAINING WHATEVER IN LOOKING AFTER THEMSELVES OUT ON THE VELDT OR PLAINS, OR IN THE BACKWOODS. BUT (A SCOUT WHO KNOWS THE GAME) KNOWS HOW TO MAKE HIMSELF COMFORTABLE IN A THOUSAND SMALL WAYS. EVEN IN THE CITY, HE CAN DO VERY MUCH MORE FOR HIMSELF THAN THE ORDINARY MORTAL, WHO HAS NEVER LEARNED TO PROVIDE FOR HIS OWN WANTS.

– B-P, in Camp Fire Yarn No. 5, *Scouting for Boys*

One hundred years ago, a revolution that would shake the foundations of the British Empire was being quietly birthed by an Indian barrister and political and social activist called Mohandas Karamchand Gandhi on a quiet stretch of the Sabarmati river in Ahmedabad. It was from the Sabarmati Ashram here – founded in June 1917 – that Gandhi launched several revolutions, including the landmark march to Dandi 13 years later. The purpose of the march, which was mainly to break an unfair British law, ended up drawing the world's attention to India's unique, non-violent struggle, and galvanizing Indians across the country to participate wholeheartedly in the freedom movement.

Sabarmati Ashram – the unassuming structure that was the birthplace of revolutions!

So yes, the Sabarmati Ashram had a lot to do with winning freedom for India, but that was not all it was about. The Ashram was in fact a social experiment, a place where Indians of all religions, castes, colours and genders came together to live as equals. There were no 'servants' or hired help of any kind on the Ashram – every resident was expected to do his own work, apart from pitching in to do community work like cooking, cleaning, farming, tending to the Ashram animals, and taking care of those who needed it – old people, ill people, disabled people, children. If the experiment worked in the Ashram, believed Gandhiji, it could be replicated across India, breaking barriers of caste and religion. And how wonderful that would be!

The cornerstone of Gandhi's Ashram, just like that of his life, was self-reliance, a quality that he felt was sorely lacking in Indians. The saddest part? A hundred years later, we still don't have it. Our country itself has become self-sufficient on so many fronts, but the average privileged Indian still expects other people to do his work – clean his home, cook his food, iron his clothes, drive his car, clean the streets that he litters, water his plants, fix his flat tyre...

What happens when others do so much of your work, a lot of which you can easily do yourself? You lose your sense of independence and control, not to mention self-esteem, since you are always leaning on other people. You lose your confidence to handle unexpected situations (to know the truth of that, you just have to look at how adults react when the maid or the cook doesn't turn up!). Worst of all, you begin to believe that people who serve you are somehow 'below' you in the hierarchy that you have constructed in your head, and that they don't therefore deserve the same privileges that you do. In short, not being able to do your own work turns you into the complete *opposite* of a WoCoTeen!

And we can't have that, can we? Let's go clean a toilet then!

WOCOTEEN MERIT BADGE 7

THE HOUSEKEEPER

> *Scouts are always tidy, whether in camp or not, as a matter of habit. If you are not tidy at home, you won't be tidy in camp; and if you're not tidy in camp, you will only be a Tenderfoot and no Scout.*
>
> **– Camp Fire Yarn No. 9, *Scouting for Boys***

The challenges involved in winning this badge – making your bed, cleaning your toilet, washing your undies, and, whether you are a boy or a girl, learning to pretty up a room – will gladden any mom's heart, so you might as well do them happily.

Actually, to make things easier, fairer, and more fun while you're trying to win this badge, get everyone at home to participate. All family members can take weekly turns at, say, laying the dinner table, washing up after dinner, making the beds – *all* the beds – each morning, and cleaning the toilet bowls and washbasins. Besides this, of course, you keep your own rooms tidy.

There's a catch, though. All this cleaning and tidying has to be done to a particular standard that *all* of you agree on before you start. What that means is that if you don't remember whose turn it was to do the dishes after dinner, you should not be able to tell who did them. *Everyone* should be washing dishes the same way, leaving the dishes – and the dishwashing area – just as dry and tidy as anyone else.

Hey, don't look so defeated already. No one said keeping house was easy!

Your room isn't the only place that looks nicer when it's clean!

PS: You may want to go give your mom or your dad or your help – whoever works hardest at keeping the house clean and tidy – a big hug before you read any further.

SKILL 26
MAKE YOUR BED – AND PERFECTLY!

Sure, making a bed isn't rocket science, but there is a world of difference between a perfectly-made bed and a casually-made one. It's the difference between a bed that looks inviting, cool and crisp, and one that looks slept-in and, well, not so inviting at all. Make it a habit to make your bed as soon as you have brushed your teeth – it will wake you up in the morning and it will make you happy to come back to it in the evening.

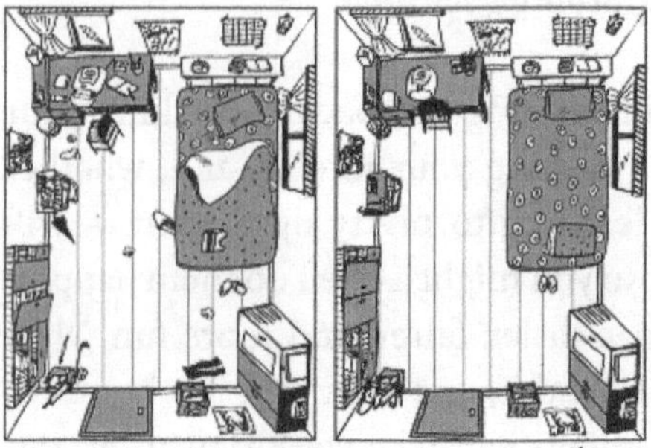

Small changes, big difference!

Here is the Bed-Making 101, in a few easy steps.

- Take everything off the bed – pillows, cushions, books, phone, crumpled clothes, the dog, and all the sheets except the one covering the mattress. If you want it to be perfect, take that one off too.
- Shake out the mattress sheet vigorously so that the wrinkles smooth out and food crumbs and hair and random other yuckies fall out. Then throw it over the bed with a flourish, like a fisherman casting his net into the sea. This will take some skill and practice.
- Smooth the sheet out on the bed, taking out wrinkles and creases as far as possible, and making sure you have enough overhang on all sides to tuck in under the mattress. Standing at the foot of the bed, tuck the sheet in neatly along the bottom edge. You may have to lift the mattress a little to do this.

■ Now gird your loins and get ready for the most important part – making four perfect 'hospital folds'. (It's tricky, this, but if you are good at origami or gift-wrapping, this should be a breeze). Once you master it (*see illustrations below*), you will have a perfectly-made bed every time!

How to make Hospital Folds: The Illustrated Guide

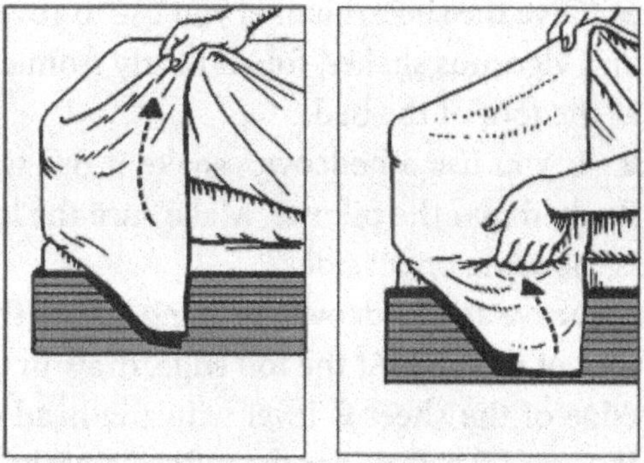

1. After tucking in the sheet at the foot of the bed, grab and lift sheet from the side about 16 inches above the bed.

2. Tuck in triangle-shaped lower drape under mattress.

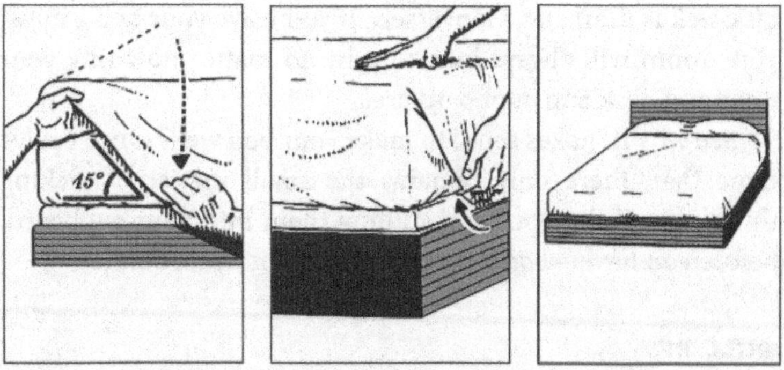

3. Hold the corner in place with one hand and fold the top drape over in a 45° angle. Repeat on the other three corners.

4. Tuck the sheet on both sides and the head of the bed.

5. Add pillows and cover the whole thing with a bedcover. Smoothen the cover – and voila!

■ Once you've tucked in both long sides using hospital folds (don't leave sheet lumps under the mattress), move to the head of the bed and tuck the sheet in there a well. Some more pulling and tucking may be necessary at this stage to make the surface really tight and stretched.

- Whack the pillows on a chair or on the bed itself to get lumps and kinks out, and land a few solid punches to their middle and sides to fluff them up. Put them at the head of your bed, neatly aligned with each other and in a straight line.
- Give the sheet/blanket you use to cover yourself a few quick and vigorous shakes, fold it neatly from edge to edge, and lay it at the foot of the bed.
- If you use a bedcover, shake it out well, and throw it over the bed *and* the pillows. Make sure the length of the overhang is the same on all sides.
- Leave the bedcover to hang down the long sides and the foot of the bed. At the top edge, draw in the overhang until the edge of the sheet is level with the head of the mattress. Tuck the extra fabric under the pillows tightly, making a long 'pillow mound'. Your bed is now made!

Yes, making a bed takes some effort, but because a bed takes up so much space in a room, the effect of just doing this one task well is dramatic. Conversely, if you leave your bed a mess, your room will always look untidy, no matter how tidy your floor and desk and cupboard are!

See why it makes sense to make your bed well? Once you've done that, there only remains the small matter of picking things up off the floor and stuffing them into your cupboard, before you have – *badabing!* – a picture-perfect room.

SKILL 27
WASH YOUR UNDIES BEFORE – YUCK! – SOMEONE ELSE DOES

Do you already wash your undies yourself? That's great! But if you are screwing up your face at the prospect of learning how to do it now, think about how unpleasant it must be for someone *else* to wash your dirty undergarments for you! Or wait, think about how you would feel if it was part of your job to wash your sibling's undergarments (here's a barf bag, just in case). Yeah, that's why the Squad considers this a mandatory skill for a WoCoTeen.

The best part is, it's easy! Here are some tips to do it right, (and quick) every time.

- The best time to wash your undies is right after your shower. Before you begin to shower, chuck them into a small bucket or mug in the bathroom, top with a teaspoon of washing powder, and run a stream of hot water into it so that the detergent foams up nicely. Let the undies soak while you take your shower.
- Once you're done, take your undies out of the water, lay them flat on the floor of the bathroom (or, if you prefer to stand while doing this, in your washbasin). Scrub the garment with a stiff-ish plastic clothes brush, making sure you do both the insides and the outsides and checking periodically to see if you've managed to scrub the grimiest bits clean.
- Throw out the soapy water in your bucket/mug (a mug is better since you will use and waste much less water that way), and fill it with clean water. Rinse your washed and scrubbed undies in it two or three times until all the soapsuds are gone and the water runs clear (you might need to change the water a couple of times for this).
- Wring your undergarments out well, until they are more damp than wet.

That's it! You're all done – and the whole process from start to finish hasn't taken more than three minutes! Remember to hang them up to dry before you head out for school.

Of course this won't work if you are the sort of person that wakes up late, rushes through leftover homework and has to zip madly through your morning activities just to be able to make it to school on time. For you, what might work better is to pile up your used undergarments

from Monday through Saturday, and wash them all together in a leisurely fashion on Sunday morning. If you choose to do this, though, make sure you use more detergent, and let the garments soak for a little longer than five minutes in hot soapy water before you wash them.

SKILL 28
CLEAN YOUR TOILET UNTIL IT GLEAMS

Gandhiji insisted that Ashram-ites take turns to clean the community toilets, never mind who had used them beforehand. You don't have to be so sweet – just cleaning the toilet that *you* use is plenty. Here are a few things to remember before we get into the actual cleaning of the toilet:

- Make sure you clean off any spray or dribble on the rim with a paper towel (or a cloth, if that's what you use in your home; if you use a cloth, remember to rinse it clean immediately after) and put the toilet seat back down as a courtesy to the next person using the toilet. If you are a boy, don't forget to lift the toilet seat when you pee, and to put it back down again.
- After you flush, check once to make sure that the water inside is clean. If not, flush again, this time using the smaller flush (which uses less water) if that option exists. For stubborn muck that will not go away, you might need to fill a bucket of water a third of the way and then pour the water into the bowl with some force to send it to kingdom come.

Now to brass tacks. How do you actually clean a toilet? Well, there is the everyday cleaning routine, and there is the once-a-week cleaning routine. For the purpose of the Housekeeper Badge, we are going to focus on the everyday cleaning. The weekly cleaning will involve toilet cleaning products that have harsh chemicals in them and are best left to a grown-up to use.

For your daily cleaning, there are a couple of basic things you will need to have within arm's reach in your bathroom.

Stash them out of plain sight, away from everything else. Here's what you need:

■ A pair of rubber gloves

■ A stiff-bristled toilet brush with its own container to rest in between uses

■ Small scrubbing brush with a long handle

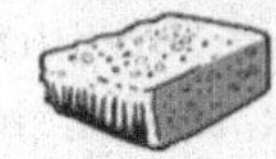

■ A sponge

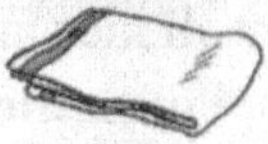

■ A wipe-down cloth

■ Some liquid hand-washing soap

Got your stuff together? Let's begin!

The Daily Cleaning Routine
(Time required: Under three minutes)

■ After ensuring that everything has been flushed away, put on your rubber gloves.

■ Squeeze a little (no more than a few drops) of hand-washing liquid into the water in the bowl.

■ Dip your sponge in hot water, squeeze it out, and run it along and just inside the rim of the bowl, the top and bottom surfaces of the toilet seat, the top and bottom of the toilet lid, and the handle of the flush, which incidentally is the dirtiest, most germ-spreading part of the whole WC. This will help loosen any caked dirt.

WC is short for Water Closet, which is the technical term for the western-style toilet – weird but true.

■ Now grab the toilet brush, dip it vigorously a few times in the water in the bowl to generate a soapsuds from the hand-washing liquid, and scrub-scrub-scrub at the insides of the bowl, paying particular attention to the underside of the rim and the area under water. Keep dipping the brush into the water at intervals to get more of the soapsuds onto it.

■ If there is still some stubborn caked dirt in the bowl or on the rim, scrub with the long-handled brush to loosen it.

■ Flush the toilet again, with your brush deep inside the bowl, so that fresh water can sluice over it.

■ With your wipe-down cloth, give all the areas that you ran your hot sponge over a quick rub-down to make them gleam. Make sure there are no water droplets anywhere and that the seat, the lid, the rim, the top of the flush tank and the handle are all nice and dry.

■ Finish the process off by placing the toilet brush back in its container, and using a cloth to wipe the bathroom floor around the WC, to soak up any water there. Put everything back in place, and wash your hands well with soap. Once or twice a week, rinse out the toilet brush container too.

■ Now step back, give the WC a quick once-over, and take a moment to feel envious of the next person who gets to use your sparkling clean toilet.

SKILL 29
DO THE FLOWERS LIKE A BOSS

So far, we've done all the grunt work that is sadly an important part of housekeeping (and remember you haven't even done the mind-numbing but vital stuff like sweeping or mopping or dusting yet!). But there is a second, equally important layer to housekeeping, and it is about making a clean and tidy place look and smell great. One of the simplest ways to make a place look pretty is to string up some fairy lights, light up a scented candle and yes, get some flowers in.

So, what do you need for 'doing the flowers'?

■ **A good sharp pair of scissors** that can shorten stalks with a quick snip. Don't try to break stalks off with your fingers – it damages the stalk and the flower.

- **A container of some sort** to hold the flowers. Don't get stuck on classic vases. Get creative – use your grandmom's brass vessels, old ceramic or other kettles, watering cans, tall steel *dabbas*, pencil holders – anything that is stable, and can hold water without leaking or rotting.
- **Flowers** (duh!), but they don't have to be expensive ones. A nice-looking bunch of asters or chrysanthemums will cost you less than ₹100 and last for a week. Buy flowers that have still not fully bloomed – they will bloom in the vase and last longer.
- **Ferns and leaves** – Flowers look best when they are arranged 'naturally', i.e., holding their heads up high to grab some sun – and your heart! – from between a sea of green stuff, just as they do in nature. So make sure you have enough of that too. Florists usually throw in green stuff for free if you ask.
- **Other stuff** – Florists use blocks of firm, water-absorbent 'foam' to stick flowers and ferns into, which makes arranging flowers a lot easier, so get a couple of foam blocks if you can. Otherwise, to hold thick flower stems in place, simply drop your collection of pebbles into the vase.

Now, how do you arrange flowers in your container so that they look good and stay fresh for as long as possible?

- **First, snip off the ends of your flowers and leafy twigs,** especially if they've been sitting in water at the florist's, so that you get a dry, fresh end to put into your vase. This gives the flower a new lease of life, and helps it last longer. Always snip the stalk diagonally.
- **Strip off all the leaves at the lower end of your flower and leaf stalks.** Only the stalk should go into the water in your vase, not the leaves. Submerged leaves will just rot in water and stink it up.
- **Decide if you want one kind of flower or several in your arrangement.** Both work. If you are using more than one kind of flower, place all flowers of the same kind in the vase before you start placing any other flowers. This technique is called layering, and it will help you 'build' your arrangement much

better than just alternating flowers of different kinds in your first layer itself. Don't forget to add the green stuff!

■ **Odds and evens:** An odd number of blooms – three, five, seven – looks much more balanced in an arrangement than an even number – two, four or six. Try it and see!

■ **Stop when you feel there's enough going on.** Less is more where flowers are concerned. Just because you have flowers, don't stuff them all into one vase. Use your leftover flowers in a different arrangement, or snip the stalks off close to the flower heads and let them float in a shallow brass bowl to create a lovely Indian-style arrangement.

■ **Change the water every couple of days** or so to keep your flowers fresh. But it, can be a real pain to dismantle the entire arrangement to change the water, especially if everything is still looking good. One cool trick to use is to stick the whole vase under a tap and let the water run into it until it overflows for 10–15 seconds. Voila! You've got the old water out and the fresh water in without disturbing anything!

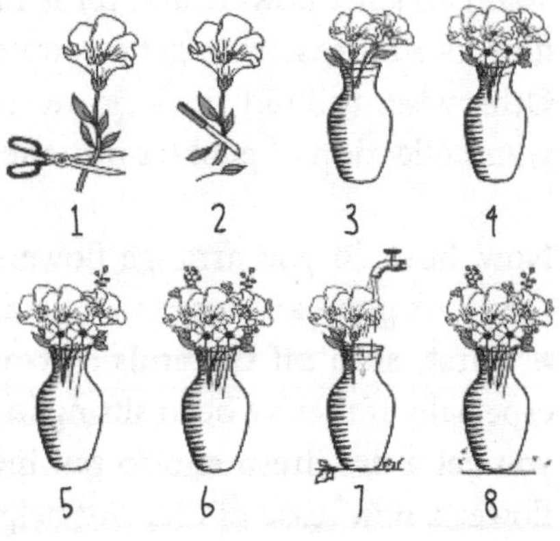

■ **Clean the surface on which you are going to place the flowers** thoroughly. Then stand back and wait for the compliments to pour in!

THE HOUSEKEEPER CHALLENGES

#26
THE MAKE-YOUR-BED CHALLENGE

There are two parts to this challenge – The Demo and The Discipline.

Part 1: The Demo – Let your Squad Leader pick a bed in her own home or one of yours for each of the Squad members to display his bed-making skills. Ideally, the bed should be a single bed that is not against a wall, and that has a mattress that isn't too heavy to lift when you tuck the sheet under (no elasticated sheets allowed!). Each Squad member brings his own set of bed linen – a bed-sheet, a pillowcase, a blanket or covering sheet, and a bedcover. In turn, each Squad member strips the bed of its linen and makes the bed again using his own linen. This will also involve slipping a pillow into a pillowcase – neatly. Then he folds the stripped linen and hands it over to whomever it belongs to.

Your Squad Leader will decide if you have mastered the skill or not. If not, you can take the challenge again another day.

Part 2: The Discipline – Make your own bed at home every morning for six successive days, and get a parent to sign off on a note (or a certificate, like in the illustration), saying you have actually done it. Only when this requirement has *also* been completed will your Squad Leader attest that you have this skill covered.

#27
THE WASH-YOUR-UNDIES CHALLENGE

No one, not even your Squad Leader, really wants to watch you washing your undies, so this challenge involves something related but a little different – hanging clothes out to dry. (However, a parent has to also confirm to your Squad Leader that you have good undie-washing skills, as demo-ed to him at home, before you are deemed to have successfully cracked this challenge).

The Squad will need:

■ A big bucket of freshly-washed laundry (which includes, ideally, a couple of shirts and trousers, a couple of kurtas, a churidar or two, a saree, and a bed-sheet)

■ Clothes pegs, around 30-40

■ Two-three long and empty clotheslines, preferably on a terrace or balcony with enough room for the Squad and Squad Leader to move about

■ A sunny, windy day

The Prep: Watch a parent – or your help – hang up your family's laundry to dry for a few days. See how she shakes out each wrung-out piece of washing vigorously to take out the kinks before she hangs them up, spacing them apart for air to circulate between them, and securing them tightly to the line with pegs.

The Challenge: Each Squad member gets three minutes, within which he or she must hang out as many clothes as possible –

perfectly. To keep it fair, each kind of garment gets a different weightage – hanging out a bed-sheet, for instance, would carry more points than doing the same with a handkerchief. The Squad Leader will decide whether you deserve a badge based both on the number of clothes you've managed to hang up (and the number of points you've thus notched up), and how well the task has been done.

#28
THE CLEAN-THE-TOILET CHALLENGE

Let your Squad Leader pick a toilet – a clean one – that you can demo your toilet-cleaning skills on. This challenge is about checking that you have the necessary skills to do it. One by one, you will go through the entire drill – putting on the gloves, dribbling a few drops of hand-washing liquid into the bowl, hot-sponging off the surfaces, including and particularly the handle, and so on. At the end of it, your Squad Leader will decide whether you are worthy of a sign-off on this challenge, and a lucky someone will have a *very* clean toilet indeed.

#29
THE DO-THE-FLOWERS CHALLENGE

Every Squad member brings his or her own bunch of flowers (costing no more than ₹100), green stuff, a container/vase to hold the arrangement, a sharp pair of scissors, and anything else that he or she needs. The flowers and greens should be in an 'unprepared' state, with all their leaves and thorns still on.

The rules are simple: You have 30 minutes to create the arrangement. Points will be given for overall look, balance of flowers and greens, and creativity (with respect to the container used, the kind of flowers and greens used, and how the words 'floral arrangement' have been interpreted).

P.S. The method of flower arranging indicated under Skill 29 is only meant as a guide – be as creative as you like!

WOCOTEEN MERIT BADGE 8

THE COOK

A Scout must be able to light a fire and make a cook-place with a few bricks or logs; cook the following dishes: Irish stew, vegetables, omelette, rice pudding; make tea, coffee, or cocoa; mix dough and bake bread in an oven; carve properly, and hand plates and dishes correctly to people at table.

– Requirements for Cook Badge, *Scout Tests and How to Pass Them*

Yeah, yeah, yeah, we know. You are already a super-chef, baking moist, yummy cupcakes and whipping up light-as-air mousses. But to be considered worthy of the WoCoTeen Cook Merit Badge, the Squad demands a very different set of skills. You need to know how to competently cook a satisfying Indian everyday vegetarian meal.

Ha! Not so cool anymore, are we?

This is not to diss any other cuisine, mind. This is just in conjunction with one of the cornerstones of Squad thought – if you don't know and respect your own, you will never be able to truly appreciate or respect any other. Plus, Indian cuisine is vast and exciting in taste and texture, nuanced and complex in flavour, beautifully balanced in terms of nutrition, stunningly diverse (for every region has its own sophisticated cuisine), and so popular worldwide – why would you not want to learn to cook it well?

So pull out that pressure cooker and that *chakla-belan*, and hunker down to some serious cooking. Make no mistake, it's going to be difficult, and it's going to take you a while before you begin to get it halfway right. But once you have, you will have acquired a skill that will keep you – and everyone around you – well-fed, healthy, happy and cared-for always. More importantly, whomever you cook for, food helps you build bonds of friendship and love. On to the first skill!

SKILL 30
IDENTIFY AND NAME INDIAN SPICES

What are spices actually? If you think about it, nothing more than a bunch of desiccated and shrunken – and yes, flavourful and aromatic – bits of various parts of plants and trees. So why are we Indians so obsessed with them?

There are many reasons, including the many health benefits of whole spices, ground spices, and an endless variety of complex spice mixes, and the fact that spices have always been easily available, since so many of them grow naturally in our fertile tropical soil. But the predominant reason is, well, that it makes food taste so good! Using spices well is the key to making a great Indian meal, so obviously, the first place to start is to learn to identify them.

Take this quiz first to see how much you know. It isn't just enough to know the name of the spice in your mother tongue or in English, you have to know it in both of them *and* in your State language. You could also learn their Hindi names – they are more commonly used throughout the country. Ready, set, go!

1. *We are tiny, spherical, black seeds used for seasoning many Indian dishes. The leaves of our parent plant are used to make a popular winter dish in Punjab. Fields of my parent plant in full bloom with yellow flowers are popular backdrops for Bollywood songs!*
2. *We are small, brown, spindle-shaped seeds used for seasoning food all over India. We've been around some five thousand years. We are used both in whole and powdered form.*
3. *I am a rhizome, a horizontal underground stem that is boiled and then dried in hot ovens before I am ground and sold as a yellow-orange powder that makes a great natural dye. I am one*

of the cheapest spices, and often used to treat wounds and skin problems like acne.

4. *I am the highly aromatic inner bark of a tree. I am used to flavour both Indian savoury dishes and Western sweet dishes. I am one of the spices that make up the famous Indian 'garam masala'.*

5. *We are flower buds that are picked before we open and then dried on palm mats until we turn rust brown. Oil made from us is good for treating toothaches. We have a strong, pleasant smell, and are used to keep moths away from stored clothes.*

6. *I am the stigma of the crocus flower, and the most expensive spice (and one of the most expensive food items in the world, by weight). My best varieties are grown in India (in the region of Kashmir) and in Spain. I was used by Buddhist monks in India as a dye for their robes, and by Alexander the Great as a bath infusion to heal battle wounds.*

7. *I am a tree resin sold as a hard gum or as powder. I have a very strong, and even unpleasant, smell that goes away with cooking. I am used to flavour curries and dals.*

8. *People in India like to eat us plain or sugarcoated after a meal to kill any bad breath. We are also good for digestion.*

9. *We are light-green, spindle-shaped seed pods that contain highly aromatic black seeds. In powdered form, our seeds are used to add a signature flavour to Indian sweet dishes. We are an important ingredient of masala chai. When you want a quick mouth-freshener, just pop us whole into your mouth and chew!*

10. *We were the Malabar Coast's most famous, and most expensive export – people often referred to us as 'black gold' – to Arabia and Europe during the heyday of the Spice Route. Europeans used us mainly, it is said, to mask the taste and smell of rotting meat. Until the chilli was introduced to India in the 16th century by European explorers who brought them back from the New World of the Americas, we were the guys who added heat to Indian food.*

Answers on page 320

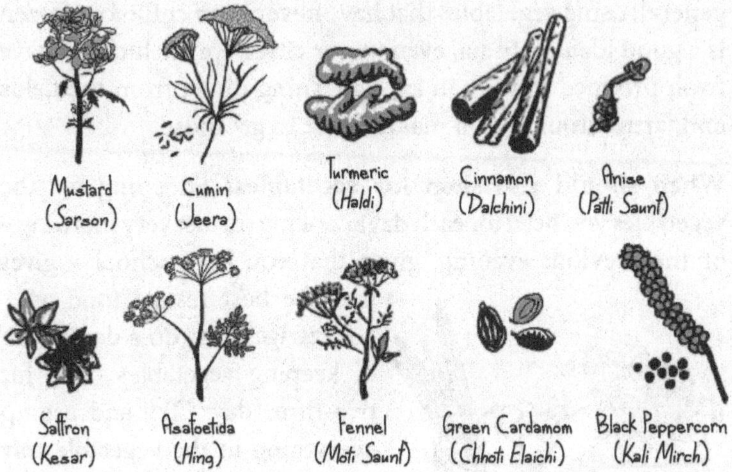

Common Indian spices

Cracked them all? Now learn to identify each by sight, and tell them apart from one another.

Done? Super! Now we can get on to the next skill, learning how to pick vegetables.

SKILL 31
PICK THE BEST VEGETABLES – USING YOUR SENSES

Fresh vegetables are good for you and taste great too. That's why the best chefs personally pick and choose the produce for their restaurant kitchens as far as possible.

There is no real manual to picking good vegetables. There are a few basics to keep in mind, of course, but it is a skill that comes from years of practice in not just picking vegetables, but also growing, cooking and eating them. Still, one must begin somewhere, so here are some tips.

Where should you shop for vegetables? You will need to do a little research in your neighbourhood to see which vendor or which market consistently has the best produce, to crack this one. Your parents or your neighbours can help with this. In general, using vegetables that have never been chilled or frozen is a good idea. In India, even in our cities, we are lucky to have fresh produce coming in each morning direct from the fields and farms around, so it makes sense to get those.

When should you shop for vegetables? Shopping for the vegetables you need for each day's cooking on that very morning – or the previous evening, given that you have school – gives you the best results food-wise, but refrigerators do a decent job of keeping vegetables fresh for two-three days. Try and use up everything in the vegetable tray every three days, so that you need to go shopping just once in the middle of the week. Of course, vegetables like onions and potatoes will keep for much longer, and outside the fridge.

With produce in so many colours, a vegetable basket is nature's work of art!

How do you pick the best vegetables?

- There are different tips to keep in mind for different vegetables, and a few are listed below, but the general rule-of-thumb is to pick plump, shiny, smooth-skinned specimens over bruised, wrinkled or dull ones. Leaves and stalks, whether attached to the vegetable or otherwise, should be a bright green, and dry and firm to the touch. Anything yellow, wilted, or slimy is a no-no. Remember that the best chance to find such specimens is when that particular vegetable is in season in your area, so cook local and seasonal produce as far as possible.
- The less your veggies have travelled to get to you, the better it is for the environment and the smaller the carbon footprint. By buying local, you are doing your bit for the environment.

'Carbon footprint' is the term environmentalists have coined for the amount of carbon dioxide released into the atmosphere as a result of the activities of a person, organization or community.

■ One last thing to keep in mind – picking vegetables is a thoroughly sensory experience – you will need to use sight, hearing (seen how people knock on watermelons and shake coconuts to hear the sound before they buy them?), touch, smell and even taste (people seldom buy grapes or peas without popping a few into their mouths to test for sweetness and tenderness) before you identify the best lot!

Here are a few quick tips for choosing individual vegetables:
■ **Onions:** Pick firm bulbs with papery skin, even colouration all over, and no sprouts. Press the root area to make sure it's firm. Turn each onion over and feel all around gently with your fingers to make sure it isn't soft or rotten anywhere.
■ **Potatoes (and any other tubers):** Should be well-shaped (odd-shaped potatoes are difficult to peel, and indicate that they haven't filled out as they should have), heavy, and have no green patches or sprouting 'eyes'.
■ **Tomatoes**: Bright red tomatoes that are firm to the touch are always good for salad. If you are planning to pulp them and use them in a curry, pick ones that give a little when gently pressed – they will be a little riper and sweeter, and will cook more quickly. Avoid wrinkled or too-green tomatoes.
■ **Green beans:** Choose slender beans, not knobbly ones. Test the bean's freshness by bending one. If it snaps with a crack, it is fresh. If it bends without snapping, not so much. The 'snap test' works for ladies' finger too. Just make sure you don't snap away at too many beans or you will attract the *sabziwallah*'s – and other customers' – wrath.
■ **Carrots:** Pick firm, smooth, well-shaped carrots without rootlets hanging off from here and there.
■ **Greens:** Should be a nice, bright green. They should also smell good and fresh – ah, the joy of sticking your nose into a bunch of fresh mint or coriander leaves and breeeeathing in! – and should not have flowers (in the case of coriander), yellow, wilting leaves, or any sign of insect damage.

SKILL 32
COOK A SIMPLE – BUT SLAP-UP – INDIAN MEAL

Indian meals can be vast, complicated affairs featuring several wonderful dishes, but we are talking here of a basic everyday meal that is wholesome, redolent of India and deeply comforting to both the stomach and the spirit. Whether you are trying to cook up a simple meal as a treat for a parent who's been working too hard or trying to keep homesickness at bay when you are studying abroad, these four 'dishes' will be absolute winners always.

Rice and dal: Guess why these two staples are clubbed under one head? Because they both involve mastery of the rock-star Indian kitchen aid called the pressure cooker. Here's the lowdown on how to cook them. (These are general pointers for rice – you will need an adult to teach you how to use the pressure cooker you have at home.)

- Put a glass or two of water into the pressure cooker, so that it covers the bottom and is at least an inch and a half deep.
- Measure out a cup (or half a cup) of rice into the flat-bottomed vessel in which you are going to cook it. Cover the rice with water. Wash the rice by scrubbing the grains between your fingers until the water turns cloudy. Drain the water off and repeat washing and draining a couple more times until the water runs clear. Now measure out some clean water – between two and three times the amount of rice you have in your vessel – pour it in, and put the vessel inside the pressure cooker.
- Close the lid of the pressure cooker securely and put it on the hob on full heat. Once the water inside has heated up nicely and steam begins to come out of the vent at the top, place the 'whistle', on it, lower the flame a little and wait for the first whistle, that familiar distinctive sound of steam being released that always lets you know there is an Indian kitchen around somewhere. Now reduce the flame further and wait for the cooker to whistle two to three more times.

■ Turn off the gas and let the cooker sit for 15–20 minutes until all the steam has slowly released. Then take the 'whistle' off the vent, open the cooker, and fluff the rice up with a fork.

■ If you were cooking *toor* dal (the most popular pan-Indian dal) instead of rice, you would follow the same procedure. Because rice and *toor* dal take similar amounts of time to cook in a pressure cooker, you can use a tiered 'vessel tower' with rice in one vessel and dal in another to get an entire meal cooked in 20 minutes. You will have to whisk the dal well and season and temper it (with ghee – yum!) before it becomes the soul food that you are craving, but all that's easy-peasy once you've cooked yourself a nice vessel of hot dal.

Chapatti: To make it easier for you, the Squad doesn't insist that you knead the wheat flour into chapatti dough yourself. But it does require you to learn how to roll out a round (or square, or triangular, or amoeba-shaped) chapatti and roast it so that it is edible. Written instructions are a little pointless for chapatti-making – it's best if you watch someone make some, or watch YouTube videos showing it, and then try it out yourself until you get good at it, but here goes, anyway.

■ **Make small rolls of the dough**, one for each chapatti, and set them aside for at least five minutes.

■ **Flour the work surface, the rolling pin and the dough *thoroughly*.** Keep a bowl of dry flour handy to plop your chapatti into as you roll it, and for you to dip into whenever you need to add more flour to the work surface.

■ **Start by flattening the ball with your palm.** This helps get the initial shape right.

■ Now **start rolling your chapatti**, trying to ensure that its thickness is the same everywhere. If you have areas that are too thick, they will not cook in the same time as the thin areas, and cooking for longer will just end up burning the thinner areas.

■ **Rotate the dough frequently** as you roll.

■ **Keep flouring & flipping** the chapatti as you flatten it, so it doesn't stick to the work surface or rolling pin.

■ If you are like most beginners, your chapatti will still look like Australia at the end of it. **To make it look perfect,** use the oldest hack in the book – with a rimmed plate or a bowl, press out a circle and roast that up instead of your original one!

■ Ask an adult who knows **how to roast a chapatti** to show you how to do it. And there you are!

A side of veggies: To keep it really simple, the Squad suggests that you learn to make a simple potato sabzi that is popular in your region. Ask an adult to show you how.

One reason that potatoes are great vegetables to cook with, apart from the fact that everyone loves them, is that they are easy to 'prepare'. All you need to do is to wash them thoroughly, scrubbing to remove soil – and that's it!

Then, for the simplest kind of sabzi, halve them, still with their peels on, and pop them into the – what else – pressure cooker, until they cook through. Once they cool, take the peel off with your fingers and chop them into even-sized cubes and toss them through some hot oil into which you've previously thrown in some cumin seeds, turmeric, coriander seed powder and red chilli powder. Season with salt, garnish with chopped coriander, and you're done!

A cup of chai: To many Indians, chai is a food group all by itself. And unlike coffee, which is simpler to prepare, chai involves brewing tea leaves in a mixture of boiling water and/or milk, for just the right amount of time. You can also get endlessly inventive with chai – flavouring it with pepper, mint, lemongrass, cardamom or ginger, adding lots of milk and boiling it until a spoon can stand up straight in it

(*kadak* chai); or leaving the milk out in favour of a squeeze of lemon and a pinch of salt (the Bengali *lebu cha*); or infusing it with cinnamon, green cardamom and a touch of saffron before adding powdered or slivered almonds (the Kashmiri *kahwa*).

Why you need to learn to make it is because a cup of well-made chai is the perfect thing to serve at any time of day to guests, or to a tired parent or grandparent. It is also a wonderfully refreshing drink, and with only a third of the caffeine that a similar amount of coffee contains, much healthier too.

Go on then, experiment, innovate, have fun, until you learn to brew up that perfect cuppa!

SKILL 33
CLEAN UP THE KITCHEN

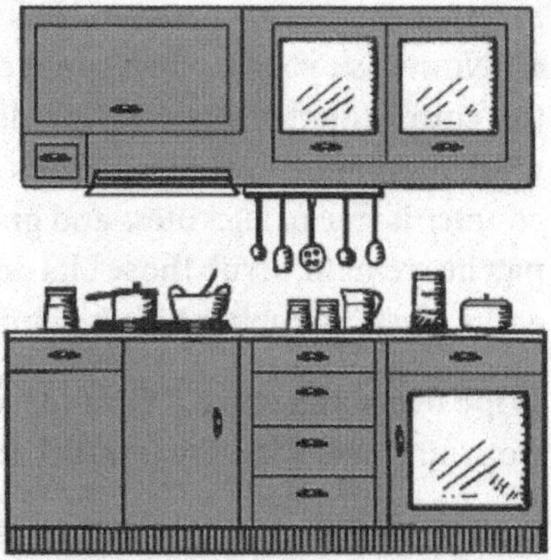

Yup, this skill is just as important as the other three required to win you the Cook Badge. As a bonus, it also earns you your parents' everlasting gratitude.

So what does cleaning up a kitchen after cooking up a meal involve? Here's a quick checklist.

Clear the work surface – This involves several steps, including:

- Collect vegetable peels and other organic debris and put them into the wet waste bin.
- Move empty plastic and paper packaging, if any, into the dry waste bin. (Don't segregate your garbage? Don't have separate bins for dry and wet waste? Start now!)
- Put the used utensils into the sink, but only after scraping off any leftover food into the wet waste bin. Make sure you stack utensils up in the sink so that you use the space efficiently. Run

some water over it all so that the food doesn't dry up on the utensils, making them difficult to clean.

- Screw lids back on all the bottles you used and put them back in their places. Close open *dabbas* and cover open vessels and put them into the pantry or the fridge as required. Give both *dabbas* and bottles a quick wipe and make sure they are all clean on the outside, i.e., don't have food, oil, or other kitchen debris sticking to them.
- Put unused vegetables and greens back into the vegetable tray inside the fridge.

Clean the work surface – Now comes the fun part!

- First dust all the dry debris – crumbs, flour, vegetable bits – off the surface and into a dust pan. For oil or egg or milk spills (that can mess up and/or stink up your wiping cloth), use newspaper or tissue paper to soak the spill up first.
- Now wash your kitchen sponge/cloth, wring it dry and give the entire counter a good wipe-down. Repeat one more time until the counter gleams. Check with your fingers that the counter is free of stickiness and grit and caked-on dirt. If some patches remain, scrub those bits down with dishwashing liquid and a plastic scrubber before wiping down again.

Wipe down the stove – Give the stove a once-over with a wet cloth, and also wipe the levers that turn the hob on and off.

Sweep the floor – With a broom, sweep all the crumbs off the kitchen floor and into a dustpan, and dump them into the bin.

And then, and only then, are you done.

THE COOK'S CHALLENGES

This is an Integrated Challenge. All four challenges are done by the Squad as a group, and completed on the same day. The idea is to practise your cooking skills, in a supervised manner, and donate the food you've cooked to a hungry person.

To whom would you donate? How many people should you cook for? Here are some ideas to get you started.

- Some charity institutions – old age homes, orphanages, and so on – will be willing to let you bring provisions and vegetables into their kitchens and help the staff there prepare a meal for their residents. The kitchen staff will discuss a menu with you, and give you a list of ingredients that you will need to bring with you to cook enough food for all their inmates. This works really well, because the kitchen there will have the industrial-sized *karahis* and cookers needed for cooking large amounts of food.
- In October 2015, a young woman in Bengaluru called Mahita Fernandez decided she wanted to feed one lakh hungry people during the nine days of Dussehra. Her idea – which she called 'Feed Your Neighbour' – was to build a sense of community by getting the whole city involved in feeding those who did not have enough to eat. Anyone who wanted to participate cooked a meal for just five people and dropped it off at a pre-decided point, from where it was distributed to five hungry people. The idea caught the city's imagination – 1,25,000 people were fed over the nine days. She repeated the effort during Dussehra 2016. You can read more about 'Feed Your Neighbour' on their Facebook page, and see if there are any such initiatives in your city to which you can contribute the meal you cook.
- Or you could, as a Squad, pick one group of disadvantaged people in your neighbourhood to whom you want to feed a good meal, and run with that. How many people can you/should you feed? Maybe you could decide to feed double the number of people in your Squad, so that each of you feeds two people. If you have five Squad members, cook for 10 hungry people. The

Squad has to lead the operation and be involved every step of the way, but you can certainly take the help of any adults who want to be part of it.

Here's how you cover all the different challenges by doing this one activity.

Before you begin, here's what you should do.

- Decide whose kitchen you will cook in.
- Draw up a menu for the meal along with your Squad Leader and a couple of other adults who want to help.
- Write down all the recipes neatly on chart paper – and hang them around the kitchen where everyone can see them.
- Calculate how much money the meal will cost – ingredients, gas, electricity, transport. Divide the number by the number of people who will be involved in cooking the meal – that will be each person's financial contribution to the effort. Or you may want to raise funds from friends and neighbours, letting them know what this is about and that you will be doing the actual cooking yourselves.
- Create a master list of all the ingredients required for all the dishes, dividing them among different headings, including: spices, vegetables, meat, rice, dals and pulses, flours (atta, *maida*, rice flour, gram flour), dry fruits and cooking oil.

#30
THE INDIAN-SPICES CHALLENGE

Assemble all the spices you will need for the entire meal into two (or three) masala *dabbas*, one containing just whole spices and the other spice powders and mixes.

#31
THE PICK-THE-VEGGIES CHALLENGE

Go shopping for all the vegetables and other ingredients you will need either on the previous evening – if you are cooking lunch, or on the morning of the cook – if you are cooking dinner. Make this a Squad trip, and use the skills you have picked up about how to choose good vegetables when you shop for them.

#35
THE IDENTIFY-THE-DALS CHALLENGE

Go to a supermarket next, and pick up all the provisions you need, including all dals and pulses. You are not allowed to ask any salesperson for help in identifying them.

Erm, yes, this is an out-of-place challenge – it is actually part of the Farmer Merit Badge challenges on page 127. But it fits perfectly here, and completing it lets you get a head-start on a different badge.

#32
THE COOK-AN-INDIAN-MEAL CHALLENGE

Cook the meal! This will also involve washing, peeling and chopping the various vegetables. Make sure you stay well fed and watered through the entire exercise. It will not do to have the cook collapse into the *sambar*!

#33
THE CLEAN-THE-KITCHEN CHALLENGE

You can't escape this! But this can be super fun too, since you will be doing it as a group, and while you are still feeling good about having pulled off a full, delicious meal by yourselves.

Now for the best part – pile everything you've cooked into large *dabbas* and take it to where the hungry people are waiting. The integrated challenge is only complete when you have also served them the meal. On your way back home, think about how good it made you feel to feed a hungry person with a meal you have cooked yourself. And promise yourself you will do it again soon.

WOCOTEEN MERIT BADGE 9

THE FARMER

> *A Scout must have a knowledge gained by practice of ploughing, cultivating, drilling, hedging, and draining. He must also have a working knowledge of farm machinery, haymaking, reaping, leading and stacking and a general acquaintance with the routine seasonal work on a farm, including the care of cattle, horses, sheep and pigs.*
>
> **– Requirements for Farmer Badge, *Scout Tests and How To Pass Them***

There are so many things that could possibly be wrong with the produce we buy at a market these days – the veggies were involved with too many chemicals while growing, either in the form of fertilizers or pesticides, the seeds themselves were genetically modified ones, the water that sustained them was polluted with human waste, yada-yada-yada – that growing your own vegetables seems like a complete no-brainer.

But that is just one of the reasons that winning the Farmer Merit Badge is so important. Another important reason is that we live in India, a still largely agrarian country that has millions of her people – many of them among her poorest – engaged in growing food for the rest of us. We are also a country still largely dependent on a good monsoon for a good crop – only about 35 per cent of India's farmland is 'irrigated', or supplied with water from rivers, wells and tanks through canals. As you can imagine, this means most of our farmers constantly live on the edge, and a bad

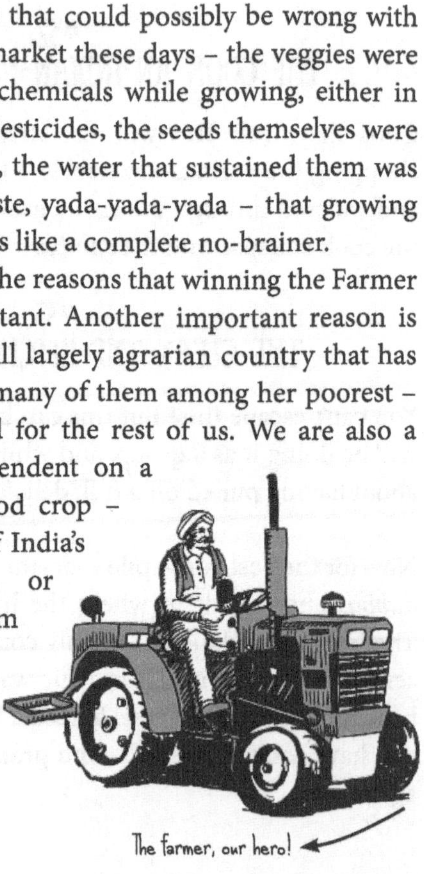

The farmer, our hero!

monsoon or a ruined crop is reflected instantly in a sudden spike in farmer suicides.

Growing your own vegetables - even just enough for a couple of meals - will give you some understanding of a farmer's life; the amount of time between planting a seed and harvesting the fruit, the number of things that could go wrong in that time, and the disproportionately small amount of money his crop brings a farmer in return for all his months of work. Sure, the effort involved in urban terrace farming (the kind you will be doing to grow your vegetables) is nowhere close to the back-breaking physical labour involved in real farming under the unforgiving Indian sun, but it's a start.

Plus, the joy of biting into a fresh, just-picked, home-grown, sun-warmed tomato is so heady that it will most likely convert you into a healthy eater for life, besides making you truly aware of and grateful for what you put into your mouth at each mealtime.

What's not to like about that?

SKILL 34
KNOW MAJOR CROPS IN YOUR PART OF INDIA

Yes, you do enough of that in Geography class, and the chapter on crops and soils is the Most Stupendously Boring of all the lessons you have. But this isn't a school lesson and what's at stake here isn't top marks in an exam - it's a WoCoTeen Merit Badge. Surely that makes knowing it worthwhile! Plus, you only have to know about crops and soils in the region of India where *you* live, and that's real and relevant and useful.

Here's a list of questions. Once you have the answers to these, you can consider yourself equipped with this particular WoCoTeen skill.

- **What are the different kinds of soils in your State?** Do you have fertile alluvial soil; mineral-rich, volcanic black soil; iron-packed, Deccan Plateau red soil; well-leached, upland laterite; forest-matter-enriched mountain soil; or sandy, saline, organic-matter-starved desert soil? What crops grow best in each kind of soil?

- **What are the crops that your State grows most of?** Which ones fall into the food crop category and which into the commercial crop one? Are there crops that your State produces more of than any other State in India?
- **How much of your State's area is dedicated to farming activities?** And where does the water for the crops come from through the year? How much of the farmland is irrigated?
- **What percentage of your State's population is involved in farming?**
- **How many cycles of planting and harvesting** do farmers in your State put their fields through? What are the main *kharif* crops ('autumn crops' harvested at the end of the south-west monsoon, around September-October)? What are the main *rabi* crops ('spring crops' harvested at the end of the north-east monsoon, in March-April)? Does your State also grow *zaid* crops (crops that depend only on irrigation and not the monsoon and therefore can be grown in the short period between the *rabi* harvest and the *kharif* planting, i.e., April-June?).

It won't be easy to find answers to all these questions, but it won't be all that difficult either, given that most of the information is available on the Internet. But just thinking about these questions, and rooting around for the answers, will give you an extra-special understanding of farming and farmers in your State.

SKILL 35
FOLLOW THE MONSOON

Again, there is a difference in studying the route of the annual monsoon as part of a Geography lesson, and as part of the skills required to win a WoCoTeen Badge.

You see, Indians – even those who are not farmers and don't depend on it for their livelihood – have a very close emotional and spiritual bond with the monsoon, coming as it does after the long, harsh summer. The sound of the first drops of a monsoon downpour hitting the roof, and the heady smell of wet earth, sends men, women and children across India dancing into the streets (admit it, you've done it too!) and improves everyone's mood one hundred percent (despite the inevitable power outage that accompanies it).

Did you know – the smell of rain has a name – it's called petrichor! Don't you just wish you could just bottle it up to take a deep sniff out of whenever you are feeling low?

If something makes you so happy, surely you should know everything there is to know about it! Here's a basic list of things you should know about the Indian monsoon to complete this skill requirement for the Farmer Badge.

- How many monsoons does India have?
- What are their names and why have they been named that?
- When does each of them arrive?
- Where does each hit the Indian coastline and how does it progress from there on?
- How long does it typically take for the monsoon to travel across the Indian landmass?
- Which monsoon has more of an impact in your State?
- How does the monsoon affect your State in terms of irrigation? In other words, which are the important man-made reservoirs, created by building dams across rivers, that the monsoon helps fill up? (It is the water in these reservoirs that will keep the fields around irrigated in the hot, dry summer months).

Also: which of these rain-fed reservoirs provides most of the drinking water for your city?

SKILL 36
IDENTIFY DIFFERENT FOODGRAINS, DALS AND PULSES

Can you say, hand on heart, that you know what rice grains look like just after they are harvested, before they are husked, cleaned and polished, when they are still called paddy and not rice? Do you actually know what wheat grains look like before they are turned into atta and *maida*? If you answered both questions in the negative, don't you think it's a bit weird that you have no idea what the food you eat on a daily basis even looks like when it first comes off a plant?

That's why the Squad included this skill as a must-have for the Farmer Badge. This is what you must be able to do.

- **Pick out unhusked wheat and paddy grains** from a selection of different foodgrains.
- **Pick out the different forms in which we use rice** – puffed rice, beaten rice, rice flour; and the different forms in which we use wheat – whole wheat flour, refined wheat flour, broken wheat, semolina. Also understand the difference between each form, and how each is processed from the original grain.
- **Identify at least five different dals** and be able to name them in three languages – English, your mother tongue and another Indian language. You should be able to identify them in their whole husked form, their whole unhusked form and

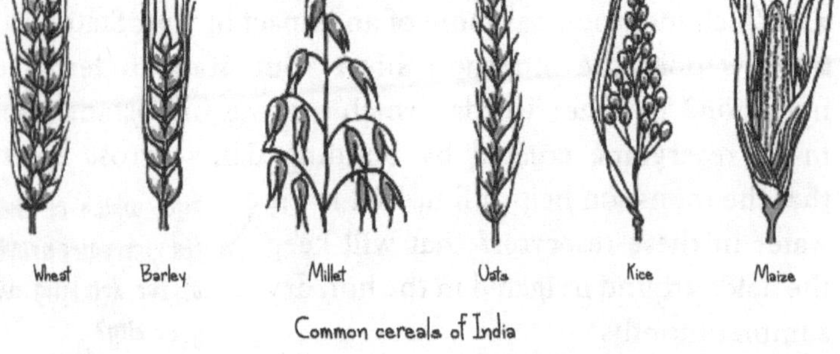

Common cereals of India

their split form. The five dals that the Squad recommends for identification are:

- Red gram
- Green gram
- Bengal gram
- Red lentils
- Black gram

(Bet that will have even your parents reaching for Google!)

- **Identify at least five different pulses** and be able to name them by in the same three languages as above. The recommended pulses are:
  - Chick peas (white)
  - Kidney beans (red)
  - Chick peas (brown)
  - Black-eyed beans (beige)
  - Chick peas (green)
- **Identify and name two flours** apart from rice flour and the two kinds of wheat flour, namely:
  - Gram flour
  - Maize flour

The best part is that most of these should be right in your kitchen at home. Yup, it takes a *lot* of *dabbas* and bottles to contain the basic ingredients for an Indian kitchen!

SKILL 37
CREATE A SQUARE FOOT GARDEN

It would of course be great to have a big kitchen garden and grow enough of all kinds of vegetables, but garden space is a limited resource in a city. If you live in an apartment it is quite likely that the only space you have for a garden is your balcony. But here's the good part – if your balcony can spare about 4 x 4 ft of space and gets good, direct sunlight for about four hours a day, you can actually grow your own vegetables!

If you don't have a large enough balcony or enough sunlight, you could work with your neighbours to set up a community kitchen garden somewhere in your apartment complex – on the terrace or in a sunny part of the garden downstairs – that is managed entirely by your Squad (if everyone else in the Squad also lives in your apartment complex). Or you could talk to your school principal to give over a part of the school grounds to you to plant a kitchen garden in. So many possibilities!

Let's say you have managed to secure a 4 x 4 sq ft gardening space for yourself. You're now ready to grow your own Square Foot Garden (SFG)! The SFG was a revolutionary concept pioneered by American engineer Mel Bartholomew, in a book of the same name, in 1981. He wrote an updated version of it, in 2006, after SFG had taken the world by storm. Mel's biggest innovation was rethinking the traditional method of growing vegetables, which was meant for commercial farming, and coming up with a new method for home gardeners that involved 80 per cent less space, 90 per cent less water, no added fertilizers, and almost no weeds.

The best part was, you could grow just enough vegetables to use up in your own kitchen. As Mel said of his gardening philosophy, 'I garden with a salad bowl in mind, not a wheelbarrow.'

SFG as a concept became hugely popular all over the world. Schools in the USA were charmed with the small amount of space it required and the fact that children could do it too, and introduced kitchen gardening as part of the curriculum. Mel Barthlomew died in May 2016, at the age of eighty-four, but his wonderful gardening concept has, in recent years, caught the urban Indian imagination too. That's why it's one of the skills you need to acquire to get your Farmer Badge!

The Beginner's Guide to growing an SFG

Gardening – especially the vegetable-growing kind – is an involved process that requires a lot of patience and experimentation and comes with no guarantees. But when you finally succeed, it is totally worth all the hard work and the heartbreak. These are just a few tips to get you started.

Step 1: The Box

Build or buy a 4 x 4 ft (or 3 x 3 ft – the size recommended for gardeners below 12 years) wooden box (discarded wooden crates work well), with a height of at least eight inches. Line the bottom and sides of the box with heavy plastic sheeting and you're ready to begin putting in the soil. (If a wooden box is hard to find, concrete blocks will do just as well. You will need more space for your SFG though, as each block is thick. You won't need a bottom for your concrete 'box', just plastic sheeting.)

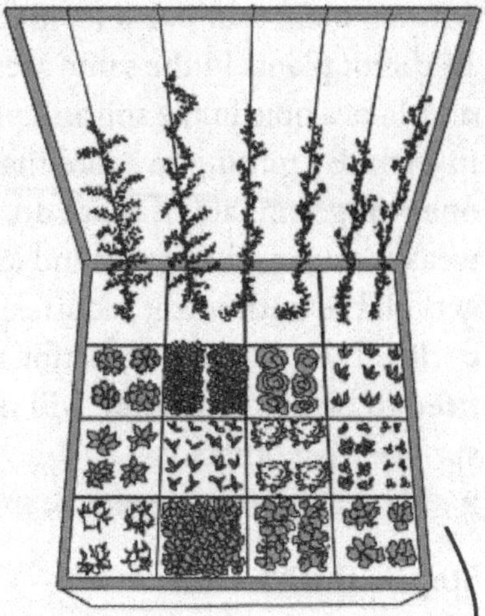

The SFG: maximum yield, minimum effort

Step 2: The Soil

Put in your soil mixture to a depth of at least six inches. The ideal mixture is one-third compost (preferably one that is a mix of leaf and animal manure) which provides the nutrients, one-third coconut coir (coco peat) or peat moss, which lightens and improves the soil, allowing it to breathe, and one-third vermiculite (or perlite), which helps the soil hold water.

Step 3: The Grid

Create a grid of nine squares (for a 3 x 3 ft box) or 16 squares (for a 4 x 4 ft box) such that each square is one square foot in size (see why it is called a 'square foot' garden?). You can create this grid simply by putting in nails at one-foot intervals on all sides of the box and then tying string across the tops. This is just to give you a visual indication of each square foot in your box.

Step 4: The Planting

Now you are ready to plant your seeds!

- Read the instructions on the back of the seed packet to see how far apart the seeds of that vegetable should be planted. That will tell you how many seeds of that vegetable you can plant in each square of your SFG. A tomato plant, for instance, requires space, so you can only plant one seed per square. But you can plant four palak (spinach) plants per square, and up to 16 carrot plants in the same area.

- Make a hole in the soil and place one (or two or three) seeds in each. By putting in more than one, you can be sure at least one will germinate. If more do, you can cut off the tops of the weaker ones as they grow and keep the strongest one, so that it gets all the nutrients it requires.
- Read the packet instructions to see at what depth the seeds need to be planted. Some will need to be planted closer to the surface than others.
- Plant a different vegetable in each adjacent square.

Step 5: The Kick-off

Water your newly planted seeds. Be careful, now and always, to ensure that you don't overwater – there should be no water visible above the soil – or under-water – the soil should not be dry and crumbly. When you pick up a handful of soil, it should be moist enough to hold together when you press it in your palm, but aerated enough to crumble between your fingers.

Once your seeds have sprouted and are doing well, try this to give your plants great nutrition: collect all the vegetable peels and waste from your kitchen (or your wet waste bin) each day, and grind them up in the blender with a little water into a smooth 'chutney'. Mix one part of the chutney with about 20 parts of water and use that mixture to water your SFG and any other plants you may have. You're welcome.

Step 6: The Long Wait

Yup, you can't escape that when it comes to growing things! Many, many factors are involved in growing good vegetables, so set your expectations low and don't give up if your first attempt fails. Talk to experienced gardeners in your family or neighbourhood to get tips. Look up gardening blogs and YouTube videos posted by enthusiasts. Give your plants a lot of love. And sooner rather than later, the magic will happen. You will have a lovely harvest of home-grown vegetables that will make you feel very proud – and very nourished – indeed!

THE FARMER'S CHALLENGES

#34
THE KNOW-YOUR-CROPS CHALLENGE

Together with the Squad, sketch out as large a map of your State as possible on paper, or on the floor of your Squad room (if you have one). Fill in the topographical details in 3-D with lots of texture – papier-mâché hills, blue-cord rivers, and so on. Divide the map into crop regions and fill each up with something symbolic of that crop. Invite parents, friends and neighbours to a presentation about your State's crops, soils, and more, using your big map as the centrepiece.

#35
THE IDENTIFY-THE-DALS CHALLENGE

See The Cook's Challenges on page 117 for details.

#36
THE FOLLOW-THE-MONSOON CHALLENGE

As a Squad group activity, read Alexander Frater's book *Chasing The Monsoon*, which recounts the author's experiences as he follows the south-west monsoon across the subcontinent from Kerala, where it makes landfall each year, all the way to Bengal, where it exits our borders. Each Squad member takes turns to read one chapter, and describes it to the others in the next meeting, in a two-three minute presentation.

#37
THE GROW-YOUR-OWN-VEGGIES CHALLENGE

Even if you don't have room for a Square Foot Garden, you can certainly grow a plant in a pot. Grow any vegetable plant from seed to fruit to finish this challenge.

WOCOTEEN MERIT BADGE 10

THE HANDYMAN

A Scout must be able to paint a door, whitewash a ceiling, repair gas-fittings, tap washers, sash lines, window and door fastenings, replace gas mantles and electric light bulbs, hang pictures and curtains, repair blinds, fix curtains and portiere rods, lay carpets, mend clothing and upholstery, do small furniture and china repairs, and sharpen knives.

– Requirements for Handyman Badge, *Scout Tests and How To Pass Them*

Of course you don't have to win WoCoTeen badges in any particular order, but say you had to. Say you had just won yourself the Housekeeper Badge and the Cook Badge and the Farmer Badge. Which means you are growing your own vegetables, cooking them yourself, and keeping a clean and tidy house (okay, okay – room). Super!

Now, say something goes kaput in your lovely, tidy, smoothly-functioning house. Maybe a bulb fuses. Or your toilet clogs. Maybe you've woken up and discovered that the shirt of your school uniform is missing a button, or maybe you want to hang a beautiful sun-catcher you just made on your window-frame. What do you do? Stare helplessly at it, and then yell for mom or dad? Moan about how everything horrible seems to happen only to you? Pick up the phone and call the apartment handyman, and then curse him and the apartment maintenance staff when he doesn't pick up the phone?

Never mind. This is not a confessional. But if any of those reactions comes close to your own, it is time you began to do things a little differently around the house. It's time to acquire the skills required to win yourself the Handyman Badge.

PS: Do keep a grown-up around for all the activities suggested in this section. It will make you feel safer and make them feel good that they can keep an eye on you!

SKILL 38
SEW ON A BUTTON

You will need:

- A sharp, shiny needle, through which you will thread...
- ... eight inches of doubled-over thread, whose ends you will knot a few times until the knot is big enough not to slip through the fabric, plus...
- ... the button – the original, or if you can't find it, one of the spare buttons you will usually find sewn on the inside of the bottom front of the shirt, and also...
- ... a 'spacer' needle (or a toothpick, or a pin), and last but not least...
- ... a pen/pencil to mark your sewing spot.

Fix that button!

1. Start by marking the spot from which your button has fallen – it's pretty easy to identify because of the holes through which the original button was sewn.

2, 3 and 4. Sew a little 'x' on the spot to give the button a lift.

5. Place your button on the spot by slipping the needle through one of its holes (use one of the top two holes in case of a four-holed button) and push down until it rests on the 'x'. You could dab a spot of fabric glue on the x to hold the button in place while you sew it on. Pull the needle and thread through all the way.

6 and 7. Then bring the needle down through the hole of the button adjacent to it and back through the fabric to the other side (if it is a two-holed button, there is only one other hole). Take the needle up again through one of the two bottom holes of your button, pull tight, and bring it back down through the last hole of the button. Now the button is anchored!

8. Push your 'spacer' needle between the button and the first layer of thread holding it down.

9. Repeat steps 6 and 7 at least three more times (at least five times if it is a two-holed button) going *over* the 'spacer' each time.

10, 11 and 12. Remove the 'spacer' and 'pull' the button up. Wrap your thread around the threads between the button and the fabric three to four times to create a shank. The shank allows the button to sit a little off the fabric, making it easier to button.
13, 14, 15 and 16. Bring your needle back down through the fabric for the last time (not through the button!). Tie off the thread by taking the needle through a loop of its own thread and pulling tight.
17. Trim off the ends of the thread with a pair of small, sharp sewing scissors.

If you'd like to further secure your knot at the back, a dab of fabric glue should do it. Or use a dot of clear nail polish just where the thread meets the button to fix the button better.
18. Make sure that all your stitches are hidden under the button so that it looks neat and professional.
You're done! Now hold the shirt away from you and admire your handiwork. Seriously, how cool are you!

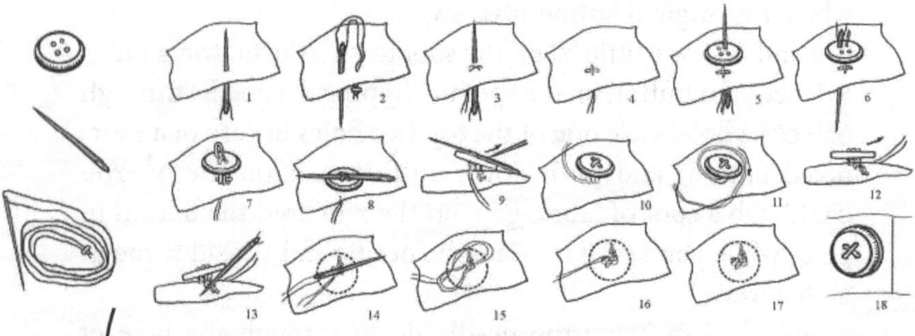

How to sew a button (Read through the steps for more detailed instructions)

SKILL 39
CHANGE A BULB

You are racing through your last revision for your test tomorrow, and pop! the bulb in the hanging lamp above your desk goes out suddenly. Luckily, it isn't something that fazes you, because you know exactly what to do.

- First, you turn off the power supply to the lamp by switching it off. The lamp is now safe to handle.
- Then you head over to where you stash your rubber chappals and put them on. Always better to be safe than sorry where electricity is concerned.
- Back in your room, you pull out the torch that is always in your desk drawer, switch it on and shine it over the bottom shelf of the cupboard where your mom stores the spare bulbs.
- You take the bulb carefully out of its packaging, knowing that it is fragile, and place it far back on your desk, not at the edge, from where you are liable to knock it off in the dark.
- Standing on a wooden chair, you reach inside the lampshade, and carefully turn the bulb anti-clockwise to ease the little metal nubs on its base out of the notch in the bulb-holder. Then you slip the kaput bulb out of the bulb-holder, and place it carefully at the back of your desk, away from the new bulb, so that you don't mix them up.
- Picking up the new bulb, you repeat the process in reverse, easing it into the holder carefully. You also give the bulb a couple of firm tugs after, to make sure it is secure.
- You get off the chair and switch the lamp on, standing well clear of it. Success!
- There's one more thing left to do – discarding the old bulb. If it is an incandescent bulb, you know it doesn't contain anything toxic and can be disposed of in your regular dry waste bin. However, since it is made of thin glass, you carefully wrap it in a couple of sheets of newspaper before you place it inside the bin, so that it doesn't hurt garbage collectors if it breaks.

If it is a CFL (Compact Fluorescent Light) bulb, you have a problem. CFLs contain toxic mercury and have to be disposed of in some other way. Organizations that collect e-waste (CDs, batteries, toner cartridges) in your city will also usually pick up your used tubelights and CFLs and dispose of them safely. If you can't find one, the kindest thing you can do for Mother Earth and your neighbours is to store your used CFLs in a carton in your loft, until the government finalizes regulations on safe CFL disposal (which should happen soon).

SKILL 40
MAKE LIKE BOB THE BUILDER – USE 'EM TOOLS!

Can. You. Fix. It? Yes. You. Can! If you have the right tools around, that is. It would also help if you, erm, knew what each tool was for, and exactly *how* to use it. Here are some tips to get you started.

REMEMBER! Do NOT use ANY of these tools unless there is an an adult present, or until an adult trusts your skills enough to let you go solo.

What are the basic tools you would need in your home toolbox? Let's see.

- **A Hammer** – Focus on three things when you go hammer-shopping. Your all-purpose, everyday hammer should have:

◆ *A medium weight* – Remember you're Bob the Builder, not Thor. So don't go for something too heavy (difficult to swing) or too light (not strong enough to pound a nail in).

◆ *A good head-to-handle weight ratio* – The hammer should be neither top-heavy (the head is heavier than the handle) or bottom-heavy. Balance is everything when you're swinging something with force.

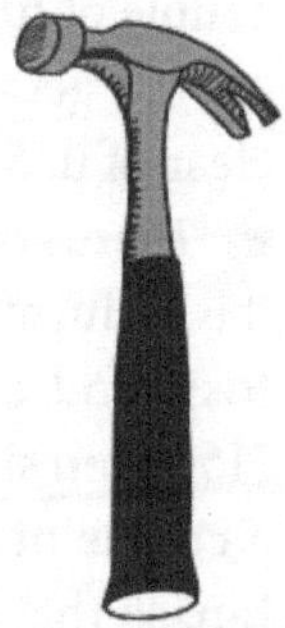

◆ *A claw* – Most regular-use hammers will have a head with a flat smooth circular face on one side to pound things in with, and a split 'claw' – which looks like a two-tined fork and is used to grab the head of a nail and rip it out of a wall – on the other side. The claw could be curved (curved claw) or straight (rip claw). Both work equally well.

- **A pair of Combination Pliers** – The basic use of a pair of pliers is to grip an object – nails, screws, nuts, bolts, wire, a metal strip – firmly. Once it is held firmly, the object can be turned or twisted or bent or manipulated in the way you want. Closer to the pivot (the point where the handles of the pliers intersect) are the serrated 'cutting faces' of the jaws, and at the tip are the flat 'gripping faces'. Here's what you should keep in mind while using pliers:

◆ *Choose the right kind of pliers for the job* – Combination pliers are very handy for most jobs around the house, but for more specialized jobs that involve holding and twisting thin wire or stripping insulation from electrical wires or reaching into narrow spaces, needle-nosed pliers are more useful.

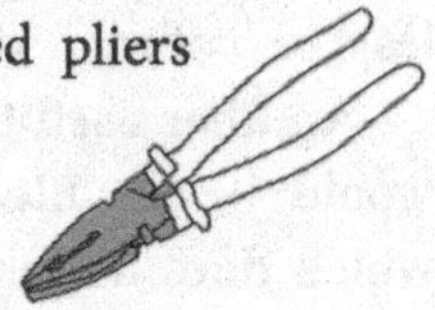

◆ *Mind your fingers* – There is a big chance of getting your fingers (or skin) pinched by the handles, pivot or jaws when you are using pliers. Some pliers come with thumb guards to prevent this – if you can find one like that in your hardware store, pick that one.

■ **An Adjustable Wrench** – This is also often called an **Adjustable Spanner**, or a **Monkey Wrench**. Wrenches are usually used to tighten or loosen nuts on furniture, bicycles and cars, or in plumbing repair jobs. An Adjustable Wrench – in which the size of the 'jaw' can be made bigger or smaller to fit snugly around the nut or bolt – is far more useful than a 'fixed-jaw' wrench (because with these, you will need different spanners for different-sized nuts). Wrenches are really a special kind of pliers.

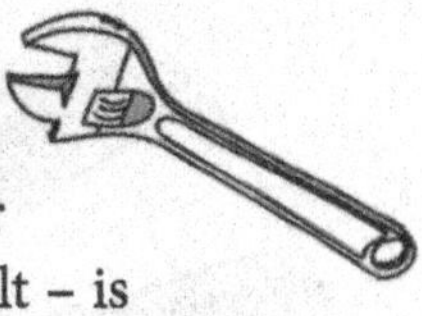

How do you operate an adjustable wrench?

◆ Identify the nut or bolt you want to tighten or loosen.

◆ Open the jaw of the wrench using the screw mechanism. When it is slightly bigger than the head of the nut, slip it over the nut and tighten the screw so that it holds the nut securely.

◆ Turn the wrench in a clockwise direction to tighten the nut, and in an anti-clockwise direction to loosen it. Keep turning until the nut is tight enough, or loose enough to unscrew with your fingers.

◆ Unscrew the jaw of the wrench until it is wide enough to be taken off the nut easily.

■ **A set of Screwdrivers** – How can any toolbox be complete without a set of screwdrivers? But how many should you get, and what kind?

Essentially, screwdrivers come in two flavours – **Flathead screwdrivers** (which are used for screwing and unscrewing screws whose heads have a single slot) and **Philips screwdrivers** (used for screws whose heads have an X-shaped slot). Get at least two of each kind, in different sizes.

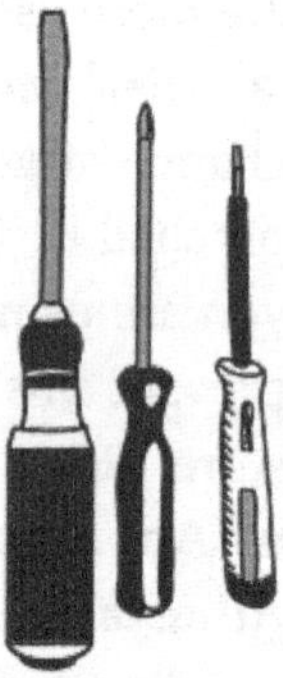

Another useful screwdriver to have around would be an **Electrical Tester Screwdriver**, which does double duty as a regular flathead and as a device to test if electricity is running through a circuit (usually by sticking it in a power socket). If the socket is live, a neon lamp inside the clear handle of the tester switches on.

■ **An Allen Key** – An Allen Key, or a **Hex Key**, doesn't look anything like a screwdriver – it is small, light and looks like a leftover piece from something you assembled recently. But it is very useful – in fact, it is the only 'driver' you can use to tighten screws that have hexagonal sockets in their heads. And where can you find such screws? In taps, and in knock-down furniture which comes in a box and is assembled in the retail store or in your home. Get a set of Allen keys in different sizes – when you whip them out to fix that faucet handle that keeps falling off or that chair with the wobbly legs, you will be a hero, no debate!

■ **A Paintbrush and Roller** – It is the easiest – and most joyful – thing in the world to dip a nice flat brush into a tin of paint (or to run a roller on a tray of paint) and start expressing yourself on a large and forgiving canvas like a wall. Experiment (with permission!) on an outside wall at the back of your house (or a friend's) with a 'safe' colour like cream first. Then, as you gain in confidence, you can paint over the same wall in darker and

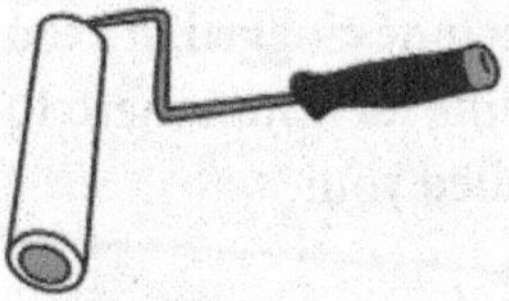

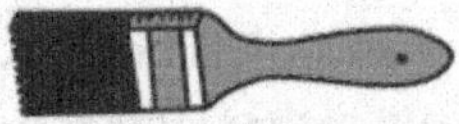

darker shades (or scrape it down and start again if you want to go back to a lighter shade). You could cut blocks of any shape that you like out of thick sponge and do some block-printing on it too!

Be warned, though – this could get really addictive. When it does, maybe you could get a group of volunteers together and start giving some neglected walls in your neighbourhood some much-needed TLC. A nicely-painted wall signals that someone cares, and prevents people from littering around it, or peeing and spitting on it. For more inspiration and guidelines, check out the Facebook page of 'The Ugly Indian'.

■ **Other Toolbox Essentials –**

◆ A spring-loaded tape measure (the 26-ft one should be good for most jobs around the house)

◆ A good flashlight with extra batteries

◆ A pair of safety goggles (make sure you wear them when you are using your handyman tools)

◆ A couple of rolls of electrical duct tape

◆ A couple of packs of M-Seal, a branded Indian 'epoxy sealant'. M-Seal looks and feels like play dough when you begin but it hardens like cement when it is exposed to air for a few hours. It's great for sealing cracks, fixing leaks in pipes, joining broken things together, and more.

Here's a fun fact – M-Seal is most often used in DIY art projects because it is so easy to use!

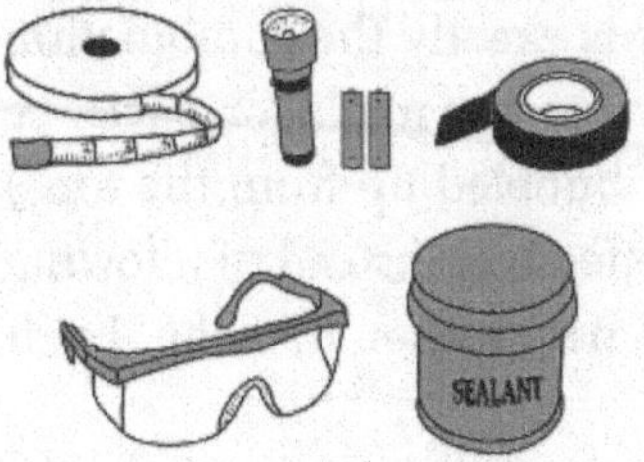

SKILL 41
UNCLOG A WASHBASIN

This is every party host's – read: parent's – nightmare. There are a bunch of guests coming to dinner and the washbasin in the nice bathroom has suddenly suddenly become clogged. It's too late in the evening to call in a plumber. Time for a superhero to step in and save the day – a superhero called you!

- **Unclogging a partly-clogged washbasin:**

If you can see that your washbasin or kitchen sink is beginning to clog, i.e., the water has begun to drain out rather slower than usual, do a quick pre-emptive strike to nip any clogging ideas the drain may have in the bud.

What you will need:

- A pot of boiling water
- A cup of vinegar
- Half a cup of baking soda
- A superhero mask and cape (optional)

How to do it:

Be careful!

- Pour a pot of boiling hot water down your drain from a height, with some force. That should hopefully loosen and push some of whatever's clogging it down the drain.
- Dump in about half a cup of baking soda. Let that sit for a few minutes.
- Then, pour a mixture of one cup vinegar and one cup very hot water on top of the baking soda.
- Cover with a drain plug if you have one. This keeps the baking soda-vinegar reaction (this is exactly the combination of ingredients you put into the volcano you made for a science project – remember how the 'lava' bubbled up from the top?) inside the drain, where it is most effective, instead of allowing it to spill out. The bubbling should help loosen the clog. Let it sit for 5–10 minutes.
- Flush one more time with a pot of boiling water.

- **Unclogging a fully-clogged washbasin:**

What you will need:

- Rubber gloves

■ A super tool called a plunger (if you don't have one at home, make your parents buy one today! Most inexpensive plungers just have a rubber 'bell' at one end, but if you can find one with an extension flange on the bell, buy that one. The flange converts the regular plunger, which works great with sink drains, into a real beast when it comes to unclogging toilet drains. When you want to use it to unclog a sink, just fold the flange in).

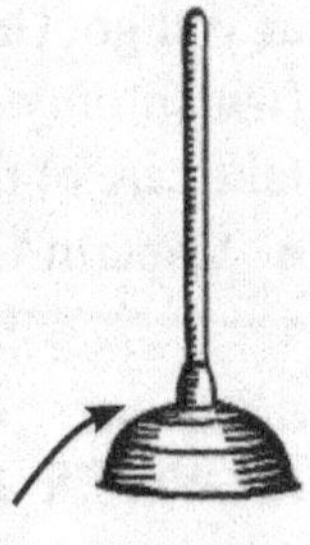

The rock-star of all tools – The Plunger!

■ A wire clothes hanger that you can open out into a long and stiff, but still manoeuvrable, wire.

How to do it:

■ Put on the gloves.

■ Plunge the plunger into the standing water in the washbasin and place the bell over the drain, making a watertight seal. Press down gently with the handle so that the concave bell collapses and becomes flat, pushing out the air inside.

■ Once you force out the air, plunge vigorously in and out, without lifting the plunger off, and ensuring that you maintain the seal. You will be forcing water in both directions in the drain – every time you plunge in, you force water into the drain, each time you pull up, you draw it up. This action will effectively loosen most clogs. Stick with it, plunging 15 to 20 times if necessary.

■ Be patient. Try alternating between steady strokes and occasional monster heaves when you 'pop' the seal and pull the plunger out, making water in the sink rush into the sudden vacuum.

■ Keep enough water in the bowl so the plunger stays covered. Trying to force air through the drain won't generate much pressure.

■ Most of the time, this is all it takes to clear the clog. If it still hasn't cleared fully, insert the opened-up wire hanger into one of the drain holes and push it all the way down, poking around as you go. Unless it is a really major clog in the external pipes (which only a professional plumber can remove), this should take care of the clog.

- Captain Unclog is now ready for his/her next mission!

SKILL 42
HAMMER SOME NAILS

No debate about it. Every WoCoTeen has to be proficient at using a hammer and banging nails straight and true into all kinds of surfaces. It is a life skill that you only get better at by doing it over and over again until you get it right. DIY household projects are a breeze when you have good nail-hammering skills.

Here are a few tips to get you started and keep you safe.

- If you've never used a hammer to nail anything into anything, start small and slow. If you don't even have a hammer at home, go to your closest hardware store and buy one first.

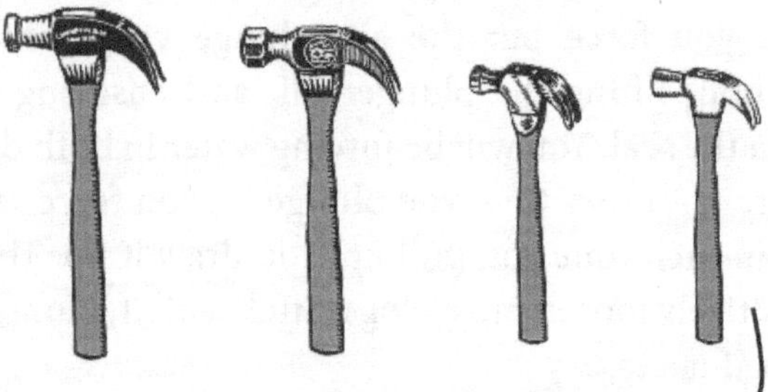

How do you pick a good hammer? Learn to nail it with Skill 40!

Since you are at the hardware store anyway, also buy a bunch of nails of different sizes/lengths. Try and get ones with broad heads and thick shafts. They're the best for practice.

Let's get hammering!

Before you start:

- Get everything you need – hammer, nails of different sizes... – and put them within easy reach.

■ Put on some safety glasses – swimming goggles will do at a pinch. This is just to protect your eyes from flying bits of the surface you are hammering at.
■ Slip on some footwear – you don't want to be stepping on nails or wood chips.

What surface should you practice hammering into?
Definitely not your walls to begin with! Indian homes are built of brick or cement blocks that are hard surfaces to hammer things into. Start with wood. No, not your study desk or dining table. Try it on a thick wooden board or plank that no one has any use for, or even better, the stump of a dead tree in the neighbourhood. (Do *not* put nails into a living tree!)

Positioning the nail
Pick a nail whose length is shorter than the thickness of your wooden block. You don't want it coming out of the other side, after you've banged it through.

Make sure the wooden block/plank you are hammering into is either heavy enough not to move around or fixed in a way that prevents it from moving when you hammer into it. Bring it up to a comfortable standing height to work with (it's best if it is at waist height – placing it on an old table would work), or squat on the ground.
■ You will now need to position the nail and hold it in place until you have driven it in far enough for it to stay in place without being held.

Scared of holding the nail between your thumb and index finger while you hammer? Here are other ideas.
■ You can hold it with pliers.
■ You can hold it with a spring-loaded clothespin.
■ You can put a thick piece of cardboard or corrugated paper on the board and push the nail

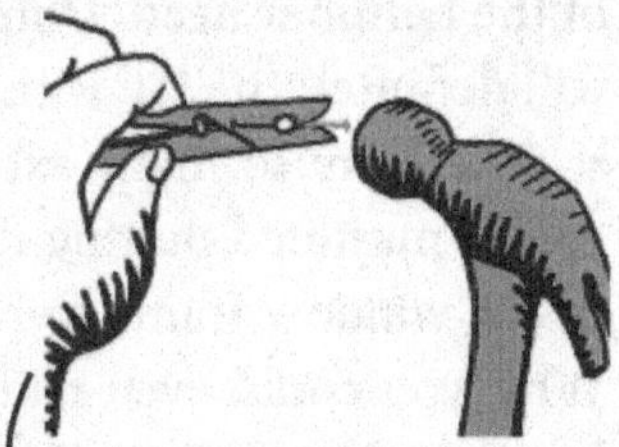

Use the clothespin, save the hand.

through that before you begin hammering. This will help the nail stay in position.

■ If the wood is quite soft, you could 'drill' a pilot hole in it by turning the nail round and round in position. That will create a groove that will 'hold' the nail while you hammer.

Whichever method you pick, hold the nail closer to the nail head rather than closer to the board surface. That way, even if you do strike your fingers with the hammer, they will be knocked aside, rather than 'crunched' against the board.

Driving the nail in

Once you've positioned your nail, you can begin driving it in. Here's how.

■ Hold the nail at right angles to the surface so that it goes in straight.

■ At first, hold the handle of the hammer nearer the hammer head for better control. Once you've got the nail in part of the way, move your grip to the other end of the hammer handle so that the weight of the hammer along with the flexing of your wrist – not your arm or shoulder – will do the work.

■ Many carpenters recommend the Two-Stroke Hammering technique. Here, each stroke of the hammer is not one hard 'bang', but a soft-hard, two-stroke, 'tap-bang'. The first soft 'tap' is to help your brain and eye and arm 'locate the nail head', the hard 'bang' immediately after is to drive it in.

■ Watch the nail to make sure it isn't bending. Tap it back to perpendicular position with the hammer if it does, and keep trying to strike the nail head as flatly as possible with the face of the hammer head. Don't worry if you fail a few times – you will definitely 'nail it' with practice.

■ There are so many exciting DIY projects you can do once you've mastered putting nails into wood! You could put a nail into a window frame to hang your craft project, for instance. Why, you could even nail wooden planks together to build a box for a Square Foot Garden (see Skill 37)!

THE HANDYMAN'S CHALLENGES

The challenges under this Badge are fairly straightforward. Each Squad member simply has to demo the skills needed to fulfil the Badge requirements.

#38 THE SEW-A-BUTTON CHALLENGE

In the presence of the Squad Leader, each Squad member is required to sew a two-holed button and a four-holed button on to a piece of fabric (you could use an old towel for this).

#39 THE CHANGE-A-BULB CHALLENGE

In the presence of the Squad Leader, each Squad member is required to unscrew a bulb from a working desk lamp or hanging lamp, taking all necessary precautions, and screw it back again into the holder.

#40 THE HANDYMAN-TOOLKIT CHALLENGE

Once you have your toolkit together, how do you store it so that you can always find what you need quickly? Most serious home handymen hang their tools on a 'tool board'. For this challenge, do some online research, in pairs, on tool boards, and create one using thick cardboard (of course, this won't actually support your tools – this is just an exercise in planning a real tool board). Draw the different tools you would have in your home toolbox on it (you can add as many and thingamajigs as you like – hairpins to spring a lock, chocolate bars to sustain you when you're working on a project – but you have to also include the ones mentioned in this book), and explain why you chose to 'hang' them in those particular positions on your tool board. Your Squad Leader will decide if your tool board is imaginative enough, practical enough, and comprehensive enough to win you and your partner the badge.

#41
THE UNCLOG-A-SINK CHALLENGE

If a sink or washbasin that needs unclogging cannot be found, Squad members simply demonstrate, one by one, all the steps involved in the process. The Squad Leader will decide if the requisite skills have been acquired.

#42
THE HAMMER-SOME-NAILS CHALLENGE

Individually or in pairs, Squad members create a piece of 'nail art' (no, not the blingy fingernail kind).

Option 1: Draw a pencil outline of your favourite cartoon character or football jersey number on a wooden plank/block and bang in shiny nails all along it. Drive the nails through so that the heads are flush with the surface of the wood (make sure that the nails are short enough or the plank is thick enough that the entire nail remains inside the wood). Points are awarded on the basis of how closely the nails follow the pencil outline.

Option 2: Bang in nails as before along a pencil outline. (This time, you can draw an abstract pattern rather than a character or a number). Instead of driving the nails all the way through, however, stop when a tiny bit of the nail shaft is still showing above the surface. String coloured string over the nails and across the design in a bright, fun pattern.

WOCOTEEN MERIT BADGE 11

THE CAREGIVER

The natural disinfectants (for the patient) are – pure air and sunshine.
The nurse should have lots of fresh air, and go for an hour's walk each day.
– Scout Tests and How to Pass Them

Sure there are nursing colleges that turn out tens of thousands of professional nurses each year to take care of the sick, and you can never take their place unless you go through nursing college too. But learning how to care for an invalid, or a family member who is recuperating after a bout of illness, is a very important part of being a WoCoTeen.

All kinds of unexpected things can happen, and it is quite possible that a family member suddenly needs prolonged care. Maybe you have a grandparent who has come to live with you for a while after he slipped in the bathroom and broke his hip; maybe your younger sibling is recovering from jaundice or chickenpox; maybe your mom has had a surgery and needs to rest for a month. Wouldn't it be amazing for your parents to have an extra pair of trustworthy hands – yours! – to help?

Knowing how to make an invalid comfortable, pitching in to help without being asked, and doing things that keep her cheerful, will certainly help the recovery along.

Ready to start boning up on those skills, then?

SKILL 43
SETTING UP THE PATIENT'S ROOM

Patients need a 'customized' room to ease things for them and help them get better. If it is going to be a long recovery, you might want to put some thought into which room would most suit the patient and everyone else at home, and move other

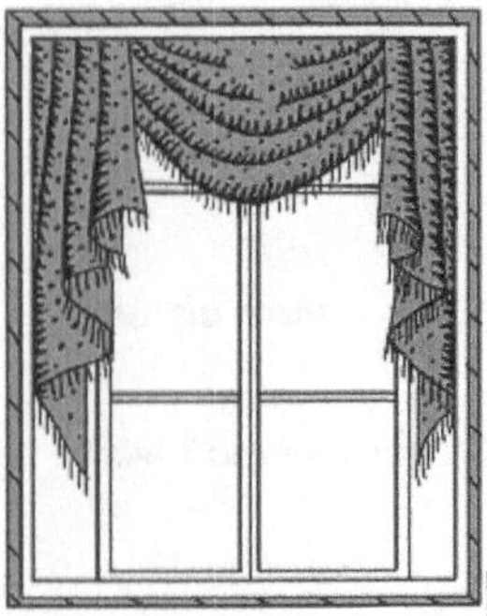

Throw open those shades and let the sun in!

people around. Since the patient is going to spend a lot of time in bed, the choice of room will play a big part in aiding recovery.

Here are some of the questions you might want to ask yourself before you pick a room.

- Does the room get enough sunlight? Is it well-ventilated? Both are important for a sickroom.
- Does the room have a comfortable temperature throughout the day?
- Is the patient the sort of person who enjoys sitting out in the open air in the evenings with a cup of tea? If yes, pick a room close to a balcony. Even better if it also has a view of some sort, for being confined to a bed, away from the sights and sounds of people going about their daily life, can get quite depressing.
- Is it an infectious disease that the patient is suffering from? Or respiratory allergies or asthma? Then pick a room with as little upholstery, curtains and carpets as possible, or move heavy furnishings out before you move the patient in. Heavy furnishings hide all kinds of germs and are proven repositories of dust. Move in plastic furniture instead, or furniture with laminated, easy-to-clean-and-disinfect surfaces.
- Is the patient so confined to bed that he needs a bed pan? Is he throwing up frequently? In these cases, it would help if the patient's room was close to a bathroom, where pans could be quickly emptied and soiled bedclothes rinsed.
- Has the patient been advised a lot of rest? If yes, pick a room that is as far away as possible from traffic noise, and from the comings and goings of various people in the house.
- Is the patient well enough to watch TV but is compelled to stay in bed because of a broken bone? Think about moving a TV into the room.
- Is the best room for the patient a different one from his usual bedroom? If yes, populate the new room with favourite

possessions from his usual bedroom – books and toys, posters, photographs of friends, trophies. Having familiar loved things around speeds up recovery, apart from keeping away boredom and depression. Also bring in a comfortable chair for the patient to sit in when he is not in bed, and another chair for visitors.

SKILL 44
MAINTAINING THE SICKROOM

Once you have picked a room and set it up, draw up a daily drill not just for yourself but for everyone else in the family. Some of the daily must-do's might involve things like the following:

- Open up the curtains each morning and let the sunlight stream in. It is important for the patient's brain to track the passage of time.
- Clear up any clutter from the previous night. Tidy away books, toys, medicine bottles, board games, used cutlery, and water glasses, and stack them up neatly in their places or take them away for washing.
- Clean up spills and bedpans. Put used hand towels and any soiled bedclothes in the wash. Bag used tissues and other disposables and remove them from the room.
- Sweep and dust the room. Mop the floor and wipe down all surfaces with a pleasant-smelling germicidal cleaner.
- When the patient is in the toilet or in the shower, make the bed, with fresh linen if necessary. Plump up the pillows and shake out the covers so that the bed looks crisp and fresh again. When the patient lies down again, make sure the pillows are placed comfortably. Nothing is more frustrating to a weak person than a bunched-up bed-sheet or a lumpy pillow that he can't fix by himself.
- Encourage the patient to freshen up with a hot shower, change her clothes, and brush her hair (or do it for her if she is too weak or is unable to do it herself). Keeping clean is important for the patient not just for hygiene reasons;

following her usual routine will also make her feel less like a sick person.

- Through the day, check the sickroom for any food items or cups or plates that need clearing.
- Bring in some fresh flowers or a potted plant (unless the doctor has advised otherwise) into the room periodically. (This may be a good time to try the flower-arranging skills you picked up in Skill 29!). Watch a TV programme or play a board game with the patient every day. If it is at a fixed time, the patient will begin to look forward to it. That will help keep her spirits up and help the time pass more quickly.
- Keep up a string of cheerful chatter with the patient when you are in the room, if she is in the mood for it. And sometimes even if she is not. Read snippets out from the news, show her a fun WhatsApp video someone forwarded to you, offer to ring a friend. It is natural for the sick person to be cranky, so don't snap back or sulk in response. It is also natural for her to be worried about her recovery. Even if you share the worries, don't let her know it. It is your job to put a cheerful face on things, so that the patient feels positive, for that will actually put her on the road to recovery.
- Keep careful track of whether the patient has taken all the medicines he needs to take. There is a proper way to do that, and that's what you will need to learn as your next skill, before you can win the Caregiver Badge.

SKILL 45
MAINTAINING A MEDICATIONS CHART

When people are recovering from serious illness or surgery, or when the patient also has health conditions like diabetes or high blood pressure that require daily medication, there are a ton of pills to pop every day. Because different people are talking to the doctor, and if it isn't always one person who is administering the medication, all kinds of unnecessary confusion could occur about which medicine was taken and when.

It is vital to keep proper track of all of the patient's medications, and that's not only because you don't want the patient to miss taking a pill that he should have. It is also because the doctor can only make a proper analysis of what medicine is working and what isn't, and decide which medicines need to be changed, when he has the correct data before him.

As a WoCoTeen caregiver, you can help keep errors to a minimum and have data readily available to the doctor all the time, simply by following these pointers. Feel free to tweak, add to, or change these suggestions as you go along, based on your experiences with your patient.

- Using your brightest markers, make a big, cheerful 'Weekly Medication Chart' (see Chart 1 on the next page) on a full sheet of chart paper, and hang/tack it up on a wall of the sickroom where everyone, including the patient, can see it.
- In the first column, fill in the names of all the drugs the patient has to take, and the dosage of each, plus any instructions – to be taken on an empty stomach / to be taken after a meal / to be washed down with plenty of water.
- In the second column, write down the times of day when each medicine has to be taken – for instance, if a tablet has to be taken three times a day, write down, say, 6 a.m., 2 p.m., 10 p.m. If another has to be taken before bedtime, just put down one timing, say 10 p.m., in the third row of the time column, so that anyone can tell at a glance that it is a pill that is only to be taken at night.
- Every time the patient takes a pill, ask her or whoever has given her the pill to place a tick in the correct row under that particular day of the week. That way, it doesn't matter who has given the patient the medicine, everyone knows, at any given time, exactly what medicines he has had. This is also a great document for the doctor to look at and get his facts at a glance.
- The chart shown on the next page has enough room to accommodate information about the medication routine of a patient taking three different medications over a week. Hopefully, your patient will not need more than these many rows. However, if he needs a bigger one, you can just add rows until you have enough.

Chart 1

Drug:_____	Time	Sun	Mon	Tues	Wed	Thu	Fri	Sat
Dose:_____								
Instruction:_____								
_____								
Drug:_____	Time	Sun	Mon	Tues	Wed	Thu	Fri	Sat
Dose:_____								
Instruction:_____								
_____								
Drug:_____	Time	Sun	Mon	Tues	Wed	Thu	Fri	Sat
Dose:_____								
Instruction:_____								
_____								

■ Another useful chart to track the patient's progress and recovery is a Medical Log (see Chart 2). Human memory is notoriously unreliable when it comes to remembering things like exactly what reaction happened due to what medicine and when, especially when people are under stress, which they usually are when someone is ill. A good way to ensure that this kind of information is accurate is to record it all as it happens, in a Medical Log. Your patient's doctor will be most pleased to have such vital data available in such a clear format when he sees your patient next.

Chart 2

Medical Log

DATE	SYMPTOM/ ISSUE	CLINIC/ DOCTOR SEEN	DRUGS/TESTS/ PROCEDURES	DRUG REACTIONS/TEST RESULTS

■ Organizing the patient's medications: When there are so many different medicines to be given by the caregiver and taken by the patient, it is possible for one or both of them to get confused. As you can imagine, it is also a real pain to have to check the label of the tablet strip each time. Sometimes the part with the name is cut off – frustrating! One way to clear this obstacle is to organize the patient's medicines in creative and easy-to-administer ways.

Here are some ideas:

◆ Take out all the pills for the entire course from their packaging, and put all pills of each kind into individual bottles. Try and get bottles of different shapes and sizes for each so that you – and anyone else – can easily tell them apart. Then stick broad white labels onto each bottle and write down, in clear block letters, the name of the medicine on it – in a different colour for each bottle.

◆ Put rubber bands around each bottle to indicate how many times a day that tablet has to be taken. Let's say there is a tablet that has to be taken three times. The bottle it is in will have three rubber bands around it. Every time one tablet is taken, take off one rubber band until, by the end of the day, they are all off. Put the rubber bands back around the bottles each night.

Or try this. Buy three pill boxes in three cheerful colours, name them Breakfast, Lunch and Dinner. Every morning (or the night before) put all the medicines your patient is supposed to have at that particular mealtime into the respective box. After each meal, check that that particular tablet box is empty. Easy-peasy!

THE CAREGIVER'S CHALLENGES

Since the Squad hopes that no one in your immediate family has been struck with an illness that involves a long recovery, and also that no one will be soon, the first two challenges only involve testing the Squad member's knowledge of the things to keep in mind should such an event actually come to pass.

#43
THE SET-UP-THE-SICKROOM CHALLENGE

The Squad Leader hands out imaginary patient profiles to each of the Squad members, along with the plan of a house, with four bedrooms marked. The patient profile includes information like whether the patient is well enough to sit up by himself or go to the bathroom on his own, whether his doctor has advised that he be surrounded by activity or not, and so on. The house plan has details like the direction each bedroom faces, which rooms are cooler or warmer than others, and which rooms have bathrooms attached. Using the patient profile handed to him, a Squad member picks the most suitable room for the patient. He then explains the reasons for his choice to the rest of the Squad.

#44
THE MAINTAIN-THE-SICKROOM CHALLENGE

Squad members recite, from memory, ten essential daily tasks involved in the maintenance of a sickroom. Both the Squad leader and the rest of the Squad are present. Each Squad member takes the stage on a different day, so that the list of tasks gets firmly imprinted in the Squad members' minds.

#45
THE MAINTAIN-A-MEDICATIONS-CHART CHALLENGE

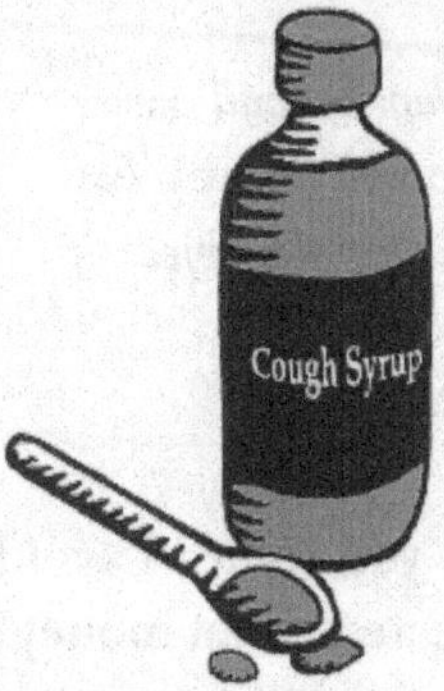

Every Squad member creates a medications chart for a grandparent or an older relative or neighbour who needs it. To do this, he either interviews the 'patient' or his caregivers – even perfectly healthy older people pop a few pills a day for various reasons. He gets the entire list of weekly medications from him or her to decide how many columns and rows the chart will require, and also finds out what each medication is for. If he interviews the caregiver, he also asks her what challenges are involved in taking care of her patient. In his presentation to the Squad, he includes an introduction to the patient and/or caregiver, the reasons why each medication has been prescribed, and the challenges of being a caregiver.

WOCOTEEN MERIT BADGE 12

THE MONEY MANAGER

Some people are fond of hoarding their money and never spending it. It is well to be thrifty, but it is also well to give away money where it is needed – in fact, that is part of the object of saving up your money.

– Camp Fire Yarn No. 20, *Scouting for Boys*

'Financial literacy' sounds like something you want to avoid at all costs, but it simply means 'being educated about money', even though it includes seemingly scary stuff like operating bank accounts, writing and signing cheques, fixed deposits, compound interest, government bonds, stocks and shares.... aaarrrrghhhhh!

But look on the bright side. Educating yourself when you're still in school about how money works, and grows, will give you a head-start in life as far as being 'financially independent' goes. Sure, right now, your parents take care of all your financial needs, and will probably to do so for several more years. But that's what makes this whole 'financially literate' thing so appealing at your age – you can *smartly* salt away *all* the money you are gifted for birthdays and festivals and simply-because-your-grandma-wants-to-give-you-some, and *all* the money you earn by making things and selling them or providing a paid service to someone (see Merit Badge 12 – The Entrepreneur) in magical things called Savings Accounts and Fixed Deposits, where it will 'grow' without your having to do any work at all!

By your eighteenth birthday, i.e., when you are getting ready to fly the coop and go off to college – you may have a small fortune. Either way, you will have an amount of money that is a good deal bigger than what you put in, which is only there because *you* decided you didn't want to miss the bus on 'financial literacy' all those years ago!

Understanding finances doesn't have to be as serious and boring as it sounds!

Inspired now, to win yourself the Money Manager Badge? Let's go open a bank account!

SKILL 46
OPEN YOUR OWN SAVINGS BANK ACCOUNT

In May 2014, the Reserve Bank of India (RBI), which is the apex bank of the country and makes all our banking rules, announced that, for the first time, children above the age of 10 would be allowed to open their own independent savings accounts in Indian banks (beforé that, 'minors', or those under the age of eighteen, were only allowed to open a savings account jointly with a parent or guardian).

The RBI also granted minors above 10 the power to operate their 'fully-loaded' account independently – they could be issued their own chequebook, and their own ATM card as well. They would have the same ability as adults to transfer money from their account to someone else via their phones using mobile banking, and buy what they wanted online, using Internet banking. It was meant, according to the State Bank of India's website, not just 'to help children learn the importance of saving money' but also 'to allow them to experiment with the buying power of money' and 'teach them the nuances of personal finance'.

All the minor needed to do to enjoy all this heady financial power was to convince his parents to let him open and operate his account. Here are some strategies to help you achieve that:

- Read the information under Skill 48 – 'Understand How You Can Make Your Money Grow' on page 159 to get your background information on how banks work.
- Google 'savings bank account minors India'. Several bank website pages, giving details of their minor savings accounts schemes, will come up in the search.
- Read them through and understand what the parent's role is in each of them, so that you can explain it clearly to yours.
- Check to see what the 'minimum balance requirement' at each bank is. If the minimum balance requirement is, say, ₹5,000, it means that your account should always have at least ₹5,000 in it. That means that if you have only about ₹600 which you earned from selling cupcakes, you can't open an account – you will need your parents to pitch in with the other ₹4,400. As you can see, the less the minimum balance required, the easier your parents will be to convince.
- Check to make sure that the bank has a branch close to your home; close enough, preferably, for you to be able to walk there yourself to operate your account.
- Make sure to also get all the same information about minor savings account 'products' (yes, banks sell you products too, only these are 'financial products') in one or two other banks.
- Invite your parents to a presentation. Begin by talking about why you think it is important for children and teens to have their own savings accounts. Then present a compare-and-contrast chart for three minor savings account products offered by three different banks. Tell them why you think a particular product would work best for you, but don't neglect to add that the final decision is theirs since you are new to all this, unlike them.
- As a show of good faith, and to reassure them, tell them that they can keep your ATM card for the first six months to a year,

accompanying you to the ATM whenever you need to draw money. Promise that you will not be using mobile or Internet banking. Inform them that you will be depending on them to show you how to deposit money into your account or to write a cheque from your account to a charity.

- Hold your breath and wait for their decision. Chances are they will agree without too much of a fuss, since they can see the benefits too, and are impressed by how professionally you've gone about your research and how earnest you are.

SKILL 47
LEARN TO KEEP ACCOUNTS

Having your own savings bank account is a great thing for many reasons. One of them is that the bank then keeps track of your money – how much you had at the beginning of the year; how much you have today; how much you took out, or 'withdrew', from it via the ATM or a cheque, and when; how much fresh money you put in, and when; how much you spent, where, and when (this only happens if you have a debit card and used it to pay for something. A debit card allows you to spend money from your account without actually withdrawing it in the form of cash).

But what if your parents decide, for whatever reason, that you cannot have your own savings account? What if they tell you, say, that they will keep all your gift money safe in a cupboard at home, and become your bank and ATM themselves – you just have to ask them for your money when you need it, instead of withdrawing it from the ATM (of course they can't really be your *bank* since your money will not 'grow' by sitting in a cupboard). What if they say they will invest your gift money in such a way that it grows well (and even share the information about its growth with you), and give you a monthly allowance to manage as you like, instead?

In each of these cases, you will have to keep accounts – that is, record all the information about how much money you have, and what you are doing with it – yourself, since there is no bank (the Bank of Mom and Dad doesn't count) to do it for you.

Which is all good, since learning how to keep accounts – also called bookkeeping – is hugely important. Not only does bookkeeping build the good habit of financial discipline for life – it takes a lot of discipline to keep a record of the money you spend each day, or week – it also helps you to know, at any given time, exactly how much money you have today, which will help you make quick and sensible decisions about how to spend it.

Most importantly, it gives you insights into your spending habits, answers to questions like:

- Are you a spender or a saver?
- What do you spend most of your money on? What percentage of your money do you typically save?
- What do you save money for? When you have saved enough, do you reward yourself for being disciplined about saving and spend that money on the thing you were saving for? Or do you suddenly become miserly, deciding that you don't actually need the thing you were saving for after all? Whichever course of action you picked, think about why you chose it.
- Do you find it more difficult to spend your own money than your parents'? Why do you think that is? Do you think it is fair that you feel that way?
- What do you do when you unexpectedly get a lot of money – maybe an aunt visiting from the USA handed over ₹1,000 as a gift? Do you spend your windfall on something extravagant and unnecessary that you've always longed for? Or do you put it away for a more sensible purchase later?

Knowing these things about yourself at an early age will help you tweak and correct any potentially undesirable behaviour – maybe you spend too little, maybe you spend too much, maybe you hate to share your money – before it becomes a habit you can't break.

Clearly, bookkeeping is an essential life skill. Here is a sample bookkeeping table that almost-WoCoTeen Enakshi Sinha kindly lent to us. Tweak it as you like to suit your needs.

Name: Enakshi Sinha

Life Goal: To be a WoCoTeen!

Date	Credit + Expenditure Description	Debit (Saving – ST*)	Debit (Saving – LT**)	Debit (Sharing)	Debit (Spending)
1/1/2017	Beginning balance	₹0 **Goal 1 – ₹258**	₹0 **Goal A – ₹7,000**	₹0	₹0
2/1/2017	Monthly allowance (₹500)	+ ₹50 = ₹50	+ ₹250 = ₹250	+ ₹50 = ₹50	+ ₹150 = ₹150
5/1/2017	Kathi Roll				– ₹50 = ₹100
18/1/2017	Chips and drink treat for BFF				– ₹80 = ₹20
2/2/2017	Monthly allowance (₹500)	+₹50 = ₹100	+ ₹250 = ₹500	+ ₹50 = ₹100	+ ₹150 = ₹170
10/2/2017	Birthday money (₹2500 – woohoo!)	+ ₹158 = ₹258 – GOAL!	+ 1500 = ₹2000	+ ₹500 = ₹600	+ ₹342 = ₹511
11/2/2017	New book	– ₹258 = ₹0 **Goal 2 – ₹440**			
12/2/2017	5 sets of markers for orphanage kids			– ₹400 = ₹200	
15/2/2017	Nail art kit				– ₹330 = ₹181
28/2/2017	Pre-finals ice cream outing with the gang				– ₹140 = ₹41
2/3/2017	Monthly allowance (₹500)	+ ₹50 = ₹50	+ ₹250 = ₹2250	+ ₹50 = ₹250	+ ₹150 = ₹191

***Enakshi's ST (Short-Term) Saving Goals**

- Goal 1 – Book (₹258)
- Goal 2 – Rainbow Loom set (₹440)

****Enakshi's LT (Long Term) Saving Goals**

- Goal A – Mountain bike (₹7,000)

The sample table records Enakshi Sinha's money management details over two months.

- In the **Credit + Expenditure Description** column, Enakshi puts down details of any money that she receives (Credit) as well as descriptions of all expenditures she makes, against the respective dates.

■ The **Debit columns** keep track of money saved, shared, and spent.

◆ **Money saved:** Enakshi has two different kinds of saving goals – an ST or Short-Term Saving Goal, and an LT or Long-Term Saving Goal. Anything that she is saving up for which costs less than ₹1,000 is considered a Short-Term Saving Goal because it won't take her very long to save up that amount, anything that she is saving for that costs more than that is a Long-Term Saving Goal. Every month, Enakshi puts aside 10 per cent (₹50) of her allowance towards her ST Saving Goals, and 50 per cent (₹250) towards her LT Saving Goals. When she gets a sudden windfall, like the ₹2,500 she received on 10/2/2017, she puts aside more under each debit column.

◆ **Money shared:** Enakshi puts aside 10 per cent of her allowance each month under a separate 'Sharing' heading. This is for giving away in charity to kids less fortunate than she is.

◆ **Money spent:** Enakshi puts aside ₹150 from her allowance every month to spend on treats for herself and her friends.

■ Every time she spends money, Enakshi records the expenditure in the appropriate column with a minus sign before it. Then she subtracts that amount from the amount that was originally available in that column, to get the new amount available.

■ Every time she receives money, Enakshi records the 'credit' in the appropriate column with a plus sign before it. Then she adds that amount to the amount previously available in that column, to get the new amount available.

■ Because she updates the amount available in each column every time she spends or receives money, Enakshi needs to look at only one row – the bottom-most one – to instantly have all the important information she needs about her financial situation. After her March allowance came in, she had ₹50 (of the ₹440 she needs) saved up towards her next short-term goal – a Rainbow Loom Set, ₹2,250 (of the ₹7,000 she needs) saved up towards her long-term goal – a mountain bike, ₹250 in her sharing account to use for someone in need and ₹191 available to spend on whatever she liked in March. Pretty cool right? You can – and should! – try it too!

SKILL 48
UNDERSTAND HOW YOU CAN MAKE YOUR MONEY GROW

There is only one way to make your money grow, and that is by lending it to someone who wants it, i.e., the borrower.

Why would anyone lend his hard-earned money to someone else, though? Classical economics tells us that it is mainly because of what's in it for the lender – a lot of money!

You see, when the borrower returns the amount he borrowed to the lender, he also pays him a 'borrowing fee' (called 'interest'). This fee is the lender's income, money he earns for himself. Essentially, therefore, anyone who lends money gets to earn money without doing any work at all (except when people lend money without charging interest, out of the goodness of their hearts).

But who would you lend your money to? No one is likely to come around asking you for a loan, are they? Ha! That's what *you* think. There are any number of 'people' around who would love to borrow your money, and will be happy to pay you interest on it too! Here are a few of them.

Banks want to borrow your money.
Yeah, that sounds weird, because banks are places that are constantly lending money to people. Anytime anyone needs a loan, one of the first places she approaches is a bank. But where do banks get the money to lend to people from? Mainly from the apex bank of the country (the RBI in our case) but also from large companies, and from – hold your breath! – *you!* Yup, the money you put in your savings account is actually money that you are *lending* to the bank!

So although it sounds a little upside-down that it's actually the bank that pays you for opening a savings account, rather than you paying the bank for keeping your money safe and doing all your bookkeeping for you, it makes sense when you realize that banks need money too. Opening a savings account, or putting your money in a fixed deposit in a bank, is a good, safe way to lend money, earn interest and grow your money. Indian banks pay about 6 per cent interest per year on money in savings bank accounts (i.e., if you put ₹500 in your account at the beginning of the year, you will have earned an extra ₹6 for every ₹100, or ₹30, by the end of the year. In December, your ₹500 will have – *ka-ching!* – become ₹530, just like that! See? Your money has grown!).

The government wants to borrow your money.
It's true! Governments need money for all kinds of public projects and one way to raise that money is to borrow it from their citizens. To do this, the government sells what are called 'government bonds'. By buying these bonds (Government bonds can cost as little as ₹101) you are lending the amount stamped on the bond to the government. The government takes your money and uses it in a project – like building a steel plant or a dam or a toll road – that they hope will be profitable and make a lot of money for them. Using the profits, they will pay you the interest due to you. Government bonds are very safe investments too – a bond is the government's promise to return your money, with interest, at the end of a particular time period, and the government's word is considered as good as gold. Investing money in Indian government bonds earns you a higher rate of interest – 8 per cent – than lending to a bank does. That means you will get an extra ₹40 instead of ₹30 on your ₹500.

Companies want to borrow your money.

Companies need tons and tons of money too, especially when they want to expand their operations – build new factories, buy new machinery, hire more people, open offices abroad. They could borrow from banks, of course, but they would rather avoid that because bank loans can be very expensive (i.e., the borrowing fee a bank will charge can be pretty high).

Instead, they borrow money from the public by allowing people to buy a small share in their company. When you buy one share, or a hundred, you become a part-owner of the company. That means you get to share in its profits too. If the company does very well, all the shareholders – people like you – stand to make a lot more money than what they first paid to buy their share. That is their reward for taking a risk in lending money to the company.

But it *is* a bit of a risk lending money to a company, because the company may not do as well as it hoped. It might even fail completely. In that situation, you will lose money. It's a bit of a gamble.

Whom you decide to lend your money to is your call to make. It is best to put your money into safe, watertight investments, with advice from your parents or a financial expert who gives sound advice.

THE MONEY MANAGER'S CHALLENGES

#46
THE OPEN-A-BANK-ACCOUNT CHALLENGE

Pool the information you and your Squad members have collected about the features of 'Minor Accounts' offered by different banks, to create a comprehensive presentation with information about Minor Accounts in 6–7 banks. Invite your parents to a Squad meeting, and share all the information with them. Sit back and watch the 'peer pressure' work on your parents to allow you to open your own account.

#47
THE BOOKKEEPING CHALLENGE

Using Enakshi Sinha's sample bookkeeping table, make one for yourself. Record all your financial 'inflows' and 'outflows' in it over the next 3–4 months, until you've got the hang of bookkeeping and acquired the discipline of recording every small detail of your income and expenditure. Don't forget to set yourself your own short-term and long-term saving goals, and work towards them. At the end of four months, make a presentation to the Squad and the Squad Leader about your experiences.

#48
THE MAKE-YOUR-MONEY-GROW CHALLENGE

If one of your parents is a stockbroker or a banker or is just a smart, informed investor, get him or her to come and talk to the Squad about the best ways to make your money grow. Discuss with your Squad members which option each of you would choose.

THE COMMUNITY COVENANT

I AM AN INFORMED, RESPONSIBLE AND VALUABLE MEMBER OF MY COMMUNITY

The Patriot

The Citizen

The Interpreter

The Volunteer

The Friend to Animals

The Cool Head in a Crisis

THE COMMUNITY COVENANT

I AM AN INFORMED, RESPONSIBLE AND VALUABLE MEMBER OF MY COMMUNITY

6

MERIT BADGES TO BE WON

The Patriot

The Citizen

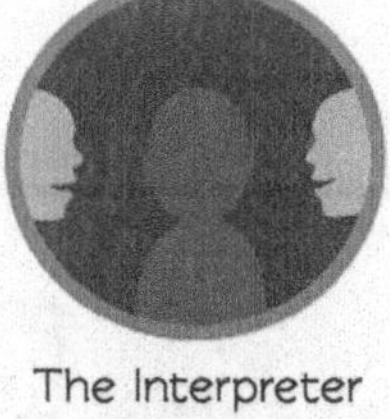

The Interpreter

The Volunteer

The Friend to Animals

The Cool Head in a Crisis

DON'T SPEND THE WHOLE OF YOUR TIME AND MONEY MERELY TO AMUSE YOURSELF, BUT THINK FIRST OF HOW YOU CAN BE OF USE TO THE COMMON GOOD.

BY DOING SO, YOU WILL BE PREPARING YOURSELF TO BE A GOOD CITIZEN NOT ONLY OF YOUR COUNTRY BUT OF THE WHOLE WORLD.

- B-P, in Camp Fire Yarn No. 2, *Scouting for Boys*

Yeah, yeah, we know. You're screwing your face up at the bunch of 'improving' lessons coming your way – love your fellow man, respect your flag, share that bar of chocolate, yada yada yada. And you're right, these are exactly the kind of lessons parents and teachers adore and approve of, which automatically makes you want to resist them.

But hey, all good things have to be earned, sometimes by doing things you don't necessarily want to do. And the 'good things' up for grabs here are six – that's right, SIX – WoCoTeen merit badges! Win these six, and you're already one-quarter of the way to your membership in the Squad.

Sure, these are not the most fun badges in terms of the challenges you have to complete to win them – you are not, for instance, required to learn sign language, go to camp, or make deductions like Sherlock. These are the 'grunt work' badges – the kind that require you to swot stuff, get out in the streets to do not necessarily 'cool' things, smile at people you may not like... yeahhh. In terms of WoCoTeen priorities, however, they rank way up on top. Rest assured, you will get far more respect from the Squad – and from your friends, family and neighbours – if you complete these challenges, and complete them with heart.

So put on that sunny WoCoTeen smile (even if it kills you), adjust your halo, and begin!

WOCOTEEN MERIT BADGE 13

THE PATRIOT

> *My country and your country did not grow of itself out of nothing. It was made by men and women by dint of hard work and hard fighting, often at the sacrifice of their lives – that is, by their whole-hearted patriotism.*
> **– Camp Fire Yarn No. 2, *Scouting for Boys***

Love for your country – it is a grand, heart-swelling emotion and an important one for every citizen to feel. After all, unless you are proud of who you are and where you come from, you cannot truly understand, respect or treat as an equal someone who is different from you but has the same pride in himself and his land and his people.

The best way to develop that love and feel that pride is to educate yourself about your country. The four essential skills you must master – and the four challenges you must crack – to win the Patriot badge will help kick-start your lifelong journey there.

Here's the thing to remember, though: Sure, a patriot loves his country more than any other, but he certainly does not believe that his country is *superior* to any other. He doesn't believe his country is always right, either. And when he finds something he disapproves of about his country? Why, the patriot works to change it, from the inside!

SKILL 49
KNOW – REALLY KNOW – YOUR NATIONAL ANTHEM

You've sung it – or mumbled it, anyway – hundreds of times. Just hearing its rousing tune makes your parents' and grandparents' eyes well up (adults are weird like that). When the tune is played at an international sports event for an Indian sportsperson or team standing on the podium, your heart feels like it might burst with pride. Yup, national anthems are pretty powerful.

Rabindranath Tagore, popularly known as 'Gurudev'.

But do you know what your National Anthem means (or even know the right lyrics)? High time you found out, don't you think?

First, though, a few fascinating facts about the Indian National Anthem.

- The song we know today as *Jana Gana Mana* was originally a 5-stanza hymn titled *Bharoto Bhagyo Bidhata*. It was written in Bengali (but with a lot of Sanskrit words included) in 1911 by Nobel Prize winner and Poet Laureate Rabindranath Tagore.
- It was first sung at the Calcutta session of the Indian National Congress on 27 December 1911.
- The song was also sung at a reception to welcome the British emperor, George V, just three days later (*fun fact*: the Gateway of India on the Mumbai waterfront, overlooking the Arabian Sea, was built to welcome him – yup, he came by ship, like everyone else in those days). Some British and Indian newspapers interpreted *Bharata Bhagya Vidhata* ('He who manages India's destiny'), and *Adhinayaka* ('Ruler of the minds of the people') to mean the emperor, when Tagore had really meant the Divine.
- To understand what the words of the National Anthem really mean, turn the page. This version is based on the official translation done by Tagore himself.
- The first stanza of the original song was adopted as the National Anthem of India by the Constituent Assembly on 24 January 1950, just two days before the first official Republic Day.

Jana Gana Mana Adhinaayaka Jaya He
You are the ruler of the minds of all people

Bhaarata Bhaagya Vidhaata
O dispenser of India's destiny

Punjab, Sindh, Gujarata, Maratha, Dravida, Utkala, Vanga,*
Your name rouses the hearts of Punjab, Sind, Gujarat and Maratha, of the Dravida and Orissa and Bengal

Vindhya, Himachala, Yamuna, Ganga, Uchchala Jaladhi Taranga
It echoes in the hills of the Vindhyas and Himalayas, mingles in the music of the Yamuna and Ganges and is chanted by the waves of the Indian sea

Tava Shubha Naame Jaage, Tava Shubha Aashish Maange, Gaahe Tava Jaya Gaatha
And they all pray for your blessings and sing your praises

Jana Gana Mangala Daayaka Jaya He Bhaarata Bhaagya Vidhaata
The happiness of all people lies in your hands, O dispenser of India's destiny

Jaya He Jaya He Jaya He Jaya Jaya Jaya Jaya He
Victory, victory, victory to you

Now commit the correct words – and the translation – to memory, so that you can sing the anthem with more feeling henceforth.

*(*In 2005, a case was filed in the Supreme Court demanding that Sindh be dropped from the song, since the region has been part of Pakistan since Independence. Others argued that the Sindhis (people of Sindh) are still a big part of India and that Sindhu was also a reference to the river Indus. The Supreme Court decided in favour of letting the wording remain unchanged.)*

SKILL 50
TREAT THE TIRANGA RIGHT

Just like the National Anthem, our national flag – the Tricolour or the Tiranga – is a powerful symbol of the promise 1.3 billion Indians make each day to each other and to their country – we belong together! Today, the Tiranga is also a very visible symbol – plastic or paper versions of it are sold at traffic lights around Independence Day, fans paint the flag colours on their faces before an international cricket match, and cars and trucks fly it whenever their drivers are feeling patriotic (like after we won that cricket match).

It didn't always used to be this way, though. In 1995, a young industrialist called Naveen Jindal returned from his studies in the USA to work his way up the family business. As president of the student government at his university, he had proudly displayed the Indian flag at every opportunity, and when he returned, he decided to fly the Tiranga from the roof of his factory. He had no idea that according to the Indian Flag Code then, Indian citizens were forbidden from flying the flag privately except on Independence Day and Republic Day. Government officials knew the rule, though, and they made him take it down.

Stung, Jindal filed a petition in the Delhi High Court against what he believed was an unjust law, arguing that the national flag belonged as much to the citizens of the country as it did to the government. Seven years of legal battle later, in 2002, Jindal won. The Union Cabinet issued a new, amended Flag Code that permitted every citizen of India to fly the Tiranga any old day he or she wanted to. In 2005, an amendment to another old law allowed the flag to be printed on clothing. In 2010, again through Jindal's efforts, Indians got the right to fly the flag through the night too (before this, the rule was that the flag had to be lowered at sunset).

And that's why you see the Tiranga everywhere you look these days! Thank you, Mr Jindal!

But just winning a right to do something doesn't complete the circle. Rights come with duties, and it is our duty to always, always safeguard our Tiranga's dignity, honour and respect.

Here are a few (but not all – look up the rest) pointers on how to do it. Swot 'em up!

- It isn't mandatory for the public to only fly flags made of khadi, but do try and use a khadi one whenever possible. It is symbolic of all the sacrifices that went into winning ourselves that flag in the first place.
- Ensure that the ratio of your flag's length to its breadth is 3:2. If the length of the flag is 18 inches, say, its breadth must be exactly 12 inches (18:12, or 18/12 is equivalent to 3:2, or 3/2).

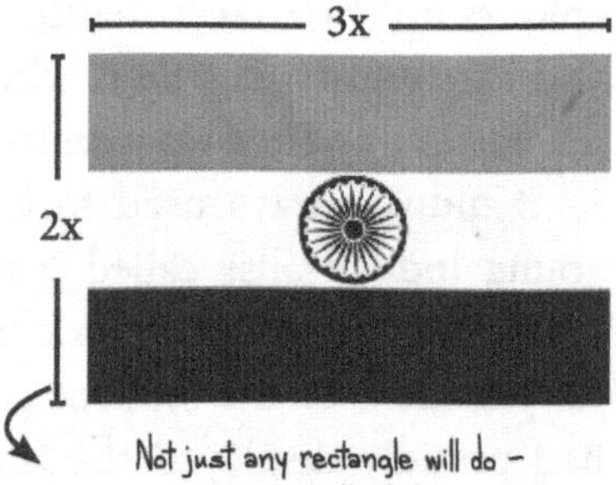

Not just any rectangle will do – it has to be 3:2.

- Never use the flag to cover tables, lecterns or buildings. Do not drape it from railings, either.
- If you don't have a flagpole to fly it from, hang the flag horizontally on a wall. If you choose to hang it vertically, the saffron stripe should be to the left of whoever's facing it.
- Never 'dip' the flag (like your school captain 'dips' the school flag to the chief guest as he marches past on Sports Day) to any person or object.
- Whenever the flag is being hoisted or lowered, and whenever it passes you in a parade, face the flag and stand at attention.
- If you want to salute the flag, do it the right way. Raise your right hand to your forehead with your arm parallel to the ground and palm facing outward. Your fingers should point to your left and the top of your index finger should be in line with the middle of your eyebrow.
- Never let the flag touch the ground, as far as possible. Make sure none of its ends is trailing in the dust or in water.
- Never put any message, inscription or lettering on the flag.

Do you know why the Army, Navy and Air Force have different salutes?

Army officers salute with the palms open, facing the person / flag being saluted, to show that they are not carrying any weapons and that they can be trusted.

The Air Force salute used to be just like the Army one, but from 2006 they salute with their palms at 45 degrees to the ground – to show the progress of humans towards the sky!

In the Navy salute the palm faces down (in olden days, the sailors constantly had to work on their ships, which got their palms dirty, and showing these dirty palms to their seniors was considered disrespectful!).

- Never use the flag as a receptacle for holding or for carrying things.
- You can print or paint the national flag on clothes, but only on those worn above the waist. And definitely not on cushion covers, handkerchiefs and other such items.
- If your flag is torn or damaged and you want to dispose of it, burn it (in private), bury it deep within the ground, or immerse it into the river Ganga (serious!). Do *not* chuck it in a dustbin. (That's why it's better never to buy those little plastic flags at traffic lights – there's no good way of disposing of them respectfully).

SKILL 51
UNCOVER THE SECRETS OF THE INDIAN CURRENCY NOTE

Actually, while it's true that each currency note holds many secrets, we're talking about just one secret here. And it isn't *really* a secret, because it is sitting there in plain view on every rupee note you've used. Now, without looking at a rupee note, answer this question, off the top of your head:

In how many languages is the value of each currency note indicated on it?

Ha! You have no idea, have you?

Now that you have failed so spectacularly, take out a currency note and look at it. On the front (the 'Gandhi side' of the note – all the currency notes now in use feature Gandhi's face, by the way), the value of the note is indicated in two languages (which have two different scripts) – Hindi and English. Now turn the note over to the side that celebrates other aspects of India – in the new ₹2,000 note, for instance, we honour the stellar work of India's home-grown space agency, ISRO, with a picture of the Mangalyaan orbiter that it developed. In a little window along the left edge, the value of the note is indicated in no less than 15 different Indian languages, which, between them, have a dozen different scripts! In all, there are 17 different languages on every note, of which 16 are official Indian languages. So what is so special about that? Well, even the Euro – which is the official currency of the Eurozone, which comprises 19 different countries – has the value of a note only written in two languages on it – English and Greek. That's partly because most Eurozone languages use only the Roman English script (bo-ring!), which makes the amount of diversity India has, all in one country, even more stunning by comparison. What is also wonderful is how inclusive India is, to acknowledge so many languages on every currency note.

China is one of the few other countries that puts more than two languages on its currency – every Yuan note has its value indicated in five languages.

Get this, though – there are actually 22 official Indian languages – in alphabetical order, they are Assamese, Bengali, Bodo, Dogri, Gujarati, Hindi, Kannada, Kashmiri, Konkani, Maithili, Malayalam, Manipuri, Marathi, Nepali, Odia, Punjabi, Sanskrit, Santali, Sindhi, Tamil, Telugu and Urdu. Which means that, right now, six of them are feeling pretty hurt that they haven't been represented on the rupee note. The general (unconfirmed) theory is that the

RBI hasn't included them not because it bears them any malice, but because of a more practical reason – there is just no more space on the note! Also, fun fact – these 22 are only the 'official languages' of India* – there are over 130 other languages and dialects that are spoken by at least 10,000 people each! That's why the Constitution of India has refrained to this day from naming any one of our languages the 'National Language' of India – instead, both Hindi and English have been given the status of 'official' languages.

The 15 languages on the Indian note besides English and Hindi.

Wooooo! Any wonder that this Tower-of-Babel country is so difficult to govern? How cool is it, though, that despite all the diversity, we've all hung together as one country, happily chattering away in 150 languages and dialects, for 70 years after Independence?

SKILL 52
EXPLAIN INDIA TO A FOREIGNER

How in heck do you begin to explain this vast, lumbering, chaotic, diverse, completely mind-boggling country-subcontinent to someone who isn't from here? Especially when you don't understand it yourself? Here are a few opening lines you may find useful.

- **We've been there, done that.** We've seen invaders come and go (or stay), seen empires rise and fall (and rise again), watched

**According to the Eighth Amendment of the Indian Constitution. However, English is also considered an official language.*

the birth and spread of new religions (and welcomed them all in), and given the world brilliant ideas, literature, science and philosophy (while absorbing those the world brought to us). When you are a 5000-year-old civilization, stuff like that comes with the territory.

- **India lives in several centuries at the same time.** When the new comes into India, the old doesn't really go away – it smiles, shrugs and makes place for the newcomer (on our streets, bullock carts sit cheek by jowl with electric cars). We learnt that from our gods – they were most accommodating too, constantly scooting over to make place for the new gods that we created.
- **We are the world's largest democracy, and we actually function as one!** Never in our history have we had a dictator, a military coup, a civil war or a hostile takeover of government. Except for a brief, dark 21-month period (1975–77) when a state of Emergency was declared, we have had regular, free and fair elections, in sharp contrast to many of our neighbours.
- **India has two major religions – Bollywood and cricket. Haha.** Actually, India has six major religions. In order of the number of people who practise them, they are Hinduism, Islam, Christianity, Sikhism, Buddhism and Jainism. Four of these religions were born in India, the other two came to us almost as soon as they were born. The first mosque in India – the Cheraman Juma Masjid in Kodungallur, Kerala – was built in 629 CE, while the Prophet was still alive, and it is believed that

St Thomas, one of the 12 apostles of Jesus, brought his teachings to us via the port of Muziris (today called Kochi, again in Kerala) in 52 CE, well before 'Christianity' was formalized under Emperor Constantine in 313 CE! *And* we have tens of thousands of people who follow other religions – Judaism, Zoroastrianism and the Bah'ai faith, to mention only three. Yup, if any country has the right to call itself 'God's Own Country', it's us.

The coolest part? Despite all this religious diversity, India's Constitution proudly declares India a secular country – religion and government are not a package deal here, and everyone is allowed to follow whatever faith they want.

The six major religions in India – can you tell which symbol belongs to which religion?

- We are a country that thrives on contrast, the kind that would confound most others. For instance:
  - People think of us as a Hindu country (and with good reason – some 80 per cent of our population practises Hinduism), but we have the world's third largest population of Muslims.
  - We are the ahimsa-loving land of the Buddha, of Ashoka and of Mahatma Gandhi, but we are also one of only eight countries in the world that have tested nuclear weapons, and we have one of the largest standing armies in the world. Go figure.
  - While a quarter of our population is completely illiterate (which is a terrible thing, but not when you consider that over three-quarters of us were illiterate when the British left), there are, among the literate, scientists so clever that they helped India launch a successful mission to Mars on her first attempt, for less than what it cost the makers of the Hollywood film *Gravity* to make their film. Not kidding.

Contrast that with the US, where women got the right to vote in 1920, which was 140 years after their country became an independent democracy!

◆ We are a pretty patriarchal country for the most part, but we've had women as Prime Minister and President – not very many other countries can boast of that. Plus, we granted voting rights to all adult women from the day we became independent!

◆ We are a society that sometimes discriminates horribly based on the caste a person belongs to, but it was a brilliant scholar, lawyer and activist from the Mahar (or Dalit) caste, one of the worst treated castes in Indian society, who was the chief architect of our country's most important document – our Constitution. His name was Dr Bhimrao Ramji Ambedkar.

By now your listener should be pretty gobsmacked. Now you can have a *real* conversation!

SKILL 53
BE A PATRIOT OF THE WORLD

While they know, love and celebrate their countries, WoCoTeens never lose sight of the fact that the borders between countries are essentially artificial ones, and that people of all nationalities are part of the human race, the big diverse family of seven billion people who share a home called Earth. As an aspiring WoCoTeen, neither should you.

Whenever there is an opportunity to interact with someone from another country – maybe she is a tourist in your city looking for directions, maybe he has come in to study at university here – make sure you make the visitor feel as welcome as possible. Ask about his country, tell him about yours. Show genuine interest and you will be surprised at the number of wonderful things you can learn. Go the extra mile for that person, without judging him on what he is wearing, the colour of his skin, the religion he practises, or the country he is from. Go, World Patriot!

THE PATRIOT'S CHALLENGES

So you think you've got those four skills done? Time to take on these challenges then!

Here's how. 'Demo' each task to your Squad Leader. He/she will decide if you've 'passed'. Make sure you have him/her tick each challenge off the 'Almost a WoCoTeen!' checklist as you complete it.

#49
THE ANTHEM CHALLENGE

- Sing the National Anthem (tunefully, mind!) and explain its meaning.
- Indian freedom fighter Subhash Chandra Bose had a national anthem written for Azad Hind, a provisional Indian government he had established in Singapore in the 1940s. This anthem was in Hindi and was based on *Jana Gana Mana.* Find out the name of this anthem, and sing its first verse to the tune of Jana Gana Mana.

#50
THE FLAG CHALLENGE

Tell your Squad Leader:

- Five things one should *not* do with the Tiranga, and follow it up with the rule for the right way to dispose of an old, dirty or torn flag.
- The official names for the shades of the orange and green used on the Tiranga.

There are so many shades of green and orange in the world, so how do you specify to someone the exact shades the Indian flag has? That's why those shades have 'official' names that everyone understands.

#51
THE CURRENCY-NOTE CHALLENGE

Tell your Squad Leader:

- The names of the 22 official Indian languages, and the six that haven't (yet) made it to the Indian currency note. Also tell her / him the names of the three languages featured on the note in which a rupee is not called anything that remotely sounds like a 'rupee'.

- The names of the five places in India where currency notes are printed, and the five places where our coins are minted. Mark all 10 places on a map of India.

#52
THE EXPLAIN-INDIA CHALLENGE

- List out five cool-weird-insane-wonderful 'It-only-happens-in-India' things that make you proud, every day, to be Indian.
- Learn to tie a saree or dhoti around yourself *properly* (which means you should be able to run 50 m in it and not have it fall off!). Then tie a sari (or dhoti) around a partner in the Squad (See pages 179 and 180 for a crash course!).
- Read up all you can about a historical monument (fort, palace, tomb, war memorial), or a heritage monument in your city (a place of worship with some historical or cultural significance, a botanical garden, the oldest part of your city). Visit and explore it for yourself, or with an official guide. Then visit again with your Squad and give them a guided tour yourself. If every member of the Squad does this activity, you will end up learning about five or six monuments in and around your city, and have a lot of fun in the bargain!

#53
THE WORLD-PATRIOT CHALLENGE

- With the help of your Squad Leader, pick six countries to research (if you have six members in your Squad). Each country must be from a different continent, and all should be countries that squad members know very little about. Pick one country each to research, by draw of lots. At the end of two weeks, present your report to the Squad. Make sure you include one cultural feature of the country and its people that is very similar to one of India's.

Here's how to tie a sari!

Take the top edge of the sari and tuck it in the petticoat – starting from the right side of your waist across your left.

Using the left hand, bring the sari around your waist from the back and centre, tucking it in.

Make 6-8 pleats, each about 5-6 inches wide, from the remaining part of the sari.

Tuck the pleats into the petticoat, facing the pleats to the left. You can pin up the pleats at the centre and tuck the sari edge at the left side of your waist.

Bring the remaining part of the sari across your back to your front from the right side, without tucking it.

Decide the length of your pallu and accordingly adjust the sari from the back and front.

Place the pallu properly on your left shoulder and pin it in place to fix it. Woohoo – you're done!

And here's how to tie a dhoti!

Hold up the dhoti behind you with most of its length to your right and just enough at the left to be able to tuck it in.

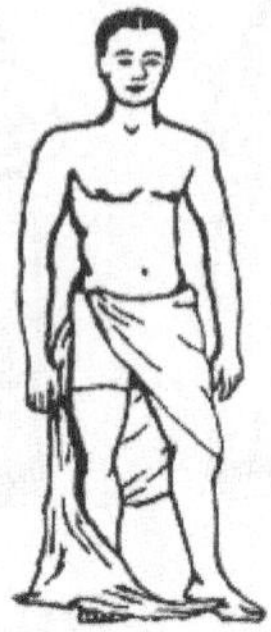

Tuck the left edge into your shorts or tie it using a square knot to a bit of the cloth on the right side.

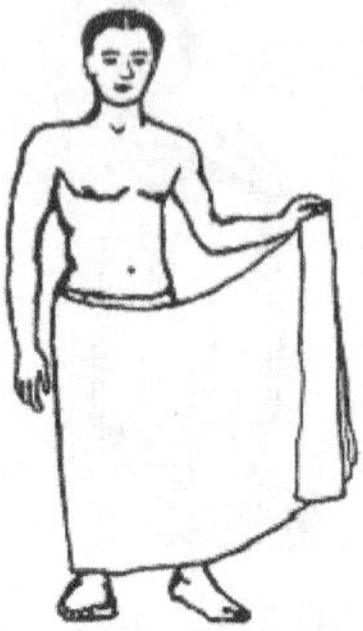

Using your left hand, bring the longer edge to your front and pleat the cloth.

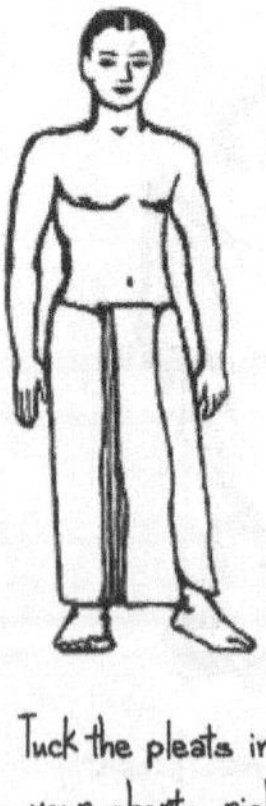

Tuck the pleats into your shorts, right under your belly button.

Grab the bottom end of the pleats and bring them up behind you from in between your legs.

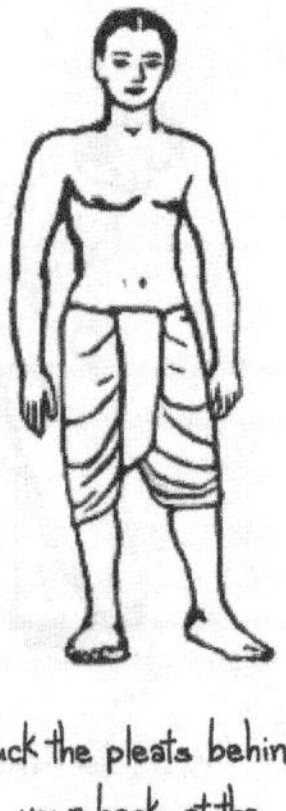

Tuck the pleats behind your back, at the centre and lo – your dhoti is ready!

WOCOTEEN MERIT BADGE 14

THE CITIZEN

Your forefathers worked hard, fought hard, and died hard, to make your country for you. Don't let them look down from heaven and see you loafing about with your hands in your pockets, doing nothing to keep it up.
– Camp Fire Yarn No. 26, *Scouting for Boys*

Who is a citizen of India? There's a simple, straightforward, technical answer to that one – anyone who has all the documents required to get himself or herself an Indian passport. Ask a different question – What does being a citizen mean? – and the answers get a little fuzzy and a little more complex. Tweak that question a little – what does being a *good, responsible* citizen mean? Hmm, bet that would lead to some serious hmm-never-thought-about-that head-scratching.

In short, though, we can all agree that as a good, responsible citizen, it is important, first of all, to educate yourself about your country – its laws, its geography, its history, its culture, its people. It also means being involved in the affairs of your country at some level – even if it is simply by informing yourself about what's going on with it, not just about things that affect you personally. It means questioning things and protesting in legal, non-violent ways against what you think is wrong. It means understanding that being a citizen isn't only about enjoying the benefits that come with it, but also about doing your bit to enrich your country in return.

Here's the best part – once you understand what being a responsible citizen of your country means, you automatically understand what it means to be a responsible citizen not only of a much smaller entity like your city, but also a much larger one like the world. Which is wonderful, for every WoCoTeen knows that that's what winning this badge is really about – getting good, solid practice for becoming an upstanding citizen of the world, who believes in the equality of all people, no matter what their colour, creed or nationality.

SKILL 54
KNOW THE 'HOLY BOOK' OF YOUR COUNTRY, AND KNOW IT WELL

A country that calls itself secular – which means a country in which religion and government are not connected – has one book that is, or should be, sacred to *all* its citizens – its Constitution.

But what exactly is the Constitution? Well, it is the ultimate rule-book for how a country should be run. The Constitution sets down rules for how a government is chosen, what it can and cannot do, how much power the Prime Minister and President have, what the responsibilities of the courts are, what rights every citizen of the country has, and so on. But the Constitution is also a country's conscience, a document that spells out the collective vision of a people of what their country stands for – justice, kindness, respect for all kinds of differences among people, and so on – and nudges people to take their cues from it.

We got lucky with our Constitution – the men and women who put it together were not only smart but also well-meaning and fair-minded people. Also, since India as a country is very young – only 70 years old – our founding fathers had the advantage of being able to study the Constitutions of other, older democracies, and cherry-pick only the best bits from all of them.

That's how we ended up with a Constitution that is considered one of the world's best, and is the world's longest to boot!

What are some other reasons for us to be proud of our Constitution?

- The Constituent Assembly – the 299 men and women that put the Constitution together – discussed and debated what the new country stood for, the values it should uphold, its dreams and aspirations for its people, and what this Most Important document should say, for a very long time – two years, 11

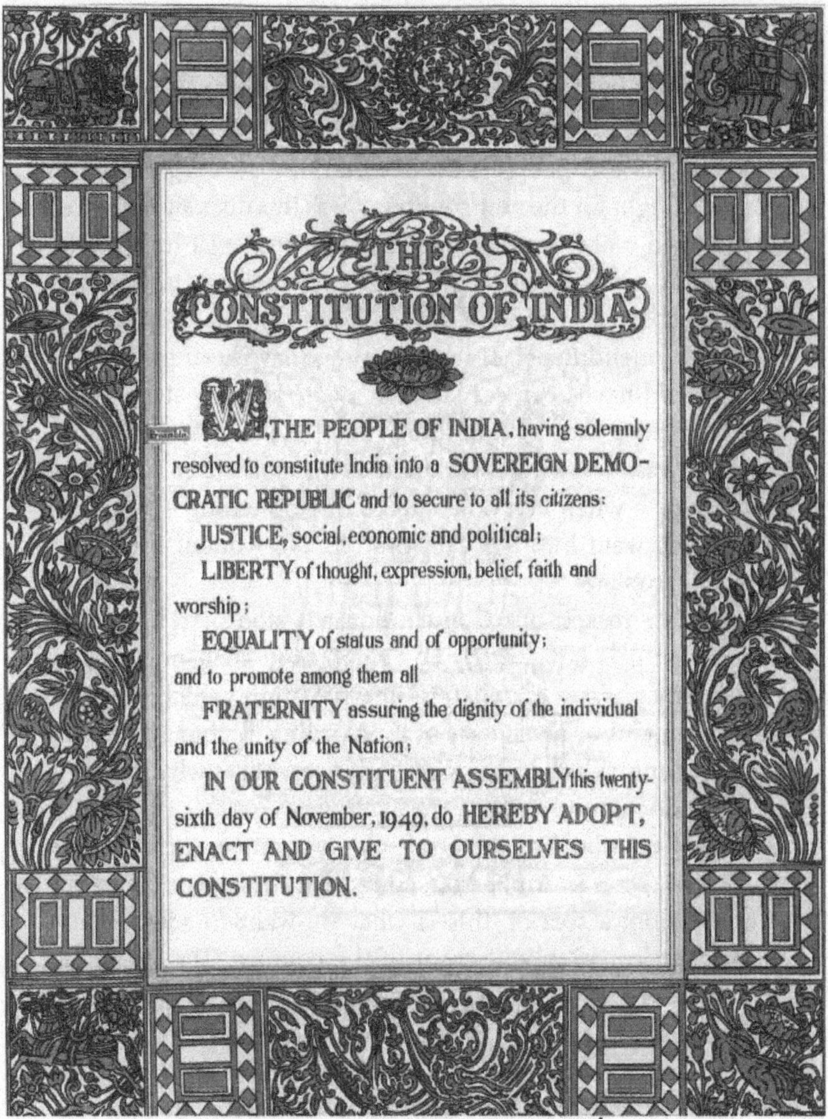

THE CONSTITUTION OF INDIA

WE, THE PEOPLE OF INDIA, having solemnly resolved to constitute India into a SOVEREIGN DEMOCRATIC REPUBLIC and to secure to all its citizens:

JUSTICE, social, economic and political;

LIBERTY of thought, expression, belief, faith and worship;

EQUALITY of status and of opportunity;

and to promote among them all

FRATERNITY assuring the dignity of the individual and the unity of the Nation;

IN OUR CONSTITUENT ASSEMBLY this twenty-sixth day of November, 1949, do HEREBY ADOPT, ENACT AND GIVE TO OURSELVES THIS CONSTITUTION.

The Preamble to the Indian Constitution.

months and 18 days, to be precise, between 9 December 1946 and 26 November 1949. That's meticulous!

■ The Constituent Assembly had a wonderfully diverse set of members. Regular citizens – elected representatives from

British provinces – worked alongside kings and queens who had agreed to give up their kingdoms and become common citizens of India. People from a vast variety of regions, castes, communities and religions sat companionably together in the assembly, as did people who had starkly opposing views on what was right for the new country. It was this diversity of voices that helped make our Constitution so inclusive (it had to take everyone's interests into account), and so robust (to this day, there has been no need to draft a 'new, improved' Constitution, although amendments, or modifications, have been made).

■ It would have been easy to take a vote at every stage of the drafting process and put in things that the majority agreed on, but that wasn't how this was done. It was *only* when there was consensus – when *everyone* agreed on something – that that something went into the Constitution. No wonder it took so long to complete!

■ Another reason our Constitution has stood strong to this day is that it is not written in a rigid, thou-shalt-not kind of way. Many phrases are open to interpretation, which makes it easy to amend or alter parts of it according to changing times and the country's changing circumstances. That's why we call it a 'living document'.

■ Seven members of the Drafting Committee, including its chairman, Dr B.R. Ambedkar, composed the 'Preamble to the Constitution', a sort of 'this-is-what-we-want-to-achieve-for-our-people' mission statement of the country. The Preamble is a work of art – and heart. In very few words, it says clearly and precisely what our Constitution is really all about. Here's a quick deconstruction of it.

'WE, THE PEOPLE OF INDIA...' – Inclusive opening line, indicating that this document belongs to us, the people, and not to the government or to the committee that drafted the Constitution.

'Having solemnly resolved to constitute India into a'

- **'SOVEREIGN'** – no one rules us but ourselves.

- **'SOCIALIST'** – means many things, including that the government owns and provides essential services like healthcare and education to its people at reduced or no charge, so that even the very poor have access to them.
- **'SECULAR'** – religion and government have nothing to do with each other. No religion will be favoured or discriminated against. People are free to practise any religion they want, worship any god they want and wear whatever symbols of their religion they wish to – Sikh turban, Muslim prayer cap, a crucifix pendant, *kumkum*.
- **'DEMOCRATIC'** – the government is elected by the people of the country – and every single citizen above the age of 18 – educated or illiterate, rich or poor, Hindu or Muslim, male or female – has the right to vote to choose their representatives in government.
- **'REPUBLIC'** – no government position is hereditary, or passed on from parent to child. All citizens have a right to try for and occupy any government position at all.

'...and to secure to all its citizens'

'JUSTICE, social, economic and political;' Not just justice of the kind that you get in a court, but also social justice – everyone is allowed to participate in society in any way he or she wants (as long as it is legal), without anyone stopping him; and economic justice – everyone is allowed to earn an income in any way she wants (as long as it isn't illegal!), and there are no restrictions on what kinds of jobs someone can do.

'LIBERTY, of thought, expression, belief, faith and worship;' You know what that means, but remember that these freedoms must be exercised with caution and kindness and sensitivity (if what you are thinking of saying or doing is going to hurt someone, or your country's dignity, don't do it – or at least think about how you can say or do it in a less insensitive way)

'EQUALITY, of status and opportunity;' Every citizen gets not just equal status under the law but also the same opportunities as everyone else – the government cannot invite applications from astronauts for a mission to the moon, for instance, specifying that only fair-skinned people may apply.

'and to promote among them all

FRATERNITY, assuring the dignity of the individual and the unity and integrity of the Nation;' Fraternity is another word for brotherhood; people must feel they are part of the Great Indian Family if you want them to stay happy and united, and the Constitution pledges to try, as far as possible, to create the circumstances for this.

'IN OUR CONSTITUENT ASSEMBLY, this 26th day of November 1949, do HEREBY ADOPT, ENACT AND GIVE TO OURSELVES THIS CONSTITUTION.'

Phew! Is that Preamble a beauty of a 'mission statement' or what? And don't you love the artful brilliance of the statement '(we) give to ourselves this Constitution' right at the very end? It basically means that the onus of ensuring that everything the Preamble says is achieved is not just on the government but also squarely on us citizens! Gulp!

SKILL 55
STAY INFORMED – GET THE 'CORRECT' NEWS

One way to be a good citizen is to stay informed about things that are happening in the country – the good stuff, the not-so-good stuff, the simple issues on which it is easy to take sides, the not-so-simple issues that require you to read and listen and talk to people and think and really understand the situation from all sides before you can make a decision. Only if you are aware of what is happening can you participate constructively in making your country a better, fairer, kinder place.

How do you stay informed?

The easiest way is to try and read at least two, if not three, newspapers each day – you can even do this online if you like. Watching news is not the same thing as reading about it in some detail, but if you only watch news, watch two-three different channels. Why? The thing is, even though news reports seem to be very objective (not taking sides), they usually are. If you examine them carefully, you will see that one news source consistently takes one side on issues, and another often takes the opposite view.

You may also notice that the same news is reported quite differently by media houses that have different positions on the same issue. A newspaper that supports development may have headlines like – 'Mega-dam to generate 1450MW for power-starved hinterland!' or 'New automobile factory to generate 1,500 local jobs!' or 'Buffer-zone wildlife resort to promote responsible tourism – with assured big cat sightings!' – while one that supports the environment will have very different headlines on the same issues – 'Mega-dam to submerge 200 villages!' and 'New automobile factory to deprive farmers of their land!' and 'Resort Scam: How was permission obtained to operate in a forest buffer zone?' Neither is lying – each has simply picked which truths to tell you and how to present them. Getting your news from two or three different sources, therefore, gives you a more balanced view on any issue.

Here's what is cool – after you're done informing yourself, you *don't* have to take either side! Information itself is power – you can now discuss issues intelligently with friends and parents, you can call out people – like TV anchors, newspaper columnists, and parents – who try to make you believe that there is only one way of looking at a particular issue, and you can win quizzes (many quiz questions are based on the news) and MUN debates!

SKILL 56
PARTICIPATE – PETITION FOR CHANGE

Skill 55 segues nicely into Skill 56 – only when you have informed yourself about what is going on in your country, and heard the arguments for and against issues from every angle, can you begin to participate in the changing of the things that you think need changing!

How do you do it? One way is to raise a petition. A petition is an old, time-honoured, legal, non-violent method to bring about change. It could be a request sent to a concerned authority for some law or practice to be changed, dropped, or included, a demand for justice when the petitioner feels he has been treated unfairly, or a request for support, when the petitioner feels he deserves it.

Let's say the government is proposing to make a new law, and you feel it is unfair to a section of society or destructive to the environment. Before a proposal becomes a Law, the government has to present it to the two houses of Parliament for their consideration. At this stage, the proposal is called a Bill. Only when a majority of Parliament members vote in favour of the Bill does it become an actual Law. By petitioning Parliament during this process, it is possible to prevent the Bill from becoming a Law. You can also petition Parliament to vote in *favour* of a Bill that you believe will be a good law. See? You're powerful!

Our Constitution expressly allows every citizen to petition the Parliament directly, which means you wield enormous power to bring about real change!

Indian citizens also have the right to petition the Supreme Court or the High Court against, say, the pulling down of a heritage building or the construction of a railway line through virgin forest, by filing what is called a PIL, or a Public Interest Litigation, against entities such as the State government or the Indian Railways.

Now, how do you get the government to take your petition seriously? You show them that there are thousands of people on your side. In the old days, it used to be done by getting people who believed in your cause to actually sign on your petition. That involved a *lot* of legwork! In the twenteens (a word we just made up, to indicate the years from 2013 to 2019), it is way easier – you can collect 'virtual signatures' online, from people a thousand miles away that you don't even

know - all they need to do is believe in your cause.

But how in heck do you make sure all these people know about your petition? Well, there are now entire websites dedicated to helping petitioners not only get the news of their petition out, but also to make sure that the petition, after it has collected its required number of 'signatures', reaches the right 'petitionee'!

Of course, it doesn't always have to be *you* starting a petition. Maybe there are already a dozen petitions online that you can support, asking the government - or a TV channel, or the board of school education - for things that you care about. (*A good place to start is www.change.org. Browse their 'Victories' section, too, to see which petitions started by a single person actually resulted in change*).

SKILL 57
LEAD BY EXAMPLE - FOLLOW THE LAW

There's no need to waste too many words on this skill - to be a good citizen and be worthy of the Citizen Badge, a WoCoTeen must abide by the laws of his country. In addition, WoCoTeens are vigilant, and ensure that their adults don't break the law either.

What kinds of laws? Well, your adults might jump red lights when they are in a rush, or lie about your age when a 'child ticket' is cheaper than an adult one. They may brush these aside as small misdemeanours which 'don't matter', but it is a WoCoTeen's duty as a good citizen to call such transgressions out when they are committed. Sooner or later, your 'pester power' will make your adults into role-model citizens themselves.

THE CITIZEN'S CHALLENGES

#54
THE CONSTITUTION CHALLENGE

■ Learn by heart the entire Preamble of the Indian Constitution, and explain to your Squad Leader what the words Sovereign, Socialist, Secular, Democratic and Republic mean.

■ How did a boy who was treated so badly in his childhood simply because he belonged to a particular caste overcome every barrier in his path and become the Architect of India's Constitution? With your entire Squad, research the life of Dr B.R. Ambedkar and present it to your Squad Leader in the form of a story, play, song or mime. Don't forget to invite friends and family to come and watch the performance!

B.R. Ambedkar – chief architect of the Indian Constitution, economist and educationist extraordinaire.

#55
THE STAY-INFORMED CHALLENGE

■ Read the daily newspaper that your parents subscribe to (and not just the comics section either!) every day for two weeks (pick one parent to monitor you). Then, choose three stories that caught your attention the most and present them to your Squad Leader and Squad.

■ Watch the primetime news on a different TV channel each day for a week (include a couple of regional language channels too). If you wish, continue doing this for another week, with the same channels. At the end, analyze how the news is presented on different channels and pick a favourite. Explain to your Squad Leader why you picked that one.

#56
THE PARTICIPATE CHALLENGE

■ With your Squad, decide on an issue that you want to start a petition about. It could be about a problem in your apartment complex (if you all live in the same one), your neighbourhood, or your city. Think about the best way to petition the authority in question and the best way to garner support for your cause. Then, along with your Squad Leader, submit the petition to the concerned authority, along with the names/signatures of your supporters. It doesn't matter whether your petition leads to the desired change – what counts is that you have participated in trying to change your community into a better place.

#57
THE FOLLOW-THE-LAW CHALLENGE

■ In your school calendar, locate the document on School Rules and read it. Over the next week, observe yourself and your schoolmates and notice how all of you break school rules in small and big ways every day. Make a list of which rules are broken most often and present it to your Squad Leader, along with your thoughts on why this is so. (You could also read the rules of your apartment complex or colony – they should be up somewhere – and do the same exercise in your apartment.)

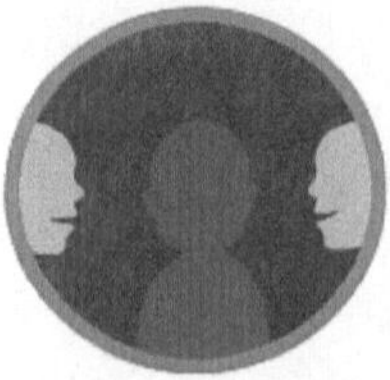

WOCOTEEN MERIT BADGE 15

THE INTERPRETER

A Scout is not only a friend to the people round him, but a 'friend of all the world'.

– Camp Fire Yarn No. 26, *Scouting for Boys*

Before we get into what goes into winning this merit badge, two questions: One, who or what is an interpreter? And two, why are interpreters important to a community?

Let's start with Question 1. In its most commonly understood form, the word 'interpreter' simply means someone who translates a language orally for someone else who cannot understand it. But in a larger sense, an interpreter is really a connector, someone who helps 'bridge the gap' – between languages, between people, between communities – thus helping one side understand the other.

Once you think of an interpreter this way, the answer to Question 2 is a no-brainer. Each community is made up of a diverse set of people who often have such different opinions on things that they might as well be speaking 10 different languages. When one side doesn't understand the other, fear and anger creep in – *What are they saying? Do they mean this thing or that other thing? Probably this – that's not very nice of them! Now they are speaking louder, almost shouting – how dare they! Do they think we will take this lying down? No way! We will shout back too! That man is smiling – is he mocking me? How dare he!*

Very quickly, these misunderstandings escalate into real conflict – *Do you see that? He is bending down to pick something up – he's going to attack! But I am quicker – I already have a stick. I will hit him before he has a chance to hit me! Take that, you brute!*

Of course our example is a little dramatic, but you do understand how this works, right? That's where an interpreter comes in, to help each side understand the other.

But that's not all an interpreter does. Sometimes, an interpreter's job in a community is simply to formally *introduce* Side 1 to Side 2, because Side 1 *simply cannot see Side 2, even though Side 2 is right in front of its face!* For instance, can you describe what your auto-driver was wearing five minutes after you have stepped out of the rickshaw with a friend? Can you pick out at least one of the construction workers who have worked on your street for the past six months, out of a random set of people? If you don't even see the other side, how can you possibly be a good and fair member of a community that includes them?

SKILL 58
SPEAK A DIFFERENT TONGUE

India is a melting pot of a hundred different languages. Actually, that's not quite accurate – India is more a salad bowl, in which each language retains its own colour, flavour and texture while still working superbly with everything else in the bowl.

The question is – how many of those languages do *you* know? Most of you probably fluently speak, read and write English (otherwise you wouldn't be reading this book) and Hindi ('NO!' – *All the terror-stricken high-schoolers south of the Vindhyas whose mother-tongue is not Hindi*). You obviously speak your mother tongue and 'father tongue' well ('Erm, okay, somewhat, sometimes...') as also the official language of your State ('This is unfair! Other countries get by fine with one language – how come we have to take this kind of pressure? Jeez!').

If you have a working knowledge of these five languages (fewer if your mother tongue, father tongue and State language are the same, and they are Hindi – lucky you!) – that means you can (a) understand most informal conversations in each language; (b) know enough phrases and sentences to carry on a halfway-decent conversation with people who only speak that language; and (c) be able to read signboards written in that language – great! Time to learn a new one, then, maybe the official language of your neighbouring State, or the State furthest away from yours. You could also learn a foreign language (although Indian languages are more fun, because you can easily practise them in real-life situations).

If you *don't* have a 'working knowledge' of at least three Indian languages (including English), well, what have you been doing all your life? The thing is, apart from all the scientific research that has proven, time and again, that knowing many languages wires the neurons in your brain in exciting and creative new ways, leading to better and faster learning of other disciplines like math and music, knowing the languages of your family and your community is vitally important to making you feel like you belong! It also gains you instant acceptance, affection and respect from your community – after all, by making the effort to learn the language, you have demonstrated that you are eager to understand and listen to what they have to say!

Also, what's not to like about being able to bargain with vegetable vendors, chat with your friends' grandparents, eavesdrop on conversations in restaurants, and read every signboard and official document in sight? Start learning/practising a new tongue today!

SKILL 59
LEARN ABOUT A DIFFERENT FAITH

Are you Hindu? – how much do you know about the life of Prophet Mohammed? Are you Christian? – do you know the broad story of the Mahabharata? Are you Muslim? – do you know five stories from the Jataka Tales, which are moral stories from the Buddhist scriptures? Are you Sikh? – have you celebrated Christmas with a Christian friend?

In a multicultural – and deeply religious – country like ours, it is vital that each of us makes the effort to know at least a little bit about the other religions that our countrymen practise. Religion and culture are inextricably linked, and to truly participate in your country's culture – its festivals, its food, its traditions, its value systems, its vibrant everyday life – you have to first educate yourself about its many religions. Equally importantly, taking the first few steps towards understanding another's religion will ensure that you are far more sensitive and thoughtful in your interactions with him than you would have been otherwise. Learning about another's religion helps to break down all kinds of barriers you didn't even know existed.

How do you start? Sure, you could first google and read up stuff, but this is just background information. The thing is, religions do not mean the same thing to all their followers – different communities across the world understand, interpret and practise what is apparently the same religion in a hundred different ways. Indian Islam and Indian Christianity, for instance, are a very different kettle of fish – in a nice way – from the Islam and Christianity practised in other parts of the world. (And you don't even have to travel out of India to experience a zillion different kinds of Hinduism, haha). That's why, to really experience how a religion is practised in your own community, you couldn't do better, or find a more fun and easy way of doing it, than to engage with your own neighbours, friends and classmates.

Ask a Christian friend if you can attend a church wedding with his family. Offer to join a Sikh neighbour in doing *seva* at his local gurdwara. Make a pact with a Muslim friend to keep the *roza* (the Ramzan fast) along with her just one day a week during Ramzan to show solidarity with her, and watch her guffaw as you struggle. Beg your Hindu friend's parent to tell you the story behind Diwali (you can keep doing this with a different Hindu friend's parent every month – and each will tell you a completely different story!). Go on a Jain diet for a week – no meat, no eggs, no root vegetables (which means no onion pakoras, no garlic bread, no potato chips, no *gaajar ka halwa*, no *mooli ka* paratha, no peanut butter) – and marvel at how food can still taste good in a very different way.

By building these cultural bridges, and experiencing other faiths and traditions in an up-close and personal way, you will never again be fooled by all the mean, misinformed things people are always spouting about other religions. That's what we call self-reliance, WoCoTeen-style!

SKILL 60
SAY HELLO TO THE OTHER SIDE OF THE TRACKS

'The other side of the tracks' is an idiom that refers to the poorer part of a town or a city. Whichever side of the tracks you think you live on, if you are reading this book, there is most certainly 'the other side', a place where there are children your age who cannot do what you are doing – either because their parents don't have enough spare money to spend on a book like this, or because they have never learnt to read English. Ever wondered what their lives are like? Ever visited one of their homes? If you haven't, well, there's no time like the present!

Why is this important, though? Well, you cannot do a fair job of working towards building a fair, kind community for everyone unless you make an effort to understand the needs, difficulties and points of view of all its different members. You may think, for instance, that the chai-*wallah* and *chaat-wallah* at the corner of your posh, clean, quiet street are an eyesore and a nuisance, because there is litter around their carts and loud conversation and laughter and fights from the men who hang around there all day. Look a little closer, though, and you will see that those laughing, loud-talking men are only the wait-staff who work at the chic café around the corner, or your neighbours' drivers or cooks, who need an inexpensive place to eat, hang out and refresh themselves when they have a spare moment.

Yup, the other side of the tracks isn't far away at all. In fact, someone from there is probably in your house or at your door each day, in the guise of your household help, the boy who delivers your newspapers, the girl who takes care of your invalid grandmother, the security guard in your apartment building – the list is endless. But that's not the surprising bit – what is truly stunning is how little we know about their lives.

Never too late to remedy that, though. Start small – smile and make eye-contact at least once a day with all the different people who serve you. Then begin to greet them – with a wave and a cheery 'Good morning!' and a 'How are you today?' As time goes by, add more to the conversation – 'You are not looking up to it today, are you unwell?' or 'It was my best friend's birthday today and I got three chocolate bars off him – please take one home for your little daughter.' Slowly, as a warm and genuine conversation develops, you will realize that another connection has been made, another bridge built. Seriously, why would you pass up on an opportunity like that?

SKILL 61
WALK A MILE IN SOMEONE ELSE'S SHOES

There are other 'different' people who live in your community, on the periphery of your vision.

Yup, we're talking about the differently-abled – an umbrella term that covers those among us who are physically and mentally disabled. Again, you will never be able to build a community that is fair to everyone in it if you don't listen to the voices of these important members.

So the next time you see a blind person on the street, take a moment to get inside his head. Watch him, really watch him, negotiate his way with his white cane. Notice what challenges he faces on that particular stretch and how skilfully he manoeuvres through the chaos of the Indian street and its pavement (if there is one!). Think about what could be changed or added to make it an easier, more pleasant experience for him.

What about a deaf person? People who work with the deaf talk about how it is an 'invisible' disability – because you can't instantly see that someone is hearing-impaired, there is less sympathy and understanding of that particular disability. What about someone in a wheelchair? What are the small ways in which you can help build sensitivity towards her within your community?

Start those conversations with yourself, with your friends and family, and with the differently-abled themselves. You will be amazed by the number of I-had-never-thought-about-that things you will discover that will lead to the all-important 'empathy'* that will form the foundations of yet another strong, shining WoCoTeen-built bridge. Just do it!

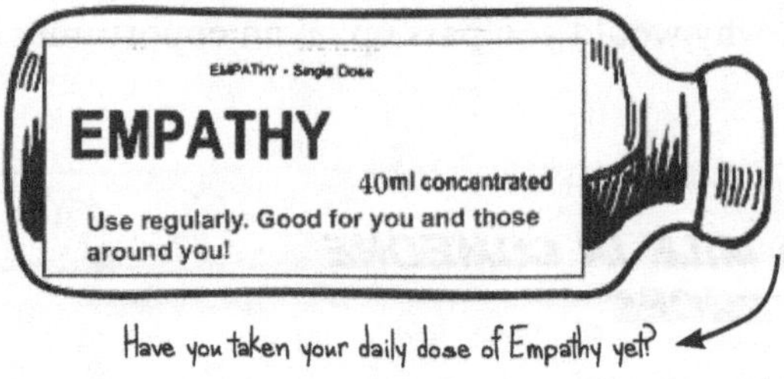

**Empathy is not the same thing as sympathy; when you feel sympathy, you feel bad for someone else and her situation, but there is still a distance between you two, a 'me' and 'her' separation. When you show empathy, however, you are getting into the other person's shoes, getting a much deeper understanding of her life by living it yourself (if only in your head). The best part? Empathy is a skill that can be learned – you don't have to be born with it.*

THE INTERPRETER'S CHALLENGES

#58
THE BUILD-A-LANGUAGE-BRIDGE CHALLENGE

■ How do you begin to learn to speak a new language? Simple! You list out a bunch of what you think are essential words and phrases to carry on a conversation in English, translate them into that language and begin to use them. Here are a bunch of word/phrase suggestions for your language starter-kit.

- Yes , no, we'll-see-how-it-goes
- The numbers: 1–100, plus fractions like quarter, half and three-quarters
- Words that help tell the time: 1:30 p.m., 10:45 a.m.
- 10 relationship nouns: mother, father, grandmother, sister, brother...
- 50 nouns which are names of vegetables, fruits, colours...
- 20 'location words': above, below, inside, outside, there, here, in front of, behind...
- 25 adjectives: good, bad, tall, short, fat, thin, big, small...
- Adverbs of time: today, tomorrow, yesterday, morning, evening, then, now
- Question words: when, where, how, who, which, why...
- Possessive pronouns: I, me, my, mine, you, yours, she, hers, he, his, we, you (the respectful plural, as in the Hindi *aap* –Very Useful and Very Important to address strangers) ours, theirs...
- Random useful words
- 25 Lines-That-Will-Fool-Everyone-Into-Thinking-I-Actually-Know-The-Language – pick these after a discussion with your Squad

Now pick a language (and you *have* to pick your mother-tongue, or your State language, if you are not comfortable speaking it, before you pick any others) and start working on mastering the elements of your starter-kit in that language. At the end of a fortnight (or, latest-latest, a month), write a couple of fun sketches / skits with your Squad, using just the words and phrases in your starter kit, and perform it, with each of you speaking your lines in the language you just learnt. The result should be hilarious!

- Learn to 'talk' using ISL, or Indian Sign Language, the most popular sign language among the hearing-impaired in India (not the same as ASL, or American Sign Language). Go to page 309 for more details on ISL.

#59
THE BUILD-A-FAITH-BRIDGE CHALLENGE

- If your Squad has members of different faiths, have each share something about their religion with the group. Or pick a religion each, and decide what aspect of 'your' religion all of you want to research – stories from mythologies, founder story, stories behind celebrations and so on. On a pre-decided day two weeks later, share these stories with the Squad. Invite parents and other friends and family to listen in too.
- Plan a Squad excursion to places of worship in your neighbourhood – Hindu temple, mosque, church, gurdwara, Parsi temple, Jain temple, Buddhist temple. Make sure you have spoken to someone at these places so that they can show you around. Dress respectfully – Indian clothes are best, and shorts best-avoided for both boys and girls. Carry a dupatta or handkerchief to cover your head with and slippers/sandals you can easily remove and put on (you will be doing that a lot). When you're back, have a group discussion on how the whole experience made you feel, and what you learnt from it.
- If you live in an apartment building, pick one festival from each of India's four main religions and talk to your Residents' Welfare Association members to organize a small celebration around a festival from each religion. During each event, take the stage with your Squad for a few minutes to talk about your experiences in the process of trying to win your Interpreter Badges.

#60
THE BUILD-A-BRIDGE-ACROSS-THE-TRACKS CHALLENGE

■ In groups of two, interview at least two people from a different economic background that you intersect with on a daily basis but don't know anything about. Ask them about their families, where they are from, a typical day in their lives, their dreams for themselves and what they wish they could change about their world. Take pictures, record short video clips of them at their work. If possible, and if they are willing to invite you, visit at least one of their homes. Then make a 'Squad Blog' of all the stories, pictures and videos the Squad has collected, and share the link over email and social media (WhatsApp, Instagram, Facebook et al).

#61
THE BUILD-EMPATHY CHALLENGE

■ With your Squad, designate one day over a weekend as 'Empathy Day'. Take turns role-playing a blind person (have a partner blindfold you and walk with you on a short stretch of street outside; after 15 minutes, switch the blindfold), a hearing-impaired person (wearing earplugs, walk through the park in your neighbourhood for half an hour, noticing how your eyes suddenly observe so much more), and a physically-disabled person – borrow a wheelchair from a friend who had needed one when he had a broken leg, and volunteer to be pushed over a 50 m distance while you're sitting in it. That short ride will give you a deep understanding of just how unsuitable our pavements and streets are for people confined to wheelchairs.

WOCOTEEN MERIT BADGE 16

THE VOLUNTEER

> *There lies a certain danger in inculcating in the individual the ambition to win prizes and scholarships ... unless there is a corresponding instruction in service for others.*
> **– Preface, *Scouting for Boys***

We all know what a volunteer is. Or do we? A volunteer is not just someone who puts his or her hand up yelling 'Pick me! Pick me!' when a magician at a birthday party asks for one to help him with a trick. A volunteer is someone who offers his time, effort, skills or ideas to someone who needs it, without wanting or expecting anything in return for his pains. It is a service offered simply because the volunteer wants to do it, because he believes that some things must be done.

Why do people volunteer? Because most of us know from experience that when we do something unforced and unselfish for someone, there is a certain quiet happiness we feel at the end of it that makes us want to do it again and again.

Volunteering within a community has other benefits. It helps inspire others to do the same and it actually makes a difference to the community as a whole. In other words, it's exactly the kind of thing WoCoTeens love to do! So what are you waiting for?

SKILL 62
VOLUNTEER YOUR SKILLS

What skills do you have? If you think you're too young to have any that are useful to anyone, you couldn't be more wrong. First off, you can read and write fluently in English; that is a HUGE and still uncommon skill in India. Maybe you are good at football or art or theatre or public speaking or writing or origami or crochet or hip-hop, and you know this because you win prizes or are part of the school team. Maybe you are an ace at using Microsoft Power Point or Excel or a particular film-editing software. Well, then, you are legitimately a Skilled Person!

Where can you volunteer your skills? Look around you. If nothing else, you can offer to help your maid's eight-year-old with his math homework twice a week. There may be a government school or an NGO-run school in your area that would love to have someone choreograph a dance or help with a Power Point presentation. An old-age home may appreciate your coming over and reading the newspapers out to residents whose eyes are now too weak to read. Talk to adults you know – someone is bound to be able to suggest ways in which you can help.

SKILL 63
VOLUNTEER YOUR TIME AND EFFORT

Time is the one resource everyone is always running out of. If you have some spare time, therefore, and are willing to put some effort into helping someone once or twice a week, you already have something that someone else will value. You don't even have to think about a particular skill to volunteer in this case! Maybe you can offer to watch a younger cousin or the neighbour's child while her mom catches up on errands or takes her older sibling to a class (but remember she will accept only if you have already proved that you can be trusted!).

There's tonnes you can do, if you only look out for where your help is needed. Is there a clean-up drive being organized in the neighbourhood park? Join in. Does your apartment complex want everyone to segregate their garbage? Volunteer to canvass from door-to-door, telling your neighbours about the benefits of segregation.

SKILL 64
VOLUNTEER AN IDEA

Of course you don't have to wait for someone else to initiate a project that you can volunteer in. The high that comes from using your own brains to come up with an idea for a project that benefits the community, and leading it to successful completion, is too feel-goody to ignore. So get cracking!

At the beginning of the summer vacation, you can initiate, for instance, a used-notebooks collection drive from all the students in your neighbourhood. Take the (huge pile of, hopefully!) books you've collected to the *raddiwallah* and donate the money that he gives you for them to a local charity, or buy colouring materials and sketchbooks for the kids of the construction crew working in your neighbourhood.

Ideas don't always have to be about fund-raising, though (when they are, think of something that doesn't necessarily involve you raising funds from your own parents!). Organize an 'Outsmart Your Smartphone' camp for senior citizens where you and your friends do one-on-one sessions to help them understand how to use their phones and apps better. Make Diwali cards for all the cleaning staff in your school, or home-made cookie packs for the children of your household help at Christmas. Basically, think about all the people in your community you don't normally think about, and how you can put a smile on their faces. That's not too tough a brief, is it?

SKILL 65
BE A MICRO-VOLUNTEER

Micro-volunteering is a new, cool way of volunteering that's getting very popular abroad. Simply put, it is a way of making a difference to someone by doing something that doesn't take any more time than you can give – even five minutes a day is enough. What's more, micro-volunteering doesn't involve any serious commitment. It is a small action done along with several other people who are also doing small actions, which together build up to something big.

For instance, in the 'Volunteer an Idea' section, we talked about making Diwali cards for the cleaning staff in your school. Just the thought of how much time and effort is involved in that kind of project may be so daunting that you drop the idea altogether. Instead, imagine that your entire class was involved in making Diwali cards. You could finish the project in one art period, and since each of you will only have to make one or two cards, you can make them really special. See how it works?

As a class, or as a school, imagine if you took charge of the street outside your school and 'owned' it. That means you would be responsible for making sure the pavements have no missing or loose stones that could trip a younger child up, the roads have no potholes, there is no garbage, there is a well-marked zebra crossing, there are 'traffic wardens' who direct traffic and ease congestion at the beginning and end of the school day and 'bus wardens' who see that younger children are safely on the bus before a bus leaves, and so on. If you had to do it alone, it would be a formidable, almost impossible task, but if you could convince your school to 'adopt' the street, this would be easy!

As a student body, you could write to or visit the authorities to petition them about the pavement and roads; senior students could take on, by turns, the roles of traffic and bus wardens as well as the 'garbage police', ensuring that the street stays clean, middle-school children could go door-to-door, letting neighbours know about the school's effort and requesting their co-operation – you could be powerful! And you would have accomplished all this during the school day, volunteering only 15–20 minutes of your time each week.

Makes you want to run out and try some micro-volunteering right away, what? Go then, think of a cracking idea, and then proceed to get your class, school, neighbours, friends and everyone you know on board. It won't be easy, but anything that is really worth doing rarely is. All the best!

THE VOLUNTEER'S CHALLENGES

Volunteering challenges have a way of merging into one another – organizing a fund-raiser involves time and effort, and some of your skills will definitely be used in any micro-volunteering project you lead. The four challenges below may have some overlaps, therefore, but they all need to be completed to win you your badge.

#62 THE FUND-RAISER CHALLENGE

Along with your Squad, think of an idea for a fund-raising activity that involves no initial investment of money. Raise at least ₹1,000 through this activity. Put this money in a bank (or a piggy bank) for the next volunteering challenge.

#63 THE MICRO-VOLUNTEERING CHALLENGE

This challenge is not just about the micro-volunteering idea itself but about your ability to sell the idea to others and get them on board. As a Squad, you win this challenge if you can each get at least 10 people to join and complete the challenge. If you are a Squad of five people, say, you need to have 50 people committed to your idea, whether it is making cards or baking something or committing 30 minutes to man a stall at a fund-raiser, whatever.

A huge inspiration for micro-volunteers in India is The Ugly Indian, an anonymous citizen movement in which people who often do not know each other come together to 'spotfix' (or clean, beautify and fix ugly spots, i.e., open garbage dumps, rubble-strewn footpaths, paan-stained walls) in their shared public spaces. By giving just two hours of their time and making a small contribution (usually ₹200) towards paints and cleaning materials, Ugly Indians all over the country have executed stunning transformations of ugly spots and ensured that they remain garbage-free and beautiful for months. Their motto? 'Kaam Chaalu, Mooh Bandh' (Stop talking, start doing)! Look up their Facebook page – The Ugly Indian – to be inspired.

#64
THE JUST-ME-VOLUNTEERING CHALLENGE

This is an individual challenge. Volunteer four times (either at the same job with the same person – like helping your granddad with gardening – or with four different people or organizations) within two months, for at least 60 minutes each time. Write down what you achieved during those four hours and get the people you volunteered with to sign off on it, for your Squad Leader's records. Remember that the Squad Leader can double-check with your grand-dad on whether you emotionally blackmailed him into signing your sheet!

#65
THE TECH-VOLUNTEER CHALLENGE

This has to be a volunteering activity with a tech twist. For instance, if you are a tech or gaming wiz, and know how to crack something that you think not many other people do, have someone make a video of you talking about and showing how it is done, and upload it on YouTube. Or you could teach someone how to use a particular software or your grandmom how to shoot videos on her phone and share them on WhatsApp. You could do this activity by yourself or in pairs. Your Squad Leader will decide whether your idea fits the brief and if it has been completed successfully.

WOCOTEEN MERIT BADGE 17

THE FRIEND TO ANIMALS

Every Boy Scout ought to know all about the tame animals he sees every day. No Scout should ever kill an animal unless there is some real reason for doing so...

– Camp Fire Yarn No. 15, *Scouting for Boys*

Every true WoCoTeen, whether he is comfortable around animals or terrified of them, believes implicitly that other creatures have as much right to the planet as we do. He understands that in the march of civilization, humans – those scary-smart beings – have colonized, exclusively for themselves, large tracts of land that they once shared with animals. Animals and birds have been pushed closer and closer together in ever-shrinking habitats, while the human footprint has grown larger and more dominant.

Whatever our own opinions on how right or wrong this is, the reality cannot be wished away: while we may imagine that we are insulated from 'them' in our barricaded homes and cities, the animals are still with us. On indulgent Indian city streets, particularly, you can't miss them – cows and buffaloes take long siestas in the middle of traffic, horses ridden by wild-haired boys suddenly gallop by, camels and elephants stride regally – if occasionally – past belching buses, pigs and dogs snuffle happily in open garbage dumps, crows, squirrels and monkeys scold and scurry and leap among dusty trees, and the rats, of course, are everywhere. It is only fair, therefore, that we count them all as bona fide members of our communities.

How should we treat these four-legged and feathered members, then? Exactly as we would treat the two-legged, non-feathered ones – with kindness, respect and dignity. And because we believe we are the superior species, the onus is on us humans to reduce conflict between the two sides and secure our own safety. How can we do that? By accepting humbly that we are the intruders who have encroached on their spaces, by educating ourselves about them and their needs, and by doing whatever needs to be done to create the kind of inclusive, non-aggressive atmosphere in which they can live their lives with dignity and without fear.

Getting a grip on these four skills should take you some part of the way there.

SKILL 66
TEACH YOURSELF SOME ANIMAL CARE BASICS

Injured animals and birds are all around us. In our cities, quite often, they have been injured because of human negligence or deliberate cruelty. Sometimes, they've been in a fight with another animal or been attacked by a predator or fallen out of a tree. It breaks your heart to see them suffering, but you don't know what to do, so you just walk on, pretending you haven't seen them. But you don't have to feel so helpless – here are a few small things you can do to help.

- **Here's the first, and easiest, and Most Important thing to do**: Find out the contact numbers of animal care and rescue organizations in your city (they actually exist!) and save them on your phone. Also save the number of the closest veterinary hospital or clinic. Even if you are comfortable handling animals and are good with caring for them, in the interests of safety, it is best to call in a professional.

If you suspect the animal is dead*, check to make sure by gently tap-tapping on a tin or tree close to its ear, creating a breeze around it with a newspaper, or stamping on the ground hard (but not too loudly) in its vicinity. If the animal blinks or makes some other movement, it is alive. Call a professional immediately. If it doesn't blink, call the City Corporation's dead animal disposal department (there is such a thing, and they're usually prompt at responding – save the number!).

****Important!** The animal could have died due to rabies or some other infectious disease. Do not touch it!*

Do not even ATTEMPT to get close if you are not comfortable around animals; animals can always sense your fear and will lash out to protect themselves.

While waiting for the professional to arrive, you may want to make the animal feel more secure. Ask for help and form a circle of stones or cardboard boxes around it so that people stay out of that space.

- Don't try to approach the animal without a grown-up experienced in animal rescue or a professional animal helper. You could stay with the animal as long as you are quiet. While around the animal, crouch low and don't make eye contact – animals see it as a challenge. Speak to them softly and soothingly. In an injured state, animals see you more as a predator than they normally would, and you don't want to agitate them further.
- For a small animal that is not dangerous, such as a baby bird, a shoebox would make a great temporary home. Line the box with paper towels or a soft handkerchief and place the injured bird inside. Make sure that the animal isn't feeling too hot or cold, and that there are holes in the box for enough air circulation. Take everything you need with you – towel, box, gloves – the first time you approach, so that you don't have to approach the animal again and again.
- Don't attempt to feed the injured animal or give it water until a professional has had a look at it. The 'professional' could also be a relative or a neighbour – make sure it is an adult! – who is an animal lover and has some experience with caring for animals and birds.

SKILL 67
LEARN THE 'WILD ANIMAL AHOY!' DRILL

Wild animals are a completely different ballgame from small, domesticated animals. While all animals can be dangerous, wild animals that are not used to humans are definitely more so. Essentially because when a wild animal strays into a human-dominated habitat, it is outside its own natural comfort zone. It is already on the defensive, and its first instinct is to attack.

Why would a wild animal stray into a city at all? Because the outskirts of constantly burgeoning cities are really encroachments on what used to be 'animal corridors' – the routes animals have taken for generations to get from one side of the jungle to another. These animals aren't really 'straying' – they are only taking the paths they've always taken, except, suddenly, there are now humans who have stationed themselves there.

More and more, therefore, especially in fast-growing cities, you hear about jackals and panthers and leopards and elephants entering schools or homes or cultivated farmland. If this happens in your school or around where you live, *do not do anything except stay inside, lock the door and call the professionals*! Google 'Wild Animal Rescue and Rehabilitation' along with the name of your city and save the numbers of all the organizations that come up, on your phone, right now.

The other kind of wild animal that is increasingly finding its way into houses in Indian cities is the snake. Warm, tropical countries are havens for snakes, and we have tons of species, including some seriously venomous ones (although 85 per cent of our snakes are non-venomous, and not all bites from venomous snakes lead to death). Here's what to do (after you've recovered from your heart attack, that is), if you spot a snake coiled under your kitchen table, or slithering across your floor.

- Retreat slowly – no running, no sudden movements – without turning your back on the snake.
- Do not attempt to kill it with a shovel or a broom. More than 80 per cent of snakebites occur during the process of trying to kill a snake.

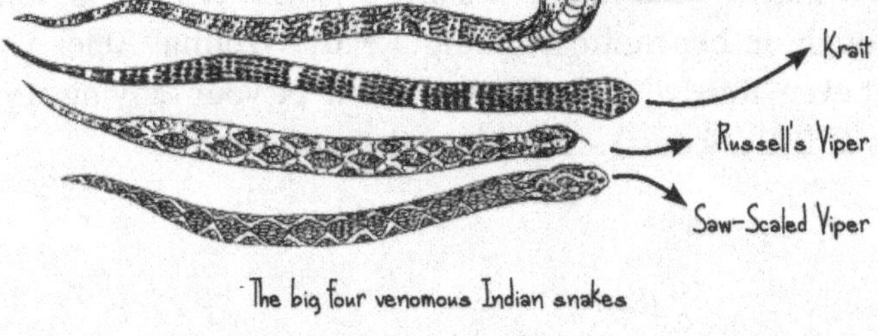

The big four venomous Indian snakes

- Allow the snake the possibility of going away by itself first, if it is near a door leading to the outside, say. If it doesn't show any signs of wanting to leave, close the door of the room or closet in which it is hiding (or maybe it isn't hiding, it's just being) tightly, and block any exits that you can see (stuff a towel across the bottom of the door, close open windows).
- Call a wildlife rescue organization such as Wildlife SOS or a professional snake catcher (make sure you have the number of a couple of snake catchers in two or three places around the house, so you are not stumped if the number is in the room where the snake is!).

If one of your family (or the family pet) is bitten by a snake (maybe they stepped on it by mistake, not knowing it was there – snakes will not attack humans unless provoked), rush them to a hospital immediately. (See facing page for some Do's and Do NOTs to keep in mind.)

The *only* cure for a venomous snakebite is anti-venom serum injection – government hospitals usually stock some, and some private hospitals in your city may have them too. Make sure you have the numbers of hospitals and pharmacies where the serum is available, BEFORE anyone you know gets bitten. (Yes, we understand your phone memory is filling up rather rapidly now, but there is no known cure for *that* yet).

You are *seriously* panicking now, aren't you? Simply by reading through this section? Calm down – this will likely never happen to you or anyone you know! But it may happen to someone in your larger community, and wouldn't it be wonderful for that person if there was someone around who knew exactly what to do? You see, a WoCoTeen cannot follow through on her motto of being 'Ready! Willing! Able!' if she isn't even 'Ready!'. So let 'Be Prepared!' be your rallying cry (as it is of B-P's Scouts) – and on to the next section!

DO NOT:

- Try and assess if the snake is venomous or non-venomous – just go to the hospital now!

- Put ice on the bite.

- Cover the bite.

- Give the victim anything to eat or drink – it will increase his metabolism and make the venom travel faster through the bloodstream.

- Use your mouth to try and suck the venom out (yes, it used to be recommended, but it has not been found to be very effective, apart from being dangerous to the sucker).

- If you are tying a tourniquet, do NOT use electric cable, string or rubber strips for the tourniquet – it will end up being too tight and may cut off blood supply completely, leading to the limb having to be amputated!

DO ensure that:

- The wound is always below heart level.

- The victim is calm (no one said this was going to be easy).

- The victim doesn't run or do anything that would increase his heart rate.

SKILL 68
KNOW THE PET-OWNER CODE

Do you have a pet? That's wonderful! Do you know the Pet Owner's Responsibility Code?

Let's pause for a clarification here. This is not about being responsible for your pet's health, comfort and happiness – (we hope like heck that) you have all that down pat. This is about the larger responsibility that you, as a pet-owner, have towards your community. A community, whether it is an apartment complex or neighbourhood, that allows you the privilege of having a pet deserves something in return. Here's a quick run-through of some of the basics of *that* Responsibility Code for dog-owners, since, most often, the only pets seen outside of a home and interacting with the larger community are dogs.

You are entirely responsible for your dog's behaviour in a public space. It is up to you to ensure that your dog does not chase, bite or attack any person.

When your dog is off your property, make sure he is on a leash. Your dog may be the gentlest creature around, but your community's public spaces are meant for everyone to enjoy, and people who are genuinely intimidated by dogs may not be at all comfortable with a dog who is not attached to its owner. Also, you cannot really control your dog's behaviour, or protect him from other, possibly aggressive, dogs if he isn't on a leash.

Do not neglect to 'stoop-and-scoop'. This is the one rule of the Pet Owner's Responsibility Code that is broken all the time, especially, sadly, in India. Think about it – if you yourself find the thought of being around your beloved dog's poop distasteful, how is it fair to other people to leave it around for them to step into? So carry a reusable plastic *dabba* and a little plastic shovel with you whenever you take your dog out, and stoop, scoop, and flush the poop away in your toilet when you get home. Don't make that face – just do it!

Rein in the barking. Of course it's natural for dogs to bark and cats to meow, but a dog's incessant barking (over 15 minutes at a stretch) is unbearable to anyone. If your dog is doing it, there must be a reason for it – exhaustion, boredom, wanting your attention, thirst, discomfort, feeling too hot or too cold. Try and figure out what it is and ensure the barking reduces, for your pet's own benefit and for everyone else's.

SKILL 69
UNDERSTAND THE STRAY DOG WELFARE ISSUE

Yes, stray dogs have a right to as dignified and comfortable a life as anyone else. But stray dogs, especially when there is a pack of them, can also be as dangerous as wild animals, or as intimidating at the very least, to several residents of the community. What is to be done about them to keep everyone – both dogs and humans – happy, and the streets safe?

In the 19th century, the British thought the best way to control the stray dog population in Indian cities and reduce the number of human deaths from rabies was to kill all of them (the dogs, not the humans). Indian municipalities continued the practice after Independence, and up to 50,000 dogs were killed each year. In 1993, the government finally admitted that the programme was a giant failure. Not only had the number of human deaths by rabies gone up, but the stray dog population had also actually increased! This is because Indian cities have open garbage dumps with plenty of food available to sustain stray dogs.

From 1994, a new idea was adopted – mass sterilization of strays, so that they could not breed any further. The government runs this programme with the help of NGOs that concern themselves with the welfare of stray dogs. This seems like the most sensible and humane thing to do, particularly because sterilization is said to reduce aggression in male dogs.

What can you do to help reduce the stray dog problem in your community while allowing them to live well as long as they are alive? You can call NGOs in your town that are helping the government with its sterilization programme, and ensure that your strays are taken away, neutered and then released back into your community. You should also make sure that everyone in the community knows what you are doing and why you are doing it – it will help reduce their fear and allow them to gradually accept the dogs as part of the community.

What should you do if you come across a stray that is injured (through human cruelty, a traffic accident, or through a fight with other dogs) or ill? Remembering that they are feral animals, and being aware that they could be carrying rabies or some other similar disease, stay well clear of the injured animal. But make sure you report the injured (or sick) animal and its location to the NGOs in your city that concern themselves with strays – they will know what to do.

One last thing. If you are one of those good Samaritans who likes to feed strays, make sure you also take the responsibility of getting them neutered and vaccinated. You can't be feeding them and enjoying their affection and helping them thrive on your streets, without also ensuring that they don't cause trouble to others who would rather not have them there at all. That's a fair ask, don't you think?

THE FRIEND-TO-ANIMALS' CHALLENGES

#66
THE INJURED-SMALL-ANIMAL-CARE CHALLENGE

- Make a list of all the animal rescue and rehabilitation centres in your city. Call each of them to find out if they are functioning, what services each provides, and whether they offer pick-up services for injured animals. Put all the information you have gathered about the functioning centres, along with their contact details, on a WhatsApp message and share it with everyone you know.
- With your Squad Leader, visit an animal shelter or an animal rescue and rehabilitation centre in your city. Before you go, list out some questions you'd like to ask the vets, volunteers, and others who work at the centre - Which is the most unusual animal or bird they have cared for? Which was the animal or bird they didn't think would survive but made it? What is a typical day in their life like? What do they love about their job? - things like that. After you've had a tour of the place, interview the staff at the centre, adding more questions that come to mind after the tour. Post the interview on the Squad Blog, along with the contact number and other details of the centre.

#67
THE WILD-ANIMAL-AHOY CHALLENGE

- Research the Big Four among Indian venomous snakes: The Indian Cobra, The Common Krait, The Russell's Viper, and the Saw-Scaled Viper. Divvy up the work among Squad members - four members research one snake each, and the fifth and sixth research, say, the ways to tell venomous and non-venomous snakes apart and recommended first aid for snakebites (for this, this Squad member could interview a doctor who has some experience in treating snakebites). Share the results of your research at the next Squad meeting.

• Contact a snake catcher in your city and invite him to do a show-and-tell about snake-catching. Share his number, and contact numbers of other snake catchers in your city, with everyone you know, via WhatsApp.

#68
THE PET-OWNER CHALLENGE

■ This is an individual challenge. If you are a pet-owner already and don't scoop your dog's poop, do it for a week. If your dog is too big for you to take for a walk, walk with whoever usually takes her, and just be the pooper-scooper. If you are not a pet-owner and are scared of animals, write a letter to all pet-owners everywhere telling them about your fears and suggesting ways in which they could be more sensitive to your needs. If you don't have your own dog, offer to walk a friend's for a week, morning and evening, doing everything a responsible pet-owner would do. At the end of the week, share your experience with your Squad. Also share your thoughts about this question: Do you want to have a pet of your own? If yes, why? If no, why not?

#69
THE STRAY-DOG-WELFARE CHALLENGE

■ Read up all you can about the stray dog 'problem' (the Welfare of Stray Dogs India website – www.wsdindia.org – has a lot of information in their FAQs section). Check out news articles on attacks by stray dogs on humans. Talk to people in your family to get their opinions on the issue. Think about how you would reduce the population of strays. On a designated day, present your solution to the Squad (every other Squad member will be doing it too).

WOCOTEEN MERIT BADGE 18

THE COOL HEAD IN A CRISIS

It is pretty certain that nearly every one of you Scouts will some day or another be present at an accident where, if you know what to do, and do it promptly, you may win for yourself the lifelong satisfaction of having rescued or helped a fellow-creature.
– Camp Fire Yarn No. 23, *Scouting for Boys*

Emergencies. Crises. Unexpected situations with unpredictable results – fire, an earthquake, a traffic accident, a medical emergency, sudden violence. They can happen anytime, in any community. And yet most of us go through life in complete denial, whistling a merry tune, thinking – 'Lighten up, people! What's the point worrying about stuff that hasn't even happened? We'll cross that bridge when it comes to it! I mean, YOLO, you know?' Others are so paralysed by their fear that *all* those things are definitely going to happen to them and their families that they do nothing practical and proactive to prepare for such eventualities.

But hey, you're a WoCoTeen, and a master at waltzing along the middle path. You dance as if no one's watching, but you've also got a whole list of emergency phone numbers in your back pocket. So that when and if something happens, you're not the one flapping about uselessly and unhelpfully, but the one actually doing stuff that helps ease the situation.

Sure, you can't prepare for every emergency that you might encounter, but these four skills should help you go some part of the way to be WoCoTeen-Ready! in a crisis.

SKILL 70
KEEP CALM AND CARRY ON

Being calm is probably The Most Important and The Most Difficult state to achieve in a crisis. When you panic, your brain gets short-circuited, and any amount of prep you've done for whatever emergency you're facing will come to nought. So it's vital that you get this one down pat. How can you do that? You practise!

Nope, we aren't suggesting that you put yourself in crisis situations voluntarily, so that you can practise staying calm. But if you think about it, you already face personal mini-crises on a daily basis – anxiety about looming exams, white-hot anger with a parent over something, heartbreak over a relationship that did not work out, burning jealousy over a friend's success. Getting past each of these requires the same techniques as the ones required in bigger crises.

Here's a quick set of tips that you can use to calm down when you're facing your next mini-crisis. That's all the practice you'll ever need for your big ones.

- **B-r-e-a-t-h-e.** Shallow breathing is your body's physical reaction to something that you're mentally or emotionally troubled by (the next time you are scared, upset, or angry, notice your breathing). So even though it sounds like the world's oldest cliché, breathe some big breaths. Inhale deeply and slowly so that your belly pushes out, exhale slowly and completely until your belly is concave. Doing this will trick your brain into thinking that everything is fine, and it will start working again.

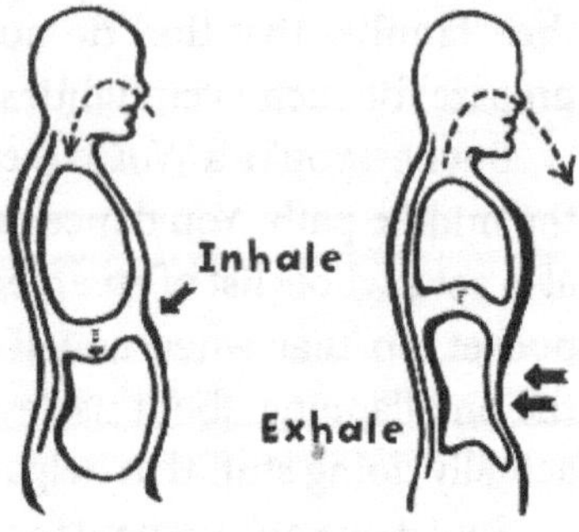

If breathing is as simple as it seems, how come so many of us are doing it wrong?

- **Step back from the problem, not away from it.** Closing your mind down to what is bothering you, saying you will 'think about it later' or pretending it doesn't exist, is just a form of denial. Instead, zoom out of the problem to see it from a larger perspective – sure your best friend's behaviour is making you mad right now, but considering all the good times you both have shared over all the years, is it worth ruining your entire friendship by saying something angry or mean that you can never take back? If the answer is no, address the problem right away – apologize, say you understand, do something nice for her that she isn't expecting. Instant calm will result – why would you want to prolong the agony by postponing thinking about the problem?

- **Fight stress with more stress.** Some people can calm down in a stressful situation by thinking about positive, joyful things. But another equally effective way to handle stress is to think about a far worse situation than the one you are in right now, or to think about how much worse this situation could have been. When you do this, you feel grateful, the problem diminishes in size, and calm results. Try it and see!
- **Don't be impulsive; think before you act.** High-stress situations release adrenalin and kick off what is called your body's 'fight or flight' response. Adrenalin gives you a brief burst of extraordinary strength and clarity, which you may decide to use to fight something or flee from it. Both are valid responses, but consciously allow yourself a few moments to think about which one is a better response in the given situation, instead of relying purely on your instinct. Practise this 'thinking-before-acting' thing consciously in dealing with your mini-crises until it becomes your body's auto-response.
- **Understand that you are not perfect, forgive yourself, and move on**. We waste too much productive time blaming ourselves with all kinds of if-only scenarios – if only I had studied regularly, if only I hadn't done that, if only I had listened to my mom... If-onlys are not only a waste of time, they take valuable mindspace away from the problem in front of you now. You can't do anything about what's done, but you certainly can take the present by the horns and do what is needed. Do it!

SKILL 71
ALWAYS BE MINDFUL, ALERT AND AWARE

This is as straightforward as it sounds. This skill is basically about being observant, and mindful, about your surroundings always, no matter how much fun you are having.

- Whether you are in a movie hall, a school bus, a mall, or a mela, **make it a habit to observe where the exits are**, and have a vague plan of the space sketched out in your head. If there is an emergency and you have to evacuate - particularly in case of fire, when the smoke could obscure your surroundings, you will not only be able to find your own way to safety but will also be able to direct others around you to the exits as well.
- **If there are fire extinguishers, make sure you have some idea where they are** as well. When you pass a fire extinguisher in a glass case, make it a habit to read the instructions for use with some concentration, and role-play the process in your head.
- When you are travelling out of town with a group of friends or family, **make sure that the vehicle you are in has a basic, well-stocked first-aid kit** in it somewhere. Also, these days, large luxury air-conditioned passenger buses - the kind that have big unopenable windows with no grilles across them to obscure the view - sometimes have a hammer in a glass case somewhere on the bus, for breaking windows open in case of an emergency - make a note of its location.
- **Pay attention in your Disaster Management class** at school. Yeah, we know, your Disaster Management textbook reads almost like a 'that-won't-happen-to-me-in-a-million-years' fantasy storybook. But the stuff in there - what to do in case of fire, flood, earthquakes, tornadoes, tsunamis, volcanoes (well, okay, maybe it doesn't talk about volcanoes) - could potentially save your life, or someone else's one day. So listen up!

SKILL 72
HAVE AN EMERGENCY PLAN AT HOME (AND SCHOOL)

Think about the places where you spend most of your days – and nights. Clearly, therefore, the probability that those are the places you will be at when an emergency occurs is pretty high. But have you ever thought about what you – and everyone else who inhabits those spaces for several hours each day – will do in such a scenario? Erm, not really, right? High time you did that, don't you think?

Let's talk about an emergency plan for the home first – you can extrapolate (nice word, that – look it up if you don't know its meaning) that to a school situation later, by yourself. What should an emergency plan for home involve? Here is a list of questions to think about. Sit down with your family and discuss these questions. You may want to add several more questions to your family's list, given your particular needs and circumstances. These discussions will give you more than the answers to your questions – they will help you understand what your family's priorities are, the kind of stuff you really care about as a family.

- **Evacuation drills:** Your school probably already conducts fire drills – it's good to also do the drill at home, with everyone who lives there, at least twice a year. That will help you find answers to questions like: How will your nearly-invalid grandmother be evacuated, and whose responsibility is that? Whose responsibility is the family pet? What are the essentials that your parents will want to take with them if you all have to leave suddenly? Are they all in one place? Does more than one person in the family know the location of these essentials? Now put together an Emergency Family Pack with only the most essential objects and documents and make sure everyone at home knows where it is.
- **Emergency numbers list:** Do you have a list of emergency

numbers – your family doctor, an ambulance service, the closest hospital, the fire station, the police control room, your grandparents, your closest uncles and aunts, your neighbours, the electricity company, the closest well-stocked pharmacy – in a place where everyone can find and access it at a moment's notice?

- **Rendezvous points:** Pre-decide two rendezvous points at which all your family members will meet in case you are separated during an emergency. One of those points can be right outside your house – if the emergency is something like a fire, which only affects your building. The other point has to be somewhere outside your area – maybe at your grandparents' if they live in your city, or a close family friend's – in case your entire neighbourhood is affected by the emergency. That way, you won't waste your time trying to find each other at a time when phone signals may be jammed.

SKILL 73
KNOW HOW TO ADMINISTER BASIC FIRST AID

There are several books – including your Disaster Management textbook – that will try and teach you, using words and diagrams, how to administer first aid. So we won't repeat those here. Also, every WoCoTeen knows well that book learning can never be a substitute for hands-on learning, so we suggest you learn how to clean a wound, or use a splint or tie a sling, by actually doing it, even if the wound is fake and there are no real broken bones to immobilize.

How do you learn practical first aid?

- There are organizations and hospitals in most Indian cities that officially offer half-day and full-day first-aid courses for the general public. A good place to start your enquiries would be with your city's branch of St John Ambulance. Sign up for one of these courses with your family or a group of friends.

Remember to keep practising once you've been through the course to keep your first-aid skills honed and ready.

- In addition, watch YouTube videos on basic first aid. Watching first aid being administered gives you a lot more insights into how it is done than reading about it does.
- Even as you do all this, understand that this is all just an exercise in being prepared. When a situation that needs urgent medical attention does arrive, you may realize that nothing you have learnt has taught you what to do in this particular situation. That's fine – simply call in a professional or an ambulance (using the numbers you've remembered to save on your phone) and wait with the injured person until help arrives, talking to him or her, letting her know help is coming, and that there is a caring human beside her. Often, that's all it takes to comfort the injured person and give her the strength to fight, hang on and not panic until professional help arrives.

THE COOL HEAD'S CHALLENGES

#70
THE KEEP-CALM CHALLENGE

■ This is an individual challenge. For a whole week, whenever you are angry, upset or anxious, practise the moves outlined under Skill 70. Record these incidents in a notebook at the end of each day, and write down your experience each time you used the moves – did the process of deep breathing, stepping back from the problem, fighting stress with stress, and so on help you? If yes, how? If not, why do you think it did not? Whether you think it helped you or not, don't stop using the moves for a week. At the end of the week, read through all the entries and write down how you feel about it now. Share your experience with the Squad and your Squad Leader.

#71
THE MINDFUL-ALERT-AWARE CHALLENGE

■ With your Squad, make a visit to a mall close to your neighbourhood. Divide yourselves into pairs and walk (do not run) around the mall for 15–30 minutes, making a note of the exits, fire extinguishers, fire hoses, sand buckets and any other safety equipment they may have. Also make a note of the fire hazards and other dangers – blocked exits, locked exits, narrow stairwells, missing lights in stairwells. Find out if there is a terrace to which people can escape to in case of a fire (even in contained fires, many people die because the stairwells to terraces are blocked with junk and the terrace door is locked). Check if the mall plan, with exits clearly marked, is posted in the lift and at several points on every floor.

Meet at a pre-decided venue at the end of your exploration.

The challenge for each pair now is to draw a plan of the mall from memory, with the *usable* exits and fire extinguisher positions marked (without referring to any pictures you might have taken on your phones!). Then have a Squad discussion around these questions – In your opinion, is your neighbourhood mall equipped to handle an emergency that will require shoppers to evacuate quickly and easily? The next time you go to a mall to shop, will you look at it differently from before?

#72
THE EMERGENCY-PLAN CHALLENGE

■ With the help of your parents, create a master-list of emergency numbers for your home and put it up in a clearly visible, easily accessible location in your house. Take a picture of it in its location and WhatsApp it to your Squad Leader (he or she should be able to see all the numbers clearly) to prove that you have completed this task.

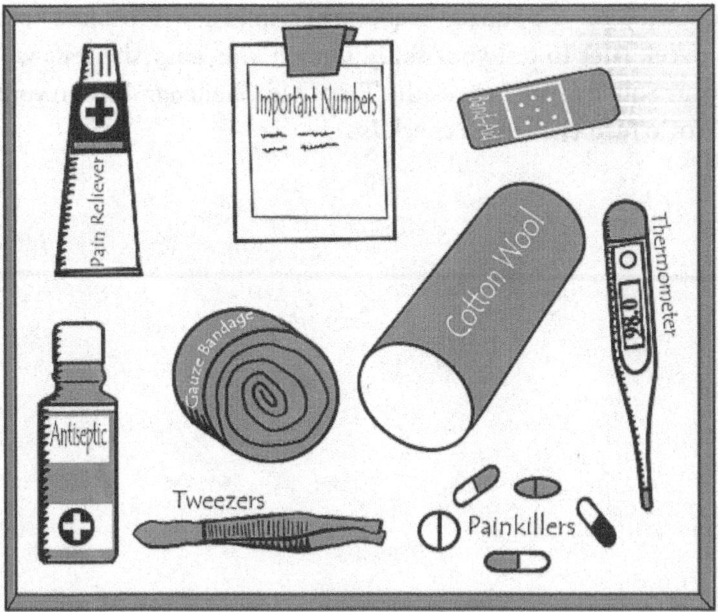

A basic first-aid kit. Have you made one yet?

- Using the suggestions in the illustration of the first-aid box, and in consultation with your parents about any special medications your family needs and trusts, put together a first-aid box for your family. Do a show-and-tell session at the next Squad meeting, where each of you shares what you put in your box, and why.
- Talk to your school's student council, your class teacher and/or school principal about the need to have an 'Emergency Plan' for the school. Offer to put a group of students together to formulate the plan in consultation with a teacher. Once it is done, present it to the school during morning assembly, and talk about why it is important for each student to know it by heart.

#73
THE FIRST-AID CHALLENGE

- With your Squad Leader, attend a class on basic first aid in your city, or invite a doctor or nurse to come over and conduct a session for the Squad. Request the professional to come back a week later to test your skills. Only if you 'pass' the tests will your Squad Leader check the 'First-Aid Challenge' box on your WoCoTeen challenges checklist.

THE GREAT OUTDOORS COVENANT

I BELIEVE I'M AN INTEGRAL PART OF THE NATURAL WORLD

The Naturalist

The Pathfinder

The Pioneer

The Camper

The Starman

The Signaller

THE GREAT OUTDOORS COVENANT

I BELIEVE I'M AN INTEGRAL PART OF THE NATURAL WORLD

6

MERIT BADGES TO BE WON

The Naturalist

The Pathfinder

The Pioneer

The Camper

The Starman

The Signaller

AN OLD CANADIAN SCOUT AND TRAPPER, OVER EIGHTY YEARS OF AGE, BILL HAMILTON, ONCE WROTE A BOOK CALLED 'MY SIXTY YEARS IN THE PLAINS' DESCRIBING THE DANGERS OF THE ADVENTUROUS LIFE OF AN EARLY PIONEER. 'I HAVE OFTEN BEEN ASKED,' HAMILTON WROTE, 'WHY WE EXPOSED OURSELVES TO SUCH DANGERS. MY ANSWER HAS ALWAYS BEEN THAT THERE WAS A CHARM IN THE OPEN-AIR LIFE OF A SCOUT FROM WHICH ONE CANNOT FREE HIMSELF AFTER HE HAS ONCE COME UNDER ITS SPELL. GIVE ME THE MAN WHO HAS BEEN RAISED AMONG THE GREAT THINGS OF NATURE. HE CULTIVATES TRUTH, INDEPENDENCE AND SELF-RELIANCE. HE HAS GENEROUS IMPULSES. HE IS TRUE TO HIS FRIENDS, AND TRUE TO THE FLAG OF HIS COUNTRY.'

I CAN FULLY ENDORSE WHAT THIS OLD SCOUT HAS SAID. I FIND THAT THOSE MEN WHO COME FROM THE FARTHEST FRONTIERS – FROM WHAT WE SHOULD CALL A RUDE AND SAVAGE LIFE – ARE AMONG THE MOST GENEROUS AND CHIVALROUS OF THEIR RACE, ESPECIALLY TOWARD WOMEN AND WEAKER FOLK. THEY BECOME 'GENTLE MEN' BY THEIR CONTACT WITH NATURE.

– B-P, in Camp Fire Yarn No. 5, *Scouting for Boys*

Ahhhh. The Great Outdoors. So desirable in theory for anyone who has always lived in a city – beautiful landscapes, star-studded skies, fresh air, a silence only broken by the rustling of leaves and the babble of a brook – but so difficult to deal with in practice – bugs, itchy grass, no air-conditioning, and, horror of horrors! – no Wi-Fi signal.

Still, there is no denying the sudden lifting of the spirits that even the most hardened city-slicker experiences in the 'lap of Nature'. And with good reason. Living in the city, we tend to forget that like every other living thing – animal, plant and tree – we are carbon-based life forms, as much a part of Nature as everything else in it. So we deliberately sequester ourselves inside our climate-controlled homes and cars, control the Nature that does make it past our gates by keeping our plants pruned and our gardens weeded and our bug spray at the ready, and choose to believe that we are somehow outside of Nature, and even – the cheek! – that we are superior to it. It's a stupid, unwise deception, and definitely not one that a WoCoTeen will let himself succumb to.

And that's why the six Merit Badges in this section are so important. Mastering the skills it takes to win them will put you back in touch with your surroundings in an elemental kind of way, even if you never leave the city. For while you may think Nature is something that you have to travel out of town to find, she is in fact all around you, just waiting to make friends.

WOCOTEEN MERIT BADGE 19

THE NATURALIST

> *Woodcraft is the knowledge of animals and nature. (Scouting) is, in a word, a school of citizenship through woodcraft.*
> **– Preface, *Scouting for Boys***

A naturalist, the dictionary tells us, is a student of natural history. And what is 'natural history'? It is 'the scientific study of animals or plants, especially as concerned with observation rather than experiment'. And that's exactly the spirit in which the Squad would like you to approach this badge.

You see, you don't need any special skills to be a naturalist. Nature has already provided you with a set of five wonderful senses to help you experience the world. She has given you a brain that can make rapid-fire connections between what you see and hear and smell and taste and feel.

All you need to do, therefore, is deploy those senses and that brain well – in this case, for *observing* things around you. Observation skills are critical for scientists, detectives, doctors, novelists, WoCoTeens who want to win the Naturalist Badge, and oh, really anyone who wants to live a life where he is never bored.

By the time you master the four skills that will win you this badge, you will have those observation skills in spades. Exciting thought, right?

SKILL 74
HONE YOUR OBSERVATION SKILLS

The good thing about observation skills? They are a learned skill, not something you are born with. Which means anyone can become an ace at observation by using some techniques and practising them regularly. Here are a few activities to get you started.

Draw something from memory. You think you know your classroom well, but how well do you really know it? How many benches and desks? How many charts on the walls? How many windows, tubelights, and shelves in the class cupboard? What kind of flooring? How many objects on the teacher's desk? If you are reading this book at home, draw your classroom out, right now, as accurately as you can remember. Check what you missed, or got wrong, in school tomorrow.

Describe someone's face and/or body structure in words. Say you've been a witness to a bag-snatching. You got a proper look at the perpetrator but did not have time to get a picture of him on your phone. You now have to describe that person to the police. Would you be able to? To check, describe someone you see often – a teacher, perhaps – to a friend who doesn't go to your school, and ask her to do a basic sketch (this works better if the friend has some drawing skills!). She will obviously have lots of questions – does your teacher have sticky-outy ears or ones that lie flat against her skull? Does she part her hair to the side or the middle? What shape is her face? Are there any 'distinguishing features' – a mole, a chipped front tooth, a scar – that make her face unique? At the end of the activity, ask yourself – Were you sure of all the answers? Does the sketch look anything like the teacher? The next day in school, really 'look' at your teacher to see how many answers you got right.

If you begin to look at people with a mind to describing them to someone, your observation skills will be ace before you know it.

Train your memory. It's all very well to observe things well, but if your memory is like a sieve, you would have forgotten all of it in the next day or two. The trick with 'deductive reasoning' is for your brain to observe *and retain* things, so that you can build on that knowledge to solve a problem later. What is called 'instinct' or 'gut feel' is not a random nerve impulse – it comes from all the subconscious knowledge your brain and body have

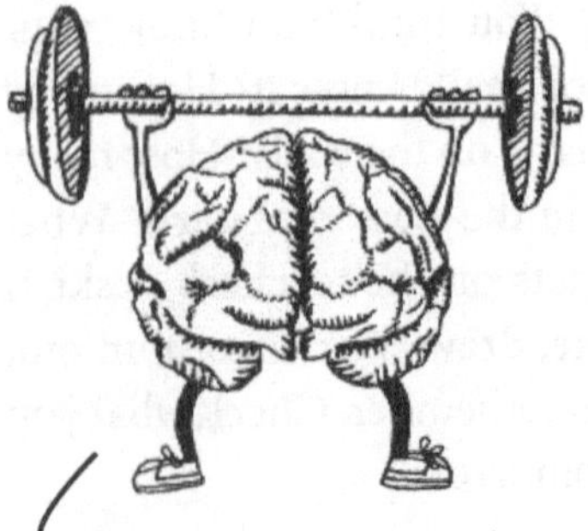

gathered not only over your lifetime but what has been passed on to you through your genes from all the knowledge humankind has gathered over its entire evolutionary history. Yup, that's why training your memory and keeping it sharp is so important.

How do you do it? You are already getting lots of memorizing practice with your school lessons, and you are surely brilliant at remembering lyrics of songs that you love (and hate – earworm!), but you could also do it with other stuff. Memorize telephone numbers instead of outsourcing the job to your phone. Memorize shopping lists and lists of random unrelated objects – all the different things inside your desk drawer, maybe, or name lists of Class XII toppers that your school has displayed on the noticeboard.

Here's a neat trick for remembering lists of objects (like 30 items on a grocery list), *in order*, and *never* missing a single one. All you have to do is to connect each of the different objects on the list to the ones adjacent to it, using the silliest associations possible. For instance, if your list reads: shoes, lipstick, cauliflower, engine oil, chocolate chips, gel pens, cricket bat, and brown wrapping paper, you could connect them this way in your head: Imagine a pair of shoes whose uppers have separated from their soles, giving them 'mouths', which are painted over with bright red lipstick, chomping on cauliflower manchurian, except the brown of the manchurian is not soya sauce but engine oil that is flowing out of the plate and turning into a chocolate river that is depositing chocolate-chip pebbles along its banks, at the feet of gel-pens that are fielding during a gel-pen cricket match where the cricket bat is constructed entirely of brown wrapping paper. You have to actually 'see' these images in your head, otherwise your memory will not retain the list, and the order. But once you do, you will never forget, and will even be able to recall the list in the same order three days later!

Do a Sherlock on people around you. This is the most fun activity in the world. Based on what someone is wearing, reading, carrying, doing, and/or who he or she is hugging, talking to (and in what language), eating with, yelling at, and/or where she is standing, sitting or going, and/or how old she looks, what can you deduce about what she does for a living, which company she probably works for, which part of the country she is from, and what her relationship is to the person she is with? Of course, you can't always confirm whether your deductions were right when you are observing strangers, but you will learn a lot simply by observing someone, and you would have spent your time at the bus stop in a far more interesting fashion than if you had been playing a game on your phone.

Do this exercise sometimes with people who aren't absolute strangers too. Maybe you can watch a TV talk show on mute – you don't know the people on the panel or the subject of the discussion, but just by looking at what they are wearing and how they look, can you tell whether they are scientists or politicians or sportsmen, and where they're from? Then turn the sound up, listen to the accents and the content of the discussion, and check if you were right.

The game, WoCoTeens, is on!

Sharpen your logic. Logic is an important part of deductive reasoning – the if-then-else loop that is running constantly in your head even though you don't realize it. Like in these cases:

- If I can smell cooking gas, then there is probably a gas leak.
- My friend has been called to the teacher's desk to get her

math marks. I can only see her back from where I am. If her shoulders tense up when she sees her paper, I must arrange my face into a sympathetic, supportive expression; if her shoulders relax, I can grin and give her a thumbs-up when she turns around.

To keep your logic sharp, make solving logic-based puzzles part of your routine. The Rubik's cube, Sudoku puzzles, cryptograms, chess, all work brilliantly as practice. Writing computer code is another great exercise.

SKILL 75
KEEP A TREE LOG

I think I shall never see
A poem lovely as a tree
– Opening lines from the poem 'Trees ' by Joyce Kilmer

Have you ever really, really looked at a tree? Not just on one day of the year when it is full of flowers, not just by casually letting your eye skim over it as you walk or drive past, but dozens of times, noticing all kinds of little details about it? It's only when you do this, in season after season, that you really get to *know* a tree; and it's only when you know a tree that you truly begin to care about it. Here are some ideas to convert you from someone who is aware that trees exist to a committed tree fan.

'Adopt' some trees. Pick five or six different species of trees that you can observe on a daily or weekly basis. If you walk to school, they could be trees on your walking route. Or they could be in a neighbourhood park or within your apartment complex or within your school compound.

Observe your trees. For the first couple of weeks, just spend time observing your trees and getting to know them, one tree at a time. Spend 15–20 minutes with each tree at your first meeting, observing little details, like:

- **Overall shape** – Tall and thin? Broad and short? Willowy?
- **Canopy** – Messy, floppy crown like a punk-rocker's (coconut tree)? Dense leafy mop that looks too heavy for the short trunk to bear (mango tree)? Big spreading umbrella-shaped hairdo with dry straggly dreadlocks hanging down everywhere (banyan tree)? Also, does the canopy throw a deep, 'solid' shadow or a 'dappled' one?
- **Trunk** – Thick or thin? Smooth or gnarled? Single or buttressed? Straight or twisted?
- **Branches** – Do they grow upwards or outwards? Where does the branching start – low on the trunk or higher up?
- **Leaves** – What shape are they? What colour? Simple (one leaf per stalk, as in mango or peepul) or compound (many leaves per stalk, as in *gulmohar* or tamarind)?
- **Buds and flowers** – What kind are they? What colour?
- **Berries and fruit** – Can you see any? Check the ground below for fallen fruit that you can open up and examine.
- **Seed pods** – Are there seed pods hanging off the tree? Have some of them burst open and fallen down? What shape are they? Do they rattle when you shake them? When you open them up, can you see the seeds inside? What 'packaging material' has the tree thoughtfully put into each seed pod to cushion the seeds and protect them?

Once you've spent time observing a tree, you will be quicker to notice any changes that happen. And changes are happening every day! You will be amazed at the amount of activity that goes on in a tree, and constantly.

Name your trees. It doesn't matter what the scientific name of the tree is, or even what its common name is. Give each of your trees your own special name based on features about them that you love or find unique. If it has a particularly striking purple flower, go to www.pantone.com/color-finder and match the purple of its flower to the exact shade in the shade card. Is your flower's colour more a *Vigorous Violet* or a *Powerful Purple*? Is the flower more trumpet-shaped or saucer-shaped?

Does it have one layer of petals or several? That will help you decide whether to name your tree 'The Powerful Trumpurple' or 'The Vigorous Violayered'.

This is just to give you an idea of how it's done (of course you don't have to name your tree only based on its flowers – many trees do not have showy flowers at all). Only after this exercise, proceed to find out what your tree is actually called (thereby making it *your* tree).

Record your observations. After 2–4 weeks of getting to know your trees, start recording information about them in a book. Populate the book with drawings or photographs of different parts of the tree, and put down your observations on new and exciting things you observe on your tree in each season. Make sure you update your tree log at least once a month.

Spread the love. As you get really close to your trees, you will start noticing other trees, comparing them to yours, seeing the ways in which they are similar and different. You will see how each is unique and important in its own way to its ecosystem – maybe bees love feeding on the nectar of the flowers of one tree, while monkeys love the fruit of another; maybe

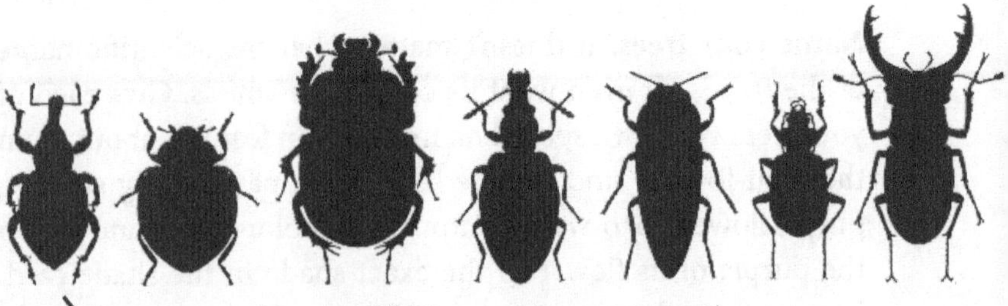

There are as many as 1,017,018 species of insects in the world.
You may pick your jaw off the floor now.

one has rather special seed pods, while another is home to a hundred different bugs; maybe one provides a dense, lovely shade in the summer, while another is just heart-liftingly beautiful. Noticing such details will make every tree dear to you, and you will now want to protect and cherish *all* of them. Tree-mendous, what?

SKILL 76
BE AN ENTOMOLOGIST

Insects and bugs are all around us, and we're always trying our hardest to get rid of them. But considering that there are, at any given time, a million trillion of them – heck, they add up, in sheer numbers, to over 50 per cent of all living things on earth! – it makes sense to get to know and understand them a little better than we might do now. Well, some of the nicer ones, at any rate.

How do you observe bugs? Earlier, it was standard practice to catch bugs in bottles and tins, and once they were dead, pin them up on a board for display and observation. But that kind of thing, thankfully, has fallen out of favour now.

What you can do instead is capture your bug in a bottle which has air-holes in the lid (or a piece of porous muslin cloth rubber-banded across its mouth) and enough moist leaves and grasses inside to make the bug feel comfortable for the couple of hours it spends there while you observe it. Of course, if you find a dead insect, there is nothing wrong in picking it up (but carefully! A dying bee or wasp can still sting you) and mounting it with a pin on a sheet of thermocol so that you can observe its parts closely before you throw it away.

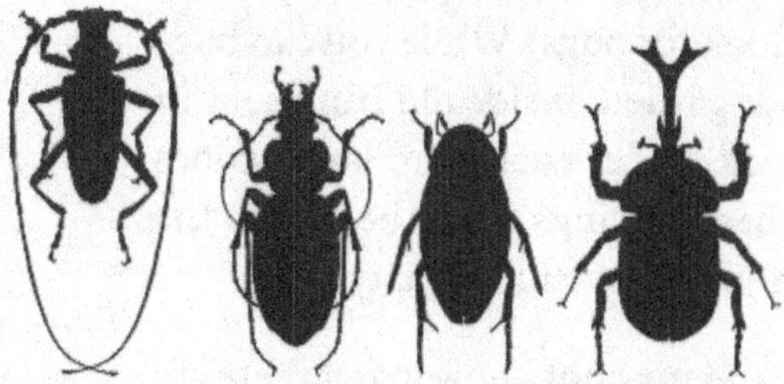

If you don't want to collect bugs at all, there are several other things you can do to get to know the bugs you share your neighbourhood with.

Bone up on some basic insect trivia. What is the difference between a bee and a wasp? What is the difference between an insect (six-legged cockroach) and an arachnid (eight-legged spider)? What are the official names of the different kinds of ants we see in our environment? Which are the different species of mosquito that are the carriers of the deadly viruses that cause malaria, dengue and chikungunya?

Maintain a Bug Book. Make a list of all the bugs you have commonly seen around you, and write their names down, one bug to a page. Most Indian city lists would include cockroaches, spiders, a variety of ants, centipedes, millipedes, caterpillars, silverfish, bees, wasps, mosquitoes, houseflies, butterflies, moths, ladybugs, praying mantises, lice, bedbugs, grasshoppers, crickets, dragonflies, and all kinds of beetles. Now start looking actively for each of them inside and outside your house and garden. Every time you find a bug that doesn't fit under any of the categories you've listed, create a new page for it.

Take pictures of every bug you spot. You will need to bring on all your 'stalking' skills to creep up really close to a bug without it noticing you or your camera. This, as you know from experience, is particularly difficult with bugs, which have compound eyes that can detect the smallest movement. But keep trying valiantly to outwit the bug – fortune favours the brave! Once you have your picture, print it out and stick it on the relevant page in your Bug Book. Use the picture to find the bug on the Internet or in a book on insects and identify it. Write down all the information you find out about it next to the picture.

What are good places to look for bugs? While you can bug-hunt through the year in your garden, inside old trunks, or in the neighbourhood park (look under rocks and large stones and dead branches), the richest pickings are to be had in the monsoon, and in wide open spaces outside the city.

Follow an Indian bug blog. You may not know it, but there are several passionate wildlife lovers across the country, who share information, expertise, experience and great photographs generously online. One of the best, and most regularly updated ones, is maintained by award-winning conservationist and educationist Karthikeyan Srinivasan, who has a special interest in insects, and blogs at *wildwanderer.com*. There are several others – pick a couple and make them part of your weekend reading. You will be bug-literate in no time!

Watch entomology documentaries. There are so many brilliant ones out there! Pick from films made by the *BBC, Discovery Channel and National Geographic*. The best part is that you can not only choose what you want to watch but *when* when to watch it too because, duh, they are all on YouTube!

SKILL 77
BE AN URBAN BIRDER

The sight of a great bird in free flight is probably one of the most spirit-lifting sights in the world. And if you think you have to go out to the top of a hill or into the country to see it, think again. Birds are everywhere around us, and they are fascinating, which is probably why so many Indian cities have so many active birdwatching groups.

So how do you actually start your birdwatching journey? Um, the first step is pretty simple, actually.

Watch birds. The next time you see or hear a bird outside your window, stop what you're doing and stare. Be very quiet, so you don't alert or alarm it in any way. Notice its size, its overall shape, its markings, its beak, its feet and its posture – each kind of bird has a signature 'silhouette', which makes it easy to identify from far away. Once the bird flies away, try and draw it from memory. You don't have to get every detail right, just the overall shape and silhouette. If you've managed to take a picture of it, you can use it to refresh your memory. (But really, don't be in a hurry to take a picture. At first, just use your eyes

Common Indian birds. You can identify every single one, can't you?

and brain to drink it in. You can find fabulous pictures of that bird online, but the opportunity to see it for yourself, from up close, comes only rarely).

Make a list of all the birds you can identify by sight. Even those who think they can't identify any birds at all can come up with quite an impressive list, actually, when they force themselves to put it all down. Let's see now – peacock, crow, sparrow, parakeet, owl, pigeon, kite (which is the correct name for the bird of prey most often seen snatching food from children's hands during lunch break at school) dove, vulture, budgerigars (often called love-birds)... You see?

One good way to quickly increase the number of birds on this list is to learn to identify the official birds of each of the Indian States (did you even know that we have official State birds?). In a matter of weeks, even days, you will know exactly what exotic birds like Mrs Hume's Pheasant (Mizoram and

Manipur), the Asian Paradise Flycatcher (Madhya Pradesh), and the Indian Roller (Karnataka and Andhra Pradesh), look like! Cool, huh?

Tune your sense station to the bird frequency. Just like we do with the trees around us, we also take the birdlife around us for granted a lot of the time. The next time you walk anywhere (if you don't walk anywhere, start today!), keep your senses on alert for any kind of avian presence – bird, bird call, bird feather, bird poop, anything. When you wake up in the morning, spend a couple of minutes actually listening to birds chirping. In the evening, when they are flying home to roost, look up and watch them. Follow this routine for a couple of weeks and you will be surprised to discover how many birds there actually are around you.

Get a pair of good binoculars. Now that you know where you might find birds, you will want to take a closer look at them when you spot them. The thing is, though, that a good pair of binoculars can cost a pretty penny. Borrow a pair from a kind aunt for a few days if you can, and see how you like the experience of watching a jumpy bird closely without her knowing you are watching her at all. It can become quite an addiction. Once it does, you can invest in your own pair.

Buy a good field guide. *Indian Birds* is a great free app for Android phones (it even has the names of the birds in Indian languages!), but there is something to be said for having a trusty pocket-sized

Did you know that peacocks shed their feathers annually? Start your own collection today! (Once you figure out where they shed them, that is!)

book of birds with bird names and brightly-coloured photos (or illustrations) that you can flip through at will. Plus, you will be using your phone for other things – taking the bird's picture, posting it on Instagram even before you have looked at it properly, and such – so using the phone to scroll through an app as well will be pretty bothersome. Ergo, get a book. Recommended ones include: *The Book of Indian Birds* by ace Indian ornithologist Dr Salim Ali (great for beginners), and *Birds of the Indian Subcontinent* by R. Grimmett, C. Inskipp, and T. Inskipp. There are also more specialized – and often cheaper – guides covering birds of a particular Indian region – South India, North India, Goa, and so on. For general tips on urban birdwatching, try British bird fanatic David Lindo's website: www.theurbanbirder.com.

Join a birdwatching group in your city. Birdwatching groups usually organize Sunday morning outings for enthusiasts and beginners to a bird-friendly 'patch' in or around the city. Join a couple of these outings. Or you can join an online group, like the public group *Indian Birds* on Facebook. The group has over 100,000 members, and just looking at the pictures that people post on it is an education.

Keep a scrapbook. Serious birders maintain what is called a 'Life List', which is a record of all the bird species they have seen and conclusively identified in all their years of birdwatching. Even if you are a 'dabbler' – an amateur enthusiast – it doesn't hurt to keep some kind of record of all the birds you see, along with your impressions about them: where you were when you spotted them, what time of day it was, how you were feeling, what else had happened that day. If nothing else, it will give you a lot of joy when you flip through it as an adult.

THE NATURALIST'S CHALLENGES

#74 THE OBSERVATION CHALLENGE

Pick a short 50-m path somewhere in your neighbourhood, preferably a quiet, tree-lined stretch with not much traffic. A route inside a park would do as well. Ask your Squad Leader to divide you into two groups. One group 'prepares' the trail by putting 12 small everyday objects – Lego blocks, a book, a steel *dabba*, a hairbrush – along the stretch you have chosen. Some things to keep in mind:

- Pick objects that do not 'belong'. That means no leaves, flowers, bugs, pebbles... If you are 'hiding' a flower in a tree, make sure it is a rose or a hibiscus, neither of which grows on trees.
- Avoid placing objects like empty tetrapacks or bottles, a half-eaten corn on the cob, or paper plates, cardboard boxes and other 'regular litter' that one normally finds (sigh!) lying around our streets and public parks.
- Make sure the object is neither too small nor too large.
- Make sure the object is not entirely concealed. This is not a treasure hunt, it is an observation challenge.
- Place objects at slightly higher or lower than eye level, or on the ground. No object should be too high.
- Make sure you have a list and location of all the objects you've strewn about.

Once the trail is ready, the other group sets off to try and find all twelve objects. They cannot dawdle or stop or climb things or pick things up – they must stroll casually from one end of the trail to the other, simply using their eyes, in under two minutes. At the end of the trail, they must make a list of everything 'out of place' that they observed. If they have located at least nine of the 12 objects, they have passed the challenge.

Then repeat the challenge with each group's roles reversed.

#75
THE TREE CHALLENGE

For this project, all Squad members pick a tree that they see everyday and maintain a tree log (or a tree blog!) through the seasons for that tree. Every week, one member shares pictures and detailed information about her tree on a Google group (this will not be too much of a chore – if you are six members in your Squad, your turn will only come once every six weeks; but make sure you observe your tree every day and take pictures whenever something interesting happens. You can share all those pictures when it is your turn to post on the group). Do this for at least two cycles (that means you get your turn at least twice).

At the end of the two cycles, your Squad Leader will quiz you not only about your tree, but also about everyone else's in the group, and decide if you are worthy. PS: You can find out the botanical and common name of the tree you've picked by referring to a tree book – good ones are Pradip Kishen's *Trees of Delhi* and *Jungle Trees of Central India*, which have lovely colour photographs and information on most Indian trees.

#76
THE BUG CHALLENGE

Believe it or not, spies have pretended to be naturalists! One of them was none other than our own B-P, Sir Robert Baden-Powell! As a British secret agent, he posed as 'one of the exceedingly stupid Englishmen who wandered about foreign countries sketching cathedrals, or catching butterflies' and made bug drawings that concealed detailed maps of enemy fortifications! (See facing page for two examples.)

Using B-P's sketches as inspiration, conceal a message, either in words or in the form of a drawing, inside a sketch of *your* favourite bug. It could be a part of your city's skyline, a hill close by, the outline of a country, whatever. Before you show your drawing and let the Squad guess what the message is, make a two-minute presentation to the Squad on the bug you've chosen – its appearance, its feeding habits, its habitat, the diseases it spreads (if any), its benefits to the environment, and so on.

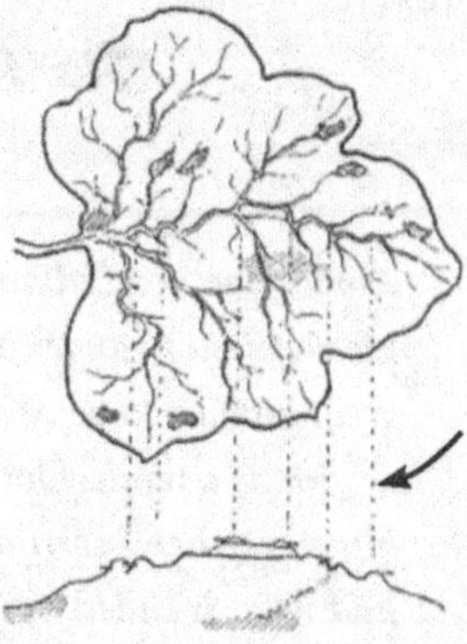

See the outline of a fort in the central vein of the leaf!

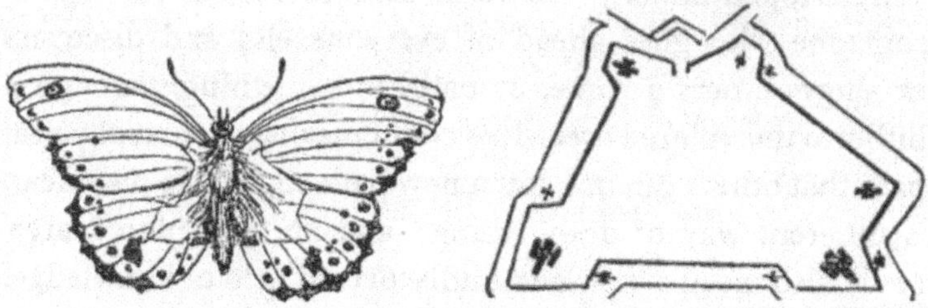

Look how there's a map of a fortress hidden in this image of a butterfly.

#77
THE BIRDER CHALLENGE

As a Squad, plan an outing with one of the birdwatching groups in your city. Or have someone from the group come over and give you a talk on urban birdlife, and tips on how and where to spot birds and become an amateur birder. If this is difficult to do, then get the Squad together one evening and watch five short documentaries related to Indian birds on YouTube. One great resource for this is birdman David Stanton's YouTube channel.

WOCOTEEN MERIT BADGE 20

THE PATHFINDER

> *Among the Red Indian scouts, the man who was good at finding his way in a strange country was termed a 'pathfinder'. It was a great honour to be called by that name.*
>
> *Many a tenderfoot has become lost in the veldt or forest, and has never been seen again, because he knew no scouting, nor had what is called an 'eye for the country'.*
>
> **– Camp Fire Yarn No. 5, *Scouting for Boys***

Who is a pathfinder? Well, in its most literal sense, it means someone who goes ahead of everyone else and discovers or shows others a route, or path, to something, through a hitherto unexplored area. This could mean an actual physical path that others can use, but a new path could also just mean 'a different way of doing things' and an 'unexplored area' could also mean a 'new and undiscovered field of knowledge'.

But we're sticking to the old-fashioned, literal meaning of pathfinder here. Sure, there can be no better literal pathfinder than The Great Google Maps, but there is a great pleasure and a wonderful sense of power and control in using your own senses and your own smarts to navigate around your neighbourhood, your city, or a new country you're visiting. Ergo, the Pathfinder skills and challenges. Rest assured, the skills you will gain while winning this badge will hold you in good stead in areas other than pathfinding as well.

SKILL 78
LEARN TO READ A 'PHYSICAL' MAP

It doesn't matter if it is one of those large, clumsy (but beautiful) fold-out maps or the Google Maps app, learning to read a map properly is one of the great life skills, and one that is in very short supply among Indians particularly. After all, why bother

to learn to read a map when you can ask someone on the street how to get where you want to? There's always someone ready and willing to give you (usually wrong) information!

As you are more likely to know how to read Google Maps, we are focusing on regular paper maps here. Because those are what you will have to turn to when your phone runs out of juice, when using mobile data is too expensive, and when, after a solar flare has hit the earth, destroying all electrical sources, you want to get somewhere (haha – let the nightmares begin!).

There are all kinds of maps, which give you all kinds of different information, but for the purposes of this book, we are sticking to learning to read what is called a Physical, or Topographical map. And not just any old physical map, either, but the topographical map of the Indian subcontinent.

A Physical map does not show you borders between States and countries (that's the job of the 'Political' map). What it does instead is give you a whole bunch of information on the physical features, or landforms – mountains, deserts, plateaus, plains – of the country, and the altutudes they are at. It allows you to trace the undulating contours of the land – its ups and downs, its hills and valleys. It lets you imagine the land in vivid 3-D, instead of in boring, flat 2-D.

Here's how you can unravel its secrets.

• **Open your atlas** (you do have one, don't you?) to the 'India – Physical' page. You see a map of India with several different colours shading random bits of it. You hate Physical maps because they are so difficult to shade and colour. Worse, the different shades make no sense to you. But stick around and you will find out exactly what they mean!

• **Track the Browns.** The colour brown dominates our northern and eastern boundaries. Different shades of brown fill Kashmir and run eastwards from there all along the border with Nepal (and fill all of Nepal too), and through Sikkim and Bhutan and Arunachal Pradesh, where they take a sharp southward turn and run like a fort wall along the length of Nagaland, Manipur and Mizoram. The darker browns are our three grand and parallel mountain ranges – the Greater Himalayas. The Lesser Himalayas, and the Siwaliks – in the north, and the Purvanchal mountain range in the east. The lighter browns appear elsewhere in the map – they run across the centre of the country where the Vindhya and Satpura mountain ranges are, parallel to the western coastline of the peninsula where the Western Ghats are, and so on.

• **Look for the Legend.** It's clear now that browns on the map indicate mountains and hills. Why the different shades though? To get the answer to that, look for the 'legend' – an information table located outside the map (in India's case, you will find it in one of the three oceans that surround the southern peninsula; our oceans make it really convenient for map-makers by offering lots of room for this kind of thing).

That's why the Vindhya and Satpura ranges in the middle of the country (between 3,500 and 4,200 m) are coloured a much lighter brown than the Greater Himalayas, and most of the Western Ghats, which are still lower, are painted an even lighter brown.

The legend we are interested in now is the table showing the different colours used on the map. Each colour fits within a number range, which is marked on a scale next to it. The numbers (usually expressed in metres) indicate the height of the landform. The darkest brown (or white, sometimes) is reserved for the highest landforms – mountains that tower between 8,000 and 9,000 m (Mt Everest, the highest point on earth at 8,880 m, is part of the darkest brown part) above sea level. As the height of the mountains decrease, the brown lightens.

• **Track the Greens.** Just below the browns, along the borders with Nepal and Pakistan, and all along the borders of the peninsula, is a band of different shades of green. The part where the band is thickest, just south of the Himalayas, is also the most fertile part of India, the Great Northern Alluvial (which means 'fed and nurtured by a river') Plain, but the legend will tell you that what the colour actually indicates, is not a lushness of vegetation but the height of the land. (Gujarat, which is coloured a lovely green, is one of the most arid parts of the country, and borders the Great Indian Desert). The green parts are, in fact, the flat lowlands, parts that are either at sea level or just a little above.

- **Track the beiges and yellows.** What about the centre of the country? You will see a gamut of lighter shades of brown all the way to a very pale yellow here. This indicates the 'tableland' – land that is higher than the plains but lower than the mountains – in other words, the Indian Plateaus. The northern plateaus are collectively called the Central Highlands, the large unbroken southern one is called the Deccan Plateau.

Do you see how, in the Deccan Plateau, the darker browns of the western part fade off to lighter shades as your eye travels east? What does that tell you? That the land slopes from west to east! See now why almost all of the peninsular rivers originate in the western hills and flow towards the east, emptying into the Bay of Bengal? Only two rivers, the Narmada and the Tapi, buck the trend, flowing into the Arabian Sea.

Look closely at the map and pick out the deltas of the big central and southern rivers – the Godavari, the Mahanadi, the Krishna, the Kaveri – on the eastern coast.

- **Find the Map Scale.** There is another vital bit of information available in another legend at the bottom of the map. This one is called a 'Map Scale', and gives you an indication of the distances between different regions on the map. A map wouldn't be much use to you if it wasn't 'drawn to scale', i.e., if it wasn't an almost perfect miniature of the actual country, every part proportionately reduced in size. The Map Scale is an indicator of that proportion. It will tell you, for instance, that a distance of one inch on the map indicates a distance of 500 km in the real world. By measuring the north-south length of the map of India in your atlas – it should measure about 16 inches – you can calculate that the actual north-south extent of India is around 16 x 500 km = 3,200 km.

• **'See' your country.** Now look at the map again, with all this information in your head. 'See' the land in your head, the lofty mountains of the north rising from the flat, inch-wide (i.e., 500 km wide) band of fertile river plains. 'See' the mighty rivers Ganga and Yamuna rushing joyfully down the heights of these mountains, bringing life, love and fertile topsoil to lay across the plains. 'See' the land rise again south of the Great Plain into a sprawling tableland in the centre and the south. 'See' the land slope from west to east in the peninsula and the rivers slip-slide and leap off cliffs as they make their long, patient way (the peninsula is three inches across at its broadest extent, which means some of these rivers travel well over 1,000 km) to the eastern sea, nurturing all the land along their way. 'See' the plateau fall away to sea level along the coasts. And think about how much one map has taught you about your country.

Yup, *that's* how you read a Physical map.

SKILL 79
KNOW THE LAY OF THE LAND

Chances are that you know exactly where your city is located in India (or not!), but, at any given time, do you know where *you* are located in your city? Ha! And you want to be a Pathfinder! Time to buck up and master this skill, then.

• **Get a fold-out map** – or a map book, if such a thing exists for your city – of your city. Open it out to its full extent on the floor and look at it for a while, noticing the following things about it:

▪ **The Grid:** The whole map is actually divided by thin lines into a grid of largish squares. The rows are perhaps named with the letters of the alphabet (look at either the right edge or the left edge of the map to spot them), and the columns with numbers starting with 1 (look along the top or bottom edge).

Think of these lines as 'city latitudes and longitudes' – they are there to help you find a locality or street or landmark.

- **The Orientation:** Somewhere on the map is a drawing of a compass, with North marked prominently pointing upwards. That tells you that the map is oriented north, i.e., the top of the map is the north of the city, and the bottom is the south. That means the right side of the map shows you the east of the city and the left side the west.
- **The Ways Out:** There are major roads, many of them numbered, leading out of your city in all directions. The numbered ones are possibly State highways or national highways, with the number indicating the official number of the highway. Highways lead to other towns and cities – they could run right through your city as well. Consult the legend at the bottom of the map to know what kind of highway each is.

- **Locate your home and your school within the map of your city.** Somewhere on the map, either on the side you are looking at or on the reverse, you will find a street and neighbourhood index – a list of every street, locality and landmark that is marked on the map. Find the street or neighbourhood where your home is located in this list. Next to it will be a two-digit alphanumeric code – A5, say, or H8. That is the grid code – it will help you zoom in on the square where your neighbourhood is. If the code is A5, it means your home is located within the square at the intersection of row A and column 5. Mark your home on the map. Repeat the process to find your school and mark it too. Here are the kinds of questions you can get answers to from this simple exercise:

- Which part of the city is your home located in – east, west, north, south? Which part of the city is your school located in?
- Where is your school located in relation to your home? To its east, south-west, north-east? Where is your home located in relation to your school?
- How far is your school from your home 'as the crow flies'? Consult the map scale at the bottom of the map and measure the shortest distance between your home and your school on

the map. If the scale of the map is 1 cm = 1 km and the distance you've measured is 5 cm, then your school is 5 km away from your home. But we don't travel through a city as the crow flies – we have to take roads, which are not often the shortest distance. You can find out how much distance you actually travel to get to school by marking the route of your school bus on the map and measuring it. Or you can ask the driver's permission to look at the odometer and see how many kilometres it clocks.

- **Look up the routes of the State and national highways** leading into and out of your city on the Internet. Which cities and towns does each touch? How far are they? Say you live in Bengaluru and want to travel to Mysuru. Which is the highway that leads out of Bengaluru and eventually takes you to Mysuru? What does that tell you about where Mysuru is located in relation to Bengaluru?*

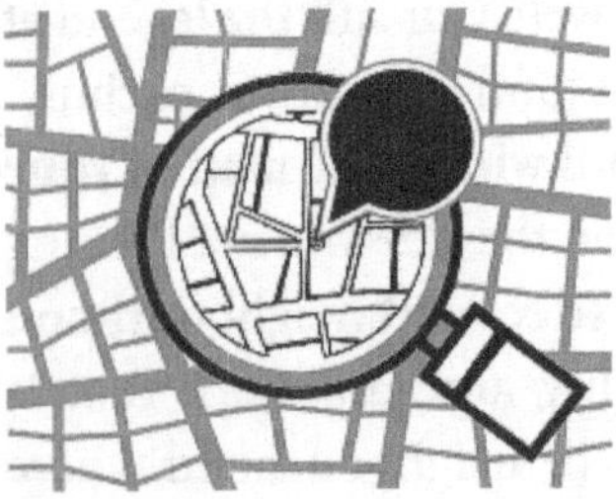

See? You are suddenly an expert on your city layout and well on your way to becoming a Pathfinder. Seriously!

SKILL 80
DRAW A MAP FROM MEMORY

On to smaller, neighbourhood maps now. On a map of your city (you can totally use Google Maps for this), zoom into an area about 1 km square, with your house being at the centre of it. Or you could pick a circular area, with your house as the centre of a circle whose radius is 1 km. (You will need to consult the Map Scale to check what distance on the map indicates 1 km on the ground). Now commit the map of that area to memory. Here are some things to keep in mind when you are memorizing a map:

- **Find the Map Legend.** It will tell you what the various symbols and markings on the map mean. Usually, a red cross indicates a

* *Ans: Mysuru is to the south-west of Bengaluru.*

hospital, an aircraft icon indicates an airport, a curvy black line scored through with perpendicular lines indicates a railway line, a coloured line punctuated by circles indicates the metro route, a blue line could indicate a river or a sewage *nallah*, and so on. When you memorize a map, memorize these landmarks too.

- **Make a mental note of the names of the streets** within the area. Some may be named after someone or something, others might just be numbered streets.
- **Make sure to note the names of the neighbourhoods** covered in that 1 square km area, and the names of any large institutions – university campuses, army bases, research establishments – that are part of your chosen area.

Now put the map away and try to draw the entire map from memory. You may or may not succeed in getting it 100 per cent right, or even 50 per cent, but the exercise would have taught you a lot about your neighbourhood. The next time you are walking (or being driven) around it, the names of the streets will have meaning – the place where you live will have suddenly come alive for you.

SKILL 81
GIVE DIRECTIONS TO YOUR HOME

The ability to give good, precise directions to someone, over the phone or otherwise, is a very useful one, and one that will earn you serious fans among your friends and relatives. It is also an astonishingly rare one, particularly in India. Here are some tips to turn you into the queen (or king) of direction-giving.

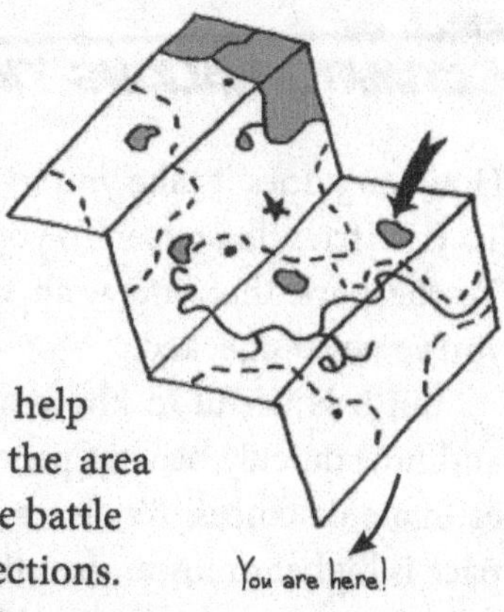

- **Master Skill 80.** That will help you become very familiar with the area around your home. That's half the battle won when it comes to giving directions.

• **Keep your eyes peeled every time you are on the road** in your neighbourhood, noting any changes in street names, stores and other landmarks. Do this often enough and it will become a habit.

• **Be precise.** Use actual numbers ('fourth right turn', 'fifth house on the left', instead of 'take a left on to the large road'), distances ('stay on the main road for about a kilometre' instead of 'you will need to keep driving for a longish while'), and easily recognizable landmarks (banks and petrol stations are great as landmarks – most people are familiar with bank and petrol pump logos and can spot them from a long way off). In the absence of a big, familiar landmark, do use a named landmark ('the A-1 Bakery' instead of 'the bakery' – there could be other bakeries on the same road). Don't give hoardings as landmarks as they keep changing! Of course you will have to have done your homework to be able to do this.

• **Find out exactly where the lost person is,** and the direction in which he is travelling. If the lost person tells you, 'I am near the GVK Hospital; can you tell me how to get to your house?' ask him more questions to zero in on his location. Is he facing the hospital? If not, is the hospital to his right, or his left? Can he tell you the names of other establishments he can see from where he is? Once you know his precise location, it will be much easier to direct him accurately.

SKILL 82
ESTIMATE WALKING TIMES AND DISTANCES

How long does it take you to walk to the closest supermarket? To your friend's house? To your favourite neighbourhood cafe? To the park that you wish was just a little closer? It's likely you've never checked.

But it is useful to know how much ground you can cover, and how quickly, at your pace of walking - it's one great way to estimate distances. It's also a good way to know whether your pace is higher or lower than the average human walking pace. If you know, say, that it takes you 10 minutes to cover the 1.2 km distance to your school, you know you walk rather quickly (the average human walking speed is 10 minutes per km). Once you know that this is your pace of walking, you can start measuring distances to different places pretty accurately simply by walking there.

Researchers have found that very few people have a good idea of how long it takes them to get anywhere at a comfortable walking pace.

- Did it take you 20 minutes to walk to your tuition teacher's house from school? That means the distance between the two is about 2.5 kilometres. Do you want to know how much ground you covered on your morning walk today? All you need to know is how many minutes you walked.
- It can work the other way around too –if you know how far something is, you can estimate how long it will take for you to walk there. If your car runs out of fuel on the highway at 5 p.m., say, and Google Maps tells you the closest petrol pump is 3 kilometres away, you know immediately that it will take you less than an hour to get there and back, which means you will be back at the car before dark.
- It will help you give precise directions to somewhere in your neighbourhood – 'Keep driving down that road for about 500 metres...' rather than just 'Keep driving for a bit'.
- And it can help you make decisions to do fun things that you may not have done otherwise. Say a friend has invited you to a chicken-tikka-and-noodles treat at a not-so-close-by cafe on a Saturday evening and your mom is not free to drop you. Normally, you would have moaned and said no, because you imagined it was too far to walk to. But now, you quickly check the distance to the café online, and discover it is only 1.3 km away. You can get there in 10 minutes if you pick up the pace a little! Woohoo!

Of course you will have done a lot of walking before you figure out your pace accurately, and what that might end up doing is converting you into someone who walks everywhere in your neighborhood, sometimes simply to test if your estimation was right. That will lead to better health for you and better health for the planet. Win-win all around!

THE PATHFINDER'S CHALLENGES

#78
THE READ-A-MAP CHALLENGE

#79
THE LAY-OF-THE-LAND CHALLENGE

#80
THE MEMORY-MAP CHALLENGE

#81
THE GIVE-DIRECTIONS CHALLENGE

#82
THE ESTIMATE-DISTANCES CHALLENGE

There is just one challenge for this badge, and it involves all the skills you should have mastered to be worthy of the Pathfinder Badge. You may need to get another adult apart from your Squad Leader into the mix for this challenge.

The Challenge: To get around your city using only public transport (or on foot, over short distances) and visit specified places of interest.

Squad Leader's task: Pick four places (P1, P2, P3 and P4) of historical or other interest in the city, with at least one or two not right next to a metro / local train station. It would also help if the four places are roughly to the east, west, north and south of city centre. Hand over the list to the Squad on the morning of the challenge (pick a Sunday to take advantage of reduced traffic), along with a city map. Give the Squad an hour to mull over the task.

Squad's tasks before setting out:

1. Find out where P1, P2, P3 and P4 are (using the Internet), and mark them on the map.
2. Figure out metro stations and bus routes that run closest to these four places. Think about how you will get from there to the place – is it close enough to make it on foot (1.5 – 2 km is a reasonable walking distance)? Will you need to take another bus, or catch an auto?
3. Plan the itinerary (decide the order in which you will visit the four P's).
4. Estimate the distances – and the time it will take to cover those distances – between the different places you will be visiting. When do you expect to be back home after visiting all four? Write down your estimates.
5. Decide if you should make and take sandwiches and other food from home, or just eat out.
6. Estimate how much money you each need to carry – taking in the cost of public transport, food and extras.
7. You will need two mobile phones for this challenge. Make sure they are fully charged.

Ready, set, go!

- The Squad Leader will ensure that there is at least one adult for every three Squad members. The adult will not aid the Squad in any logistical way – she or he is just there as chaperone and supervisor.
- When there is walking involved from the bus stop to the destination, one half of the Squad, accompanied by an adult, will go ahead as pathfinders, taking the map with them. Once they reach the destination, they will call the other half and give precise directions to the place, including the approximate distance to be walked, which they have estimated themselves based on the length of their stride and the number of steps taken. The second group is not allowed to use their GPS or e-maps, they will simply follow the first's directions to get there,

from memory (they are not allowed to write the directions down). If there are two such places, the groups can switch places at the second, with the former 'followers' taking on the pathfinder role.

- As they go from one destination to the next, Squad members keep an eye out for landmarks passed along the way and mark them on the map. At the end of the day, they will plot these different landmarks and try and figure out the route they took to get from one place to another on Google maps.
- At each destination, the entire Squad takes a selfie for the archives. Members also keep a record of steps walked, money spent, time taken and modes of transport used (including bus numbers).
- The point of this exercise is not to visit the destination itself – that can be done if time and energy levels permit, but it isn't mandatory – but simply to get there.

WOCOTEEN MERIT BADGE 21

THE PIONEER

Theodore Roosevelt, President of the United States of America, inspected some Boy Scouts in London, and expressed great admiration for them. He wrote – 'I believe in outdoor games, and I do not mind in the least that they are rough games (...) I have no sympathy with the overwrought sentiment that would keep a young man in cotton-wool. The out-of-doors man must always prove the better in life's contest.'

– Camp Fire Yarn No. 5, *Scouting for Boys*

The Pioneer Badge is one of the most basic and the most celebrated among the Scout badges, so of course the Squad had to put it in. Today, we understand the word 'pioneer' as an innovator, someone who comes up with a new and exciting way of doing things. Historically, however, a 'pioneer' was someone who first discovered, explored, or 'settled' a new country.

The Scout activity called 'Pioneering' leans more towards the historical meaning. Scouts imagine their summer campsite as a new land in which they have to 'settle' by building all the 'camp gadgets' they need for a comfortable life in camp.

Scout camps could last for up to two months.

What kind of 'camp gadgets' might they build? Rain shelters, camp tables, dish drying and clothes drying racks, camp kitchens, hand-wash stations, garbage bag holders (hey, this is the 21st century!), bridges across water bodies (seriously!) – things like that. As a fun and challenging team activity during camp, they might also build bigger and more complex gadgets – lookout towers, trebuchets (giant wheeled catapults that were used to lob fireballs over fort walls in ancient times), even ferris wheels! Whatever they build is required to be strong (you can't have a bridge collapsing when people are walking across it), durable (all gadgets should last the length of camp at least), and aesthetically pleasing (because a product becomes truly great when it is not only useful but also nice-looking and neatly finished).

What do Scouts build camp gadgets with? As far as possible, they use local materials - bamboo poles, spars (or thick, strong poles) of natural wood, and staves (thinner wooden sticks) - which they bind or 'lash' together in different ways using ropes and twine made of natural fibre before securing them with suitable knots.

Why is this skill considered a Life Skill? Because the ability to build a shelter and a stove using materials that are freely available in nature is one of the oldest and most basic human skills!

The best part is, all you need to learn before you start experimenting are a few lashing techniques (to 'lash' means to bind two poles together with some sort of rope) and a few basic knots (vital for 'finishing' a lashing so that the poles stay lashed). But it isn't easy to describe how to tie knots in words (try to write code to teach a computer how to tie shoelaces and see how many lines of code that runs into), or to convince your parents about the life benefits you will receive by building a bamboo shelter in the middle of your living room, so we'll handle the skill-learning and challenges in this section a little differently. You'll see how as you read on. Go on, be a Pioneer!

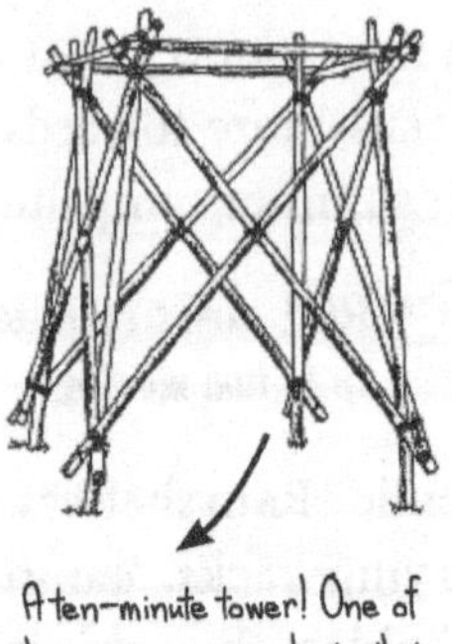

A ten-minute tower! One of the many camp gadgets that may be part of a Scout camp.

SKILL 83
GET YOURSELF A STAFF

'The Scout staff,' wrote B-P, in Scouting for Boys, 'is a useful addition to the kit of the Scout.' And that's why the WoCoTeen Squad, which owes a great deal of its inspiration to B-P's philosophy, decided to include the Scout staff as part of the essential WoCoTeen kit as well. But what can a WoCoTeen do with a staff? Listen to B-P's thoughts on the matter.

> *'Personally, I have found it an invaluable assistant when traversing mountains or boulder-strewn country and especially in night work in forest or bush. Also, by carving upon it various signs representing his achievements, the staff gradually becomes a record as well as a treasured companion to the Scout.'*

Fine, but what is this staff anyway? What does it look like?

> *'The Scout staff is a strong stick about as high as your nose, marked in feet and inches for measuring. The staff is useful for all kinds of things, such as making a stretcher, keeping back a crowd, jumping over a ditch, testing the depth of a river, keeping in touch with the rest of your Patrol in the dark. You can help another Scout over a high wall if you hold your staff horizontally between your hands and make a step for him; he can then give you a hand from above. Several staffs together can be used for building a light bridge, a hut, or a flag staff.*
>
> *'There are many other uses for the staff. In fact, you will soon find that if you don't have your staff with you, you will always be wanting it.'*

Excited at the possibilities? Let's add a few more uses for a good staff in an urban situation. To chase a pack of fighting strays away from a scared child; to put a flag at the end of and tramp around the neighbourhood on Independence Day; to use to practise your golf swing or your batting strokes; to poke into the leaves of a tree to dislodge the shuttlecock that is stuck there – you can do so many cool things with a stick!

Where can you find a stick suitable for you? What kind of stick should it be?

- A bamboo pole of about 1.5 inches in diameter at its thicker end would work well. Or you can pick up a fallen tree branch (keep your eyes peeled when you are walking through your park after a storm or when you are out of the city on holiday) of a similar diameter, which is reasonably straight and of a similar thickness throughout. If the municipality is cutting a tree in your neighbourhood, you may find some nice pickings there.
- If you are using a branch, trim off all the sticking-out twigs and leaves using a sharp knife (or hacksaw). Make sure there is a responsible adult present when you do this. Then with a blunt knife, strip off the bark (this will take time and patience) until the moist green 'flesh' below is revealed.
- Let the stick dry out slowly in a cool place for 3–4 weeks – don't bake it in hot sunlight or it will become brittle.
- When it is nice and dry, smooth down its surface by giving it a good rub with sandpaper. If it is longer than you need, cut it to the required length (to the height of your nose). Your staff is ready to decorate!
- Using a knife and going up from the base, mark off 12-inch intervals on your staff. Let's say your staff measures 4 feet, 6 inches. After you've marked off four feet, you are left with only 6 inches on the top. Mark off 1-inch intervals in this part. Your staff is now a measuring instrument!
- Rub some linseed oil into your staff to 'treat' the wood and keep it from cracking. You may need to do it a few times, at month-long intervals, to keep your stick looking good.
- At the height where it is comfortable to hold when you are walking, wrap something rough-textured to give you a good grip. You can be clever and make sure that what you wrap there is useful too. Maybe you can wrap thin cotton rope that you can unwind and use when you need it, or several rounds of thick duct tape, or a whole bunch of colourful rubber-bands.
- Use your staff as a record-keeper. Put a notch in it for every week that you stuck to a promise you made to yourself, or for every one of your new pup's 'month-birthdays'.

- Of course, you can always decorate your staff too. Paint bands around it, put stickers on it – make it yours!

SKILL 84
KNOW YOUR KNOTS

As we said before, it is insanely difficult to write down in words exactly how a knot is to be tied. So we are just going to give you a few tips about different knots, show you what the final knot looks like with a diagram, and then direct you to good knot-tying demo videos on the Internet. Deal? Deal.

Why is it important to know how to tie knots? Of all the skills you will need in a survival situation, knot-tying is one of the most useful ones. Whether it is about lowering food to someone trapped on a ledge or hauling that person up, knowing how to tie a good knot, and the right knot, can make the difference between life and death.

Knots are useful in everyday urban situations too. Maybe your car just broke down on the highway and a passing motorist has kindly offered to tow it to the nearest service station. It would help then if you knew which knot to use (the bowline) to tie the bumpers of the two cars together. (Erm, it would also help if you had a rope – make sure there are always a couple of coils of rope of different thicknesses in your car boot). Maybe you just want to send a basket down from your third-floor apartment to the balcony of the lovely aunty on the ground floor who wants to send you a couple of just-baked brownies. Maybe you want to tie a bunch of books to your bicycle carrier. Knots are everywhere!

Knot-tying is not difficult to learn, but the key is practice. Do it often enough and your fingers will be able to do it by themselves, leaving your brain free to handle other things, which is particularly useful in a crisis situation.

REMEMBER! This section is just to help you learn how to tie a few everyday knots for simple everyday situations. These are not suitable for life-saving rescue situations or for carrying really heavy loads. If you want to lower your TV over your balcony to the ground floor, please get professional help!

What you need for practice:

■ Two thick shoelaces will work fine; but if you have twisted nylon rope lying around (the kind used in washing lines) that will work as well.

■ The Internet, to watch your knot-tying demos. One of the nicest websites for demos is www.animatedknots.com. Click on the Scouting icon on the home page to get demos not only on knot-tying but also on different kinds of lashings.

TYING PACKAGES AND BANDAGES – REEF KNOT (or SQUARE KNOT)

Strong, simple to tie, easy to undo, and with a flat, pleasingly-symmetrical end result, this basic 'binding knot' – a binding knot is one that is used to tie a bunch of loose items together – is the most useful knot for tying two ends of a rope together.

The Reef Knot is a double knot, and you can remember how to tie it using the mnemonic 'Right over left, left over right/Makes a knot both tidy and tight.'

Great for:

■ Tying your taekwondo belt – or a dupatta – around your waist.

■ Tying the mouth of a plastic garbage bag – the knot will create a nice flat handle to carry the bag and won't slip. However, if you remember at the last minute that there was one last bit of garbage to put in, it is also easy enough to untie.

■ Tying your shoelaces (if your shoelaces are always getting untied, chances are you are tying them in a 'granny knot'. Tie them instead in a square knot – and you'll see that they will never untie themselves again!).

■ Tying bandages – particularly useful in tying a triangular bandage as a sling for a broken arm – since the knot is flat, it will sit comfortably on the patient's neck, and since the knot is easy to untie, it causes minimum trouble to him when you want to remove the sling.

Not so great for: Tying two different ropes together to make a long rope (chances of the knot slipping when there is a load at one end is high). For this, you will need to use what is called a 'bend knot' on page 269.

ATTACHING A ROPE TO SOMETHING – THE HITCHES

Half-hitch: One of the simplest knots, and great to use when only a light load needs to be carried.

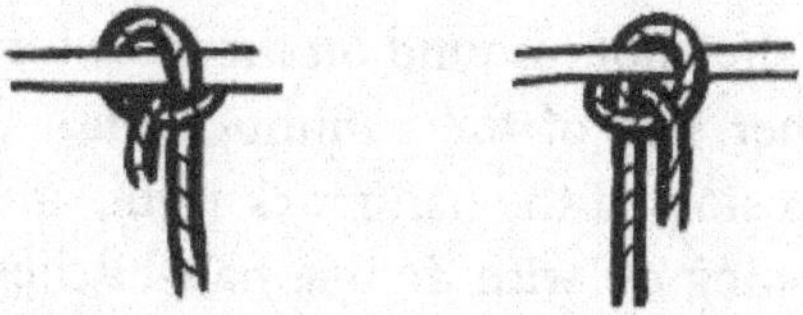

Double half-hitch: A stronger version of the half-hitch, this has one extra loop to make the knot more secure. Make sure you hold the short end of the rope as you tighten the knot or it will slip. Works best when you are tying something to a horizontal rail.

Clove hitch: Very useful for hitching your cow or your prisoner (haha), to a vertical post. The advantage of this knot is that its location on the rope can be adjusted by feeding in rope from either side, which makes it is a useful knot in situations where you may want that kind of convenience. But it is for that very reason that it is also a little unreliable – the knot slips from its position when it isn't 'under load' i.e., when the rope isn't stretched tight. If the knot has been off load for a bit, test and tighten it before you put a load on it.

Great for:

■ Tying a lightly loaded shopping bag to your bicycle handlebars (the half-hitch).

■ Tying a new washing line from one horizontal post to another (the double half-hitch).

■ Tying a garbage bag to the top rail of your gate to keep it out of reach of street dogs until the garbage collector arrives to take it away (the double half-hitch).

■ Tying your dog's leash to a bench in the park or outside the supermarket while you pop in for biscuits (half-hitch for a small, docile dog, double half-hitch for a big, active one).

■ Tying a hammock between two trees (the clove hitch). Keep moving the knots around on the trees (or other vertical posts) on either side of the hammock until you've got the height and 'tension' of the hammock right, and then 'fix' the knots by finishing off with double half-hitches on the short ends of the rope – have an adult check it's securely tied.

■ Pioneering (or, in other words, structure building) – the clove hitch is used to start and finish all kinds of lashings. (Refer to *Skill 85- Learn To Lash* to find out how.)

MAKING A FIXED LOOP (OR LASSO) – THE BOWLINE

Often called the 'King of Knots', the bowline is an old, old knot used to form a fixed loop at the end of a rope. The basic knot is itself pretty secure – it will not slip – but there are many variations on it that are even more reliable. The 'one-handed bowline' became very popular in America as a 'lifesaving knot' when it was demonstrated how it was possible for even a blind person or a one-armed person (or someone who had an injured arm) to tie a bowline around himself, so that he could be hauled to safety.

Great for:

■ Tying your boat (or any other heavy load) to a post.

■ Anchoring your rope to a tree before throwing the other end to a drowning person (the other end can be tied in a bowline loop too – the person can slip his shoulders into the loop and hold on to the rope to be more secure as he is hauled in).

- Suspending a heavy flowerpot from a ceiling hook.
- Making a makeshift lasso-style leash for your dog or cow with a piece of rope (since the knot will not slip, there is no danger of it strangling the animal).
- Tying the bumpers of two cars together so that one can tow the other.

TYING TWO ROPES TOGETHER – SHEET BEND (or WEAVER'S KNOT)

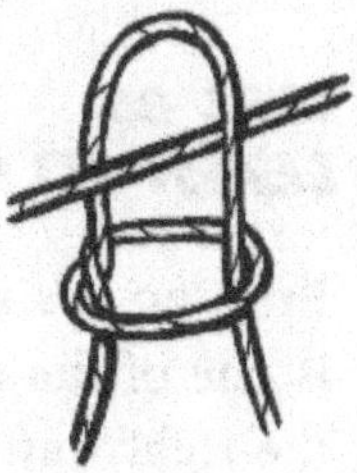

Like all 'bend' knots, the sheet bend is also used to tie two different ropes together. It works best when the ropes are of different thicknesses. It is also called a weaver's knot because it was traditionally used by weavers to join broken threads in a warp, the horizontal threads stretched tight on a weaver's loom.

The sheet bend is more secure when the short ends of the two ropes end up on the same side of the knot. When the ropes are of different thicknesses, use the thicker one to make the starting 'bight' (a bight is just the technical name for a loop of rope). When in doubt, tie a doubled sheet bend instead of a simple one to make the knot stronger.

Great for:

– When you have two ropes but each by itself is too short for the purpose required. Say you want to pull a load (like a heavy box of equipment) across a playground or a corridor. You have two short lengths of rope. You use up most of the first one just going around the crate and tying a reef knot to secure it. Now there's too little of the rope left to pull the box along. That's when you use the sheet bend to tie the longer end of the first rope to the second one. Ta-da! You can now pull your box along.

- When you want to suspend something heavy from a horizontal tree branch, while standing on the ground below.

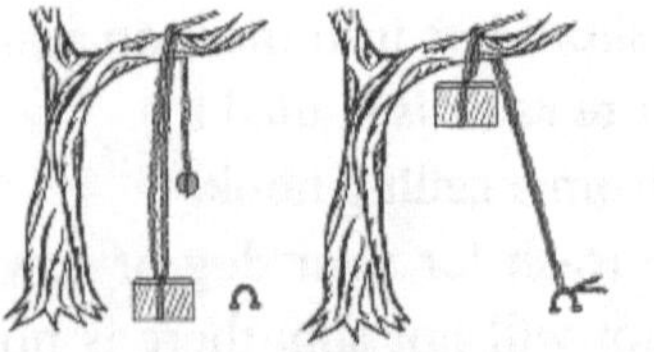

Tie the thick load-carrying rope to a thinner rope using a sheet bend. Weight the free end of the thin rope with a stone and throw it over the branch (this is way easier to do than throwing the thick rope carrying the load over the branch). Pull the thin rope down from the other side – it will bring the thicker one along with it over the branch. Then haul the load attached to the other end of the thick rope to the required height, and tie off the thick rope to a peg driven into the ground with a bowline knot.

SKILL 85
LEARN TO LASH

Erm, no, it's not what you're thinking. Our kind of lashing is one of the most basic pioneering skills. If you don't know the right way to lash two poles (or wooden spars*) together, you cannot build structures that will hold, stay strong, and be durable, and if you don't know how to do that, it means that you can't win the Pioneer Badge at all.

There are many different kinds of lashings, but we're going to deal with five basic types here. Each type is meant for one specific purpose. Most types of lashings begin and end with a clove hitch (if you need to refresh your memory about the clove hitch, go look it up under Skill 84 now!).

What kind of rope should you use for lashing? Scout websites recommend manila rope of a quarter-inch diameter, but pure manila hemp is not easily available in Indian stores. Other pioneering experts highly recommend jute twine, which is most easily accessible here. So jute twine it is!

What kind of spars should you use? Refer to 'Skill 83: Get Yourself A Staff' – the same tips for picking a good staff apply to picking a good spar. Make sure the surface of the spars is

* *We will use the words poles, spars and staves interchangeably through this section.*

not too smooth or they will slip against each other. Plus, the lashing is less likely to slip against a rough, textured surface.

Enough with the preliminaries – let's get lashing! *(Detailed videos – both animated and accompanied by voice instructions – on* www.animatedknots.com. *Click on the 'Scouting' icon to get all the info you need on knots and lashings.)*

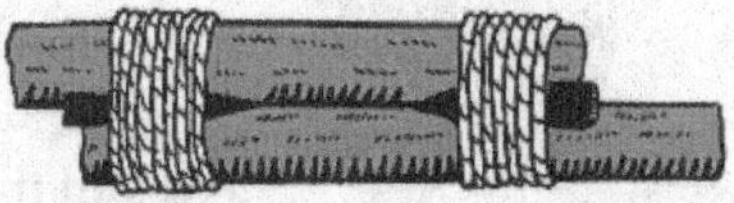

Round lashing: This is the lashing to use when you want to join the ends of two spars that are parallel to each other, to make a longer pole, for instance. Start with a clove hitch around both poles. Wrap about eight turns of the cord around both poles, pulling tight each time, and end with another clove hitch. Easy-peasy!

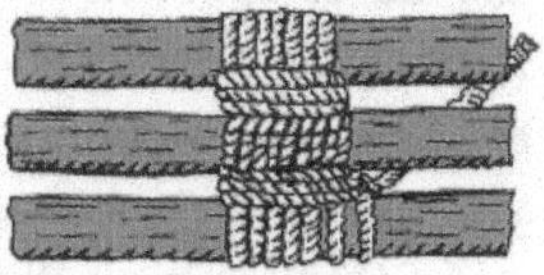

Shear lashing: Also meant for lashing together two or more poles that are parallel to each other, as in a raft-building situation. Start with a clove hitch around *one* of the poles. Wrap several turns of rope around both poles, then make two or three tight 'frapping turns' around the lashing between the two poles (a frapping turn is when the rope is wound around the lashing and perpendicular to it; frapping turns make the whole lashing tighter and more secure). Finish off with another clove hitch.

Square lashing: Meant for binding two staves that are at right angles to each other. Useful when you are making a square frame for something, or building scaffolding or a simple bamboo ladder. Start with a clove hitch around one of the poles. Twist the short end of the rope around the long one before you take the long end around both the poles, going over one of them and under the other on both sides of the join. Then make a few frapping turns around the lashings on both sides of the join. Finish off with a double half-hitch on the same pole as the one you tied the starting clove hitch on.

Diagonal lashing: Meant for binding two staves that cross each other at an angle other than a right angle (if they crossed at a right angle, you would use a square lashing to bind them). Useful for creating extra support for a large square or rectangular frame (like a tabletop or a roof for a shelter). Start with a simple timber hitch around both poles, then wrap several turns of the rope, first in one axis and then in another. Follow it up with several frapping turns around the lashings to tighten them and finish with a clove hitch.

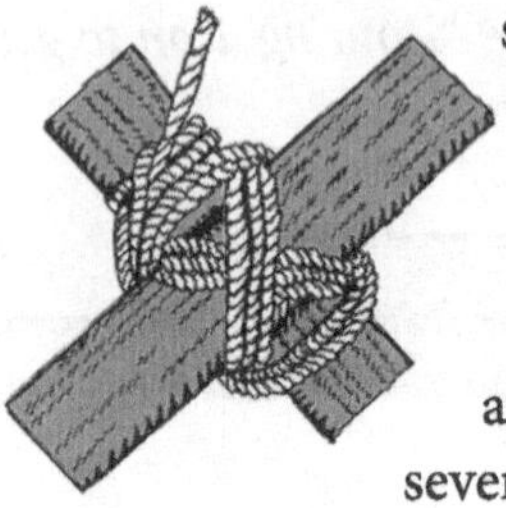

Tripod lashing: Meant for lashing the tops of three parallel staves together, and once it is done, spreading the bottoms of the staves apart to create a three-legged stable structure, the tripod. The tripod can work two ways:

- As a stand-alone structure – if the staves are tall enough, you can tack a sheet around the poles and create a hide-away tepee for a younger sibling in the garden (you can even use this technique to lash four staves together, to create a more roomy 'square' tepee).
- As a support base for something else (many of our street-side chana-chaat vendors support their entire livelihood on a bamboo tripod!). Two such tripods can support a horizontal pole (or your WoCoTeen staff) between them (and you can hang your kettle off it and make chai; of course you must also light a fire below); four such, placed at the ends of a rectangle, can support a wooden board to make an instant dining table.

For tripod lashing, start with a clove hitch on one pole, lash the three poles together by going over and under each alternately with the rope for several turns, then make a couple of frapping turns around the lashings between each pair of poles, and finish off with another clove hitch.

MUST-WATCH!

- British-Australian teenager Alex Chorley's wonderfully entertaining – and enlightening – demonstration of tripod, square and round lashings, all in one simple but useful project, at https://www.youtube.com/watch?v=lKzDbPaR7z4. Alex was only 10 when he featured in this 2011 video.
- The building of any puja or wedding pandal in India, which involves nothing more than an open field, truckloads of bamboo poles, bales of jute twine, and dozens of skilled labourers lashing the poles together using every kind of lashing style known and unknown. As these magicians drape the frame they've built in gaily-patterned cloth and wrap each individual pole in coloured strips of fabric to boot, the open field transforms, right before your incredulous eyes, into an all-weather venue for hundreds of people to enjoy. Next time a pandal starts coming up in your neighbourhood, stop and stare!

SKILL 86
BE A MINI PIONEER!

Yes, we know. By now, you're really, really excited about pioneering. You wish you could go off and live in the wilderness for a bit with your Squad and your Squad Leader, collecting fallen branches for staves, stripping them of their bark, lashing them with jute twine, building a rough shelter, being Robinson Crusoe. But there are too many logistical difficulties on the way – you don't have the tools to chop or strip branches, bamboo poles are not easily available, and your parents are not very keen on the idea of setting you adrift in the sea so you can go find yourself a desert island. You are in deep despair – how are you ever going to be a pioneer then, or practise your skills for the day when you might need them?

Never fear, Miniature Pioneering is here!

And it means exactly what it sounds like – you can still be a pioneer, but in an intense mini form. Here are some ideas:

- Instead of bamboo poles, lash bamboo skewers (available online for about ₹90 for a pack of 100 skewers) or sticks from a coconut broom with wool or cotton string to build miniature prototypes of tripods, huts, bridges, anything you want.
- Or just use a bunch of pencils for a sturdier construction. To feel more pioneer-like, shave off the 'bark' of each pencil with a knife or a blade, they will look more rugged and be more rough-textured, which is always better (the string will not slip then). Don't throw away pencil stubs that are too small to use or whose leads keep breaking – colour-code the 'staves' that are approximately the same length (draw a thick band around each with a coloured marker, using a different colour for each length) – you will need all sizes in your projects. Then practise your lashings on these staves using some kind of natural cordage (cotton thread, jute twine) as you build different structures with them. After you have gazed proudly upon your finished project for long enough and taken enough selfies with it, dismantle it so you can reuse your staves again on another project. WoCoTeens reduce, reuse, recycle or repurpose – always!
- Search online for great pioneering and miniature pioneering (also called model pioneering) project ideas.
- Start thinking like a pioneer and an engineer; think about the design and construction of the structures you see every day. What makes a structure stable? What makes it strong? What makes something light enough to be portable? Keep your eyes open and notice things around you – the chaat-*wallah's* tripod, the bamboo scaffolding around buildings under construction, the knot in the rope that the milkman is leading his cow by. Your pioneering skills will get much better simply by keeping your eyes peeled!

Here's one great idea for building a trebuchet using just bamboo skewers and marshmallows (you can substitute lumps of play dough for marshmallows) – http://www.itsalwaysautumn.com/2013/5/31/easy-marshmallow-catapults-summer-fun-for-kids.html.

THE PIONEER'S CHALLENGES

#83
THE DESIGN-A-STAFF CHALLENGE

This challenge is straightforward enough. Pick any stick, pole or rod that you think would make a great staff (it doesn't have to be a branch or a twig or even be made of wood) and do it up as cleverly and creatively as you can. Your Squad Leader will judge it on its good looks and neatness, of course, but what will count more is how functional is it, and that will depend on all the innovations you make to it. Do a 'staff presentation' to the Squad where you explain all the different uses you can put your staff to, and all the things you are carrying on it that will help you in your daily life. Don't be afraid to come up with a couple of completely wacky uses for it too!

#84
THE KNOW-YOUR-KNOTS CHALLENGE

Display your knowledge of knots – and not necessarily only the ones listed in this section – to the Squad, by using them in a practical application. Also, display at least *one* new knot you have learnt from someone in your neighbourhood who actually uses it in his or her work. For instance, learn from the flower seller the knot she uses to tie jasmine flowers together, or from the mechanic the knot he would use to tow a car, or from the cobbler the knot he uses to finish a piece of stitching. You will actually have to demonstrate how this knot works, mind, by stringing a bunch of flowers yourself, or tying a rope between the bumpers of two cars!

#85
THE LEARN-TO-LASH CHALLENGE

Split the Squad into groups of two or three. Each group then builds a 'camp gadget' of some kind – a clothes drying rack, a garbage-bag holder, a chana-*jor-garam* tripod – using bamboo poles lashed together in different ways. Lots of ideas and step-by-step instruction guides are available on the Internet, so you've no excuse!

#86
THE MINI-PIONEER CHALLENGE

This is an individual challenge. Create a 'mini' camp gadget, using shaved pencils or twigs instead of bamboo poles, and rough cord instead of twine. Post all the different mini gadgets on a Facebook page or a blog, so that others may be inspired to try it for themselves!

WOCOTEEN MERIT BADGE 22

THE CAMPER

Camping is the joyous part of a Scout's life. Living out in God's open air, among the hills and the trees, and the birds and the beasts, and the sea and the rivers – all this brings health and happiness such as you can never get among the bricks and smoke of the town.
– Camp Fire Yarn No. 9, *Scouting for Boys*

B-P was always big on camping, and when he put together the Scouts organization, he made sure that camping and the outdoor life was a huge part of what it meant to be a modern Scout. He felt rather keenly that the natural connection that humans had always had with the outdoors had been lost with urbanization, and the only way to cultivate it once again was to spend a lot of time away from modern-day comforts, 'in the wild'.

Naturally, seeing as how heavily inspired it is by B-P, the WoCoTeen Squad also sets great store by camping as a Squad activity. After all, it combines health benefits with all kinds of mental, emotional and spiritual benefits like...

Actually, never mind all that. Camping is actually just super fun! And that's why you must do it! But to have the best time while you are out there, it helps if you are somewhat prepared. Here are some skills you need to nail down.

SKILL 87
PREPARE FOR CAMP

You're going to camp! Maybe you are going with your family, maybe you're going with your Squad, maybe you have signed up for a summer camp where you are going to be surrounded by people you don't know. You're all excited, but you're also a little nervous – this is your first time. Here are a few things you can do even before you leave home to ensure that you – and the people you're going camping with – have a reasonably good time.

- **Calibrate your attitude.** Like in so many other things, your attitude counts for a whole lot when it comes to camping. If you are naturally a positive, sunny-tempered kind of guy or girl, good for you. If you aren't, you might want to work on that a little. In the weeks leading to camp, make a genuine effort to stop whining, even to yourself, when things don't go exactly to plan. Try to stay positive when, say, you miss the school bus, don't get picked for the cricket team, or can't go out to play one evening because your grandparents dropped in unexpectedly. The thing is, life in the outdoors is unpredictable, and the best-laid plans are likely to go awry. The better prepared you are – attitude-wise – to accommodate sudden changes, the better you will enjoy the camping experience.
- **Read the brochure – but don't believe it.** Familiarity with the terrain – and everything else about the place you are going to – creates anticipation (always a good thing), helps you pack sensibly, and is a vital part of your mental prep for the outdoor adventure at hand. So read everything you can get your hands on. But remember that brochures always feature the sunniest skies and the most smiley campers and only tell you the best bits about camp – it's their job to get you excited! They don't tell you how many campers got terribly homesick, or that many of them hated the food, or that it rained for three of the five days of camp, bringing the creepy-crawlies out in force.
- **Neutralize your fears**. Make a list of all the things you're worried about. Things rarely look as scary on paper as they do in your imagination. Plus, now that they are out of your head, you can actually start doing something about them. Are you worried you won't like the food? Start trying out different kinds of weird yucky vegetables – eggplant, bitter gourd, sweet potato – in the safety of your home. Are you worried about

your competence in taking care of yourself? Start doing your own tasks at home – make your bed, pack your own lunch, walk or take a bus to school instead of having a parent drop you. Are you worried you won't be able to use an Indian-style toilet? Practise squatting on the ground, in position, for 15 minutes a day, and get one part of the problem out of the way. Identify your demons, and systematically demolish them.

- **Get into training.** Even if the camp you have signed up for is not entirely about hiking or trekking, you can safely assume that you will be doing a lot more walking and running and being on your feet in camp than you would in your daily home-school-home life. To prepare for it, start walking or exercising or climbing up and down stairs a lot more than you normally do, a few weeks before camp. Cut down on the junky snacks and the fizzy drinks – there won't be a lot of those around in camp, especially if it is in a remote area. Set yourself small challenges – like the five-days-without-junk-food challenge – and complete them. They may be completely unrelated to the kinds of challenges you will face in camp, but completing a challenge, any challenge, will give you the confidence to handle others.
- **Set all your antennae to 'Receive'.** In other words, consciously open yourself – your mind, your heart, your senses – to new experiences. You will be getting a lot of those in camp. You will be meeting new people (who may or may not be like you), eating food different from what you eat at home, having to follow instructions from unfamiliar adults (who you may or may not like). You will also be doing many things that you have probably never done before, and you may find that you don't enjoy some of them very much at all. But the best way to deal with all of that new stuff is to receive it all without pre-judging it. Otherwise you might end up missing out on adding some great experiences, and some wonderfully different people, to your life.

Watching the amazing Bear Grylls (who is currently the Chief Scout of the World!) in a few episodes of 'Man Vs Wild' should serve as the best inspiration.

- **Believe that it is a beautiful world – and it will be.** This doesn't mean you go traipsing 'into the wild' with your eyes wide shut. It means that you go in (or out!) expecting the worst (and fully prepared to deal with it), while at the same time trusting implicitly that things will work out well in the end. So go, get camping! Bet it turns out to be the most fun you've ever had!

SKILL 88
PACK FOR CAMP

Packing for camp is a whole science by itself. Because each camping trip is different – Are you going to be camping in the hills or by the sea? Is it going to be hot or cold? Is it a stationary camp or do you move camp each day? – what you pack for each will also be different. Still, here are a few basic rules to keep in mind.

The Backpack: As a general rule of thumb, you should definitely not be carrying more than 30 per cent of your body weight on your back (don't even dream of carrying a duffel bag or a suitcase to camp). If you weigh 45 kilos, say, your backpack should not weigh more than 14 kilos. And that's including the weight of the backpack itself. While a 17-kilo load may not seem so bad when you first heft the bag to your shoulders, it can get really heavy a couple of kilometres into a trek, and actually cause injury.

Make sure you buy (or borrow) a good, waterproof backpack, even if you have to pay a little more for it. Nothing can be worse that having a strap rip or the seams of your bag come apart when you are on a trek. Think about the kinds of camps you are likely to go on over the next 2–3

years and buy a backpack suitable for that – no point buying a giant one with a hundred straps and all kinds of bells and whistles if you're not planning on scaling Everest anytime soon.

Apart from making sure that the backpack, when empty, is as light as it can be without losing out on strength, here are some features to look out for when choosing a hiking backpack:

- Straps that clip around your waist (which take some of the load off your shoulder straps and keep the bag stable).
- Side (usually netted) pockets large enough to fit a one-litre bottle of water each. Make sure the pocket openings can be tightened too – you may have a large flashlight structure building) a knife in one of the pockets instead of a bottle of water, and you don't want them falling out of the bag.
- At least a couple of big zippered pockets on the front of the bag to hold items that you may need to access quickly and easily
- Under-bag straps that can hold a sleeping bag outside the backpack.

The Shoes: The most important rule with shoes is that they should have been 'broken in' well before you set off for camp. That means you don't take the new fancy shoes you insisted your parents buy you two days before camp. Either buy your fancy shoes a month before camp and walk around in them every day until your feet have got used to them or wear your beat-up old comfort shoes that you've worn forever. Make sure you have the cobbler give them a quick once-over, though, before you go. The absolutely *worst* thing that can happen in camp or on a hiking trip is having something go wrong with your shoes (carrying a spare pair is a waste of space and adds unnecessary weight to your backpack).

The Sleeping Bag: Make sure you pack not just your sleeping bag but also a waterproof camp mat for spreading under it. It will not only help keep the sleeping bag dry but will also provide extra cushioning. Even if it adds to the volume, pack a small, crushable pillow too. It can be torture to not have a pillow to sleep on if you are used to one. Or take a pillowcase in which you can stack / roll some of your softest t-shirts each night to use as a pillow. Practise unrolling and rolling up your sleeping bag several times before you leave for camp (that will also help you test the zipper), so you don't have to struggle once you get there. Carry a couple of soft cotton bed-sheets too – sleeping directly on a synthetic sleeping bag isn't much fun, especially on a hot night.

The Must-Haves:

- Drinking water: Take at least two one-litre bottles and refill them wherever clean drinking water is available. So much liquid adds weight, sure, but water is a lifesaver.
- Powerful flashlight (with extra batteries).
- A loud whistle (to call attention to yourself in case you get separated from your group) that you wear on a lanyard around your neck.
- A good multi-purpose knife (like a Swiss Army knife).
- Bug repellent, and calamine lotion to soothe any bug bites that you still end up getting.
- A large-brimmed sun hat, and sun-block cream.
- First-aid kit with all the medications that you are on, along with medicines to treat allergies, motion-sickness (particularly if you have to take a long, and hilly, bus ride to your camp-site), vomiting and a loose stomach. Also band-aids, cotton, gauze, Dettol, pain-relieving spray and antiseptic cream.
- Energy snacks: Mix all kinds of nuts and dry fruit to make a 'trail mix' and bag portions of it in small Ziploc bags, for a quick burst of energy when you need it. Bite-sized chocolate bars are great too, as well as dried fruit, like *aam papad*.
- Toilet paper: Get comfortable with using it before you leave home if you aren't already.
- Hand sanitizer.
- Extra pairs of undies and socks. Wearing wet socks and undies just because you didn't bring spares is no fun (unlike your impulsive dip in the stream you just passed).

■ Comfortable clothes that are light, soft, wrinkle-free, and dry easily. Include a rain jacket with a hood and cotton cargo pants with many pockets, rather than jeans. Pack a couple of light sweaters even if it is summer – it could get cold outdoors after the sun goes down. Carry well-worn clothes and towels and sheets that you don't mind losing, or getting very dirty.

■ A waist pouch – or a small bag that hangs around your neck – to hold things that you may want to quickly and easily access while walking – money, your phone (if you're carrying one), a map, a compass (make sure you know how to use it) and a small notebook and pen (to make notes or a drawing of something interesting).

■ Your own reusable plate, bowl, glass and cutlery (which you are responsible for washing and putting away after each meal).

■ A small shovel (if you're going to poop in the wild, you will want to dig a hole to poop into, and a shovel will help; more details under Skill 89).

■ Recyclable garbage bags to carry your trash until you reach the next waste bin, where you can dispose of it properly.

SKILL 89
POOPING IN THE WILD

It is most tempting to get behind a rock, do your business, wipe up or wash up, and walk away as if nothing had happened. After all, that's what millions of people in India do each day, as a matter of course, in the fields, on railway tracks, or on the beach for the sea to (hopefully) wash away. But most of those millions do it because they have no toilets, or running water, in their homes. As an aware and responsible WoCoTeen,

who subscribes to the 'Leave No Trace' credo of all good campers, you have no such excuse. After all, your poop is just as disgusting to everyone else as it is to you, but since it came out of you, it is your responsibility to do the right thing with it.

The international 'Leave No Trace' guidelines have four rules about pooping outdoors –

- **Minimize the chance for water pollution:** Do your business at least 200 feet away from any water source, natural or man-made (also make sure it is at least 200 feet away from where you have set up camp, and 200 feet away from the trail). Even if you only want to wash yourself or your dishes, the rule is to carry water from the stream or river 200 feet away and do your washing there, rather than in the stream itself. Pooping in the river, however tempting and logical it may seem ('but the river will carry it away to the sea') is a strict no-no – disease germs, if any, in your poop could infect people who live downstream.
- **Reduce the spread of disease:** One way to do this is to poop far from a water source. Another is to bury your poop, so that no one steps on it by mistake. Carrying a little shovel with you will help greatly in the process. Just dig a hole about six inches deep and five inches in diameter. Pile up the dirt you dig out on the side of the hole so that you can use it to cover up the hole once you're done. If you are camping in a group or are going to be in the same place for a few days, save yourselves the trouble of having to dig a hole each time by getting your campmates together and digging a six-foot long, six-inch deep trench. That becomes the designated camp loo. Campers start pooping from one end of the pit, covering up their own poop each time. You may even decide to hang up a sheet as a screen between two trees to give the poopers extra privacy.
- **Minimize aesthetic impact:** Burying usually takes care of the non-aesthetic impact of the poop. You can also scatter leaves over it to disguise it completely. Make sure you leave no used toilet paper behind – all that, along with any feminine hygiene products, should be bagged and carried to the next regular garbage disposal option. If you are in a rocky area or

somewhere where the ground is frozen solid, and it is impossible to bury your poop, the next best option is to smear your poop *thinly* on a rock exposed to direct sunlight, with your shovel. The sunlight will dry it and sterilize it quicker this way, and the elements will take care of the rest. Do make sure, however, that you don't smear it in a place where someone might want to lean or may place his hand on to support himself while climbing.

- **Maximize decomposition:** Both burying and smearing work to ensure this happens.

SKILL 90
LEAVE NO TRACE

Leave No Trace, when it comes to backpacking or camping or adventuring in the outdoors, simply means that you try and leave as little impact as possible on the environments you pass through. The earth is already overburdened with human impact in high-density population clusters like cities, and we can't help that now, but we can at least try and leave as subtle a footprint as possible when we traverse through environments that still belong to other creatures more than they do to us.

What can you do to ensure that you leave no trace? Here are a few guidelines.

- **Leave nothing behind:** The most obvious of them all – leave no litter, no poop (at least not in a visible place – see Skill 89), no leftover food. Inspect your campsite and each rest stop you make on the way for any kind of litter you've left behind before you continue on your merry way.
- **Respect the trails and the laws:** If you are driving or walking through a national park, stick to the designated buffer zone on the periphery of the protected forest area instead of trying to sneak in for an up-close-and-personal with the animals. This is not only dangerous for you but harmful to the conservation environment – that area is marked protected for a reason!
- **Take extra care when you light a fire:** Make sure you build your fire away from vegetation and trees and on a dry piece of

ground with no grass or dry vegetation on it. When you collect twigs and branches for kindling, make sure you only pick up what is fallen on the ground and only branches thin enough to be broken by hand. That will ensure that your fire – and its impact on the vegetation around – remains small.

- **Respect wildlife:** Don't feed wild animals, not even monkeys or deer. Don't approach too close to any animal in the wild. Make sure you secure your food and trash well to avoid animals getting to them – they could be dangerous for the wildlife. If you are travelling with your pet, make sure you control him or her so that the wildlife is safe.
- **Take nothing away with you:** Look, observe, photograph, enjoy, but don't remove things from the environment around you. Don't carve your initials into trees and rocks, don't move rocks or pick mushrooms or wildflowers to take away.
- **Respect other visitors – and the sound of silence:** Be courteous to other people you meet on the trail and respect their right to an enjoyable experience. Don't ruin it for them by talking or singing or playing music loudly. If you are in a big school group, make sure your group is not blocking everyone else's way up a hill, for instance – instead, walk in single file.
- **Be sensitive to the local culture:** Leaving no trace also means fitting so well into the environment that you draw no attention to yourself. If local people in the area that you are passing through dress conservatively, so should you. If the area is backward and poor, don't flaunt expensive electronics and jewellery. If local custom demands that you walk barefoot through a sacred grove or cover your head while visiting a shrine, do it. Ask permission before you take photographs or climb on to someone's tractor to take a selfie. You are passing through someone else's home, and the least you can do is to show them some respect.

THE CAMPER'S CHALLENGES

#87 THE PREPARE-FOR-CAMP CHALLENGE

#88 THE PACK-FOR-CAMP CHALLENGE

#89 THE POOP-IN-THE-WILD CHALLENGE

#90 THE LEAVE-NO-TRACE CHALLENGE

Once again, all the different challenges are combined into one big, fat challenge, and it involves the Squad actually going camping! Your Squad Leader could organize the whole thing, or he could accompany you on a camping trip organized by an adventure travel company in your city. Here are some basic conditions for completing this challenge successfully:

1. You must spend at least one night outdoors, in a tent that you have helped pitch. The campsite doesn't have to be remote or difficult to access – you could even do this on someone's farm (but only after taking the owner's permission).
2. Getting to the campsite must involve a trek / long walk of some kind (at least 5 km), even if it is through the farm or on the highway leading to the farm. Or it could involve a bicycle ride (at least 10–12 km).
3. The group must cook at least one proper meal in the outdoors. One round of chai must also be made on the camp stove / portable gas cylinder with single burner.

4. Each of you must carry your own backpacks. Apart from your personal items, the backpack will also have a part of the food, water, groceries, utensils and equipment needed for a night out. Plan everything you will need beforehand and divide the common items between the Squad's backpacks.
5. Pooping outside the 'right way' – i.e., into a hole in the ground which you will cover up once you finish the 'job' – gets extra bonus points – but do use a regular toilet if there is one close by!
6. You must make sure you leave nothing – except buried poop! – behind when you leave.
7. Anyone who whines about camping not being fun because of bugs, heat, cold or rain / hunger because the meal is taking too long to cook / body ache from all the walking / backpack being too heavy, and so on and so forth will become immediately ineligible for the Camper Badge.
8. You must create your own 'Camp Album' – with photographs, drawings, pressed flowers if any, leaf and seed and grass samples, empty instant noodle packets, and any other memories – along with captions for each and a brief account of your camp experience, within a week of returning from camp, and submit it to your Squad Leader.

WOCOTEEN MERIT BADGE 23

THE STARMAN

All scouts should know how to guide themselves by the stars.
– Camp Fire Yarn No. 5, *Scouting for Boys*

What would you say if we told you that time-travel is not a distant dream? That humans have been able to do it ever since humankind began? That you can do it any day you like, that it doesn't require a time machine, and that – here's the best part – it's absolutely free, no strings attached? You'd probably scoff and say we were spinning you a ripping good yarn, the kind old B-P was famous for. And you'd be wrong. Because all you need to go whizzing back into the past is to tip your head back and look at the night sky.

Want to feel really awestruck while feeling really insignificant? Try a spot of stargazing!

Our universe is so large and the celestial bodies that populate it are so far away from each other that a new unit of measurement had to be created to measure interstellar and intergalactic distances. That unit is called a 'light year' and is a measure of the distance that light travels in a year. When you remember that light travels almost 300,000 km in one SECOND, you will see how mind-bogglingly vast a distance a 'light year' is.

It's true! When you look up into the night sky, what you are actually looking at – besides the moon and any stars you can see despite the light pollution* – is the history of the universe itself. How come?

Well, for one thing, the stars that you see are so far away that the light

* It's actually a thing! Too much light generated by man-made sources like street lights brightens the night sky in cities and obscures our view of the stars.

you see as their starlight actually left the star a very long time ago. For example, Proxima Centauri (PC), the closest star to us after the sun, is about four light-years away from us. That means that when you see PC in the sky, the twinkle is actually light that left PC four years ago! If PC exploded (or imploded) today, we will not find out for another four years (at least not just by watching its light)! Even the light from our closest star, the sun (which is a mere 150 million km away) takes about eight minutes to reach us.

Secondly, the current most popular theory about the beginning of the universe is the Big Bang theory, which hypothesises that about 14 billion years ago, the universe was way smaller, way denser, and way, way hotter than it is today. Then, say scientists, that small, dense, hot mass exploded (there's your Big Bang), and all the little shards and fragments that resulted began racing away from each other in all directions. In other words, the universe began to expand, and at a pretty rapid clip.

As the extreme heat dissipated over the large distances, some particles from the explosion began to come together and condense, congeal or simply swirl together, forming spheres of hot gases, dust or rock that became stars, planets, natural satellites and other celestial bodies. Several of these, caught up in each others' gravitational fields, bonded into star systems and galaxies. Our own blue-green rock, and our life-giving solar orb, were welcomed into the family rather recently, a mere 4.5 billion years ago. You see now how looking up into the night sky is like looking into a family album, except that this one goes somewhat further back than your own?

Thirdly, as the rock-star astronomer Carl Sagan said in his groundbreaking book *Cosmos*, the nitrogen, calcium, carbon and iron in our bodies and in everything around us were made in the interiors of collapsing stars. Yup, we share more than our history with the stars; we *are* the stars.

Fourthly, all our real human ancestors looked up to the stars a lot – to help them find their way across vast unmarked seas, mountains and deserts, to mark the passage of time and the seasons, to predict the future, and to – yes! – create all the wonderful stories and mythologies we have inherited. If you want to feel your ancestors' heartbeats, and feel a deep connection with all humanity – past, present and future – all you need to do is lie down flat on your back on the ground in open country in absolute silence, and gaze at the sequinned, twinkling underside of the dark upturned bowl that is the night sky.

And that's why the Squad thought it was so important to include the Starman Badge as one of the 24 basic eligibility badges to be a WoCoTeen. Get into your time-machine, and go win it!

SKILL 91
IDENTIFY STARS AND CONSTELLATIONS

The night sky is not constant. It changes depending on:

- **Where you live**: What you see if you live in the northern hemisphere is quite different from what you see if you look up at the sky from Australia. If you lived in the North Pole (or the South Pole) and never left it, you would only ever see 50 per cent of all the stars visible from the earth. If you lived at the Equator, however, you would theoretically be able to see all the stars that can be seen, over the course of a full year.
- **What part of the year it is:** The night sky changes from season to season because of the revolution of the Earth around the sun, as well as the stars' own motion (although this is negligible).
- **What part of the night it is:** Just like the sun and the moon rise and set, the stars too appear to move from one part of the sky to the other in the course of a night, but it is actually because the Earth is itself rotating from west to east that stars enter our field of vision in the east and leave it in the west.
- **How much moonlight there is:** The amount of moonlight doesn't cause the night sky to 'change', really, but it certainly affects how many stars you can see. Pick a dark, moonless

night over a bright moonlit one for stargazing – you can see many more celestial objects that way.

Given that the night sky is so changeable, where should you look for the constellations you are trying to identify? Earlier generations of WoCoTeens had to depend on star charts inscribed on paper and use their eyes and, if they were lucky, a telescope, to locate and identify stars and constellations. Now, there's an app for that! But while Android apps like Sky Map and Star Chart are fabulous and very useful, looking at a bright phone screen in the middle of looking up at the night sky could ruin the 'dark adaptation' of your eyes for several hours. Sometimes, the old ways are still the best ways.

So get out of town to the top of a hill or out in a field far away from the city lights, and get stargazing. You will be deemed to have mastered this skill when you can identify the following stars and constellations.

The Pole Star (Dhruva Tara): When we say Pole Star or North Star, we are usually talking about Polaris, which is the star (more or less) directly above the geographic North Pole (i.e., the place where Santa lives; not the magnetic North Pole, where the compass points – there is a difference between the two because the earth's north-south axis is tilted at a 23.5 degree angle away from the true north-south axis). While the other stars appear to move across the sky in the course of the night, the Pole Star is more or less still, which is why it was so important to ancient mariners who fixed course by the stars. In India, we know Polaris as Dhruva Tara – Hindu mythology believes it to be the manifestation of the steadfast Prince Dhruva, who did not lose focus even for a moment in his penances to gain access to Lord Vishnu.

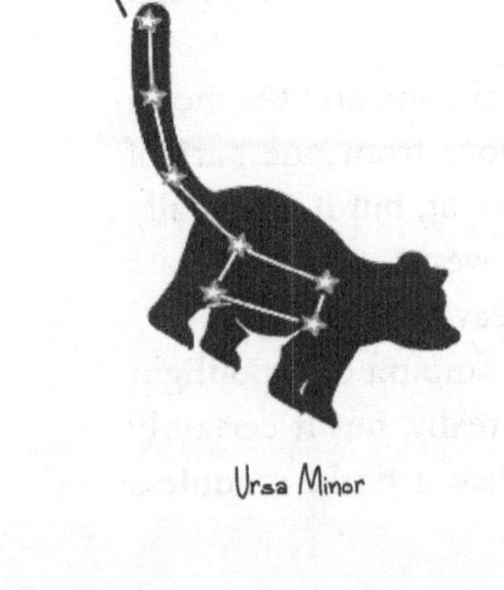

The Pole Star is also the brightest star in the constellation **Ursa Minor** (Little Bear with the long tail) or the

Little Dipper. Look due north in the sky to find it.

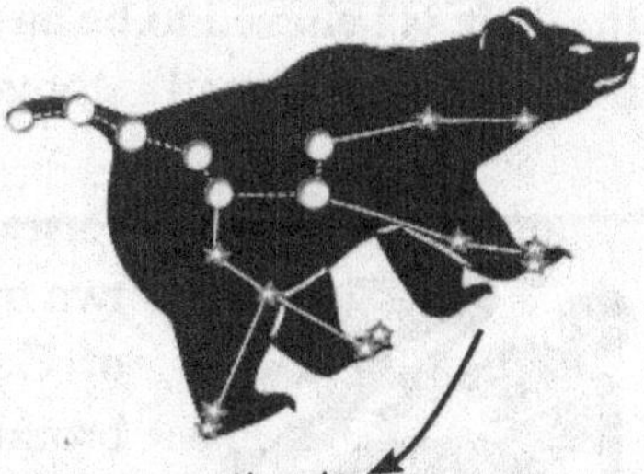

The Big Dipper / The Plough (Saptarishis) – Part of the larger constellation of **Ursa Major** (Great Bear), the seven stars in the Big Dipper form a clear panhandle in the sky. If you join the two stars that form the outer edge of the 'pan' or 'bowl' of the dipper and extend that line up into the sky, it will lead you straight to Polaris, the North Star, and to Ursa Minor, the Little Bear (Polaris is at the tip of the Little Bear's tail). In Indian mythology, the seven stars in the Big Dipper are the Saptarishis, the seven wise sages of old who were carried to safety through the Great Flood by Vishnu in his *Matsya* (Great Fish) avatar.

Find the Saptarishis in the northern sky, low on the horizon in October through March and higher up thereafter.

Orion the Hunter (Prajapati): One of the best-known constellations (it can be seen from both the Northern and Southern hemisphere, although the hunter is seen as standing on his head or lying on his side in the latter), Orion has several important stars in it and is one of the easiest to identify. The giant red star **Betelguese** marks the hunter's right shoulder (his right arm is raised, holding the club), a white star, **Rigel**, his raised left foot; **Bellatrix** marks his left arm, which holds the shield, and three bright stars in a straight line (a dead giveaway to the location of Orion) cinch his waist in a belt that he wears at a jaunty angle. From his belt hangs his sword, in the middle of which is the fuzzy bright cloud of stars called the Orion nebula. In Indian mythology,

the 'belt' is believed to be an arrow shot by an angry **Vyadha** (Sirius) into Prajapati's stomach.

Castor and Pollux (Punarvasu): The two brightest stars in the constellation of Gemini are named after the two brothers of Helen of Troy, the mythical twins Castor and Pollux. These stars mark the heads of the twins, and both can be found to the upper left of Orion.

Sirius (Vyadha the Butcher): The brightest star in the sky, Sirius or the Dog Star is part of the constellation **Canis Major** (the Great Dog). When the ancient Egyptians saw Sirius begin to rise in the eastern horizon just before sunrise (after it had disappeared over the western horizon for over two months), they knew it was time for the annual flooding of the Nile. The ancient Greeks dreaded the time of year when Sirius began to rise almost with the sun (between July and September), because those were the hottest, most sultry days of the year. That period is referred to, in literature, as the 'dog days' of summer. See why?

To find Sirius in the night sky, join the three stars of the belt of Orion and extend the imaginary line south-west for a bit (about eight times the length of the belt) until it points to the brightest star in the sky.

Canis Major (Svana): Named in Indian mythology after Yudhishthira's dog, which accompanied the Pandava brothers on their long and dangerous journey to heaven, this is a constellation of 13 stars. Four of them are particularly bright, and Sirius, at the dog's mouth, is the brightest in the sky.

Cassiopeia (Sharmishtha): An inverted version of the Golden Arches, (remember them from a certain hugely popular American fast-food chain?), this starry W is once again easy to pick out in the night sky. Think of the five stars in the W as a slightly wonky throne for Queen Cassiopeia of ancient Greece.

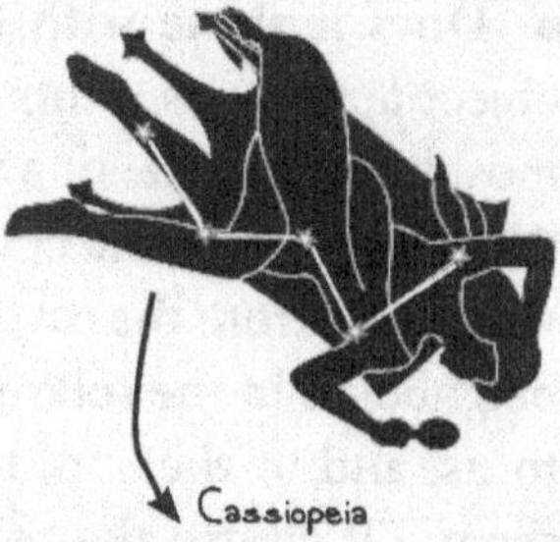

How do you find Cassiopeia? Look for it on the opposite side of Polaris from the Big Dipper.

Pegasus (Maha-ashwa): Beyond Cassiopeia lies Pegasus, the winged horse. You can't see too much of it with the naked eye except the four stars that form the Great Square of Pegasus, outlining the horse's torso.

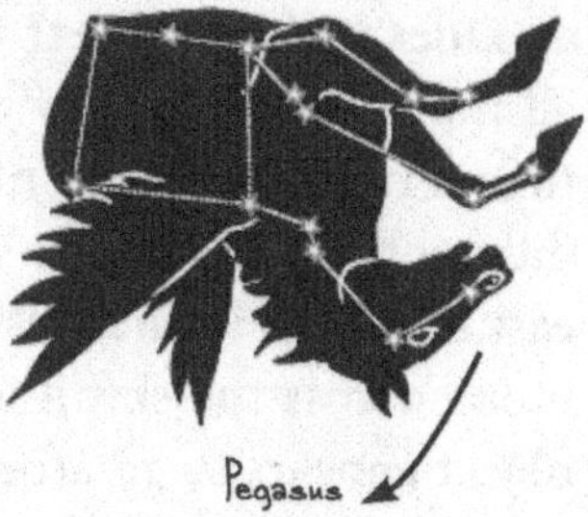

SKILL 92
TELL STARS FROM PLANETS

When you look up into the night sky, you can see all manner of celestial bodies – stars, planets, satellites, meteors, even the occasional comet. How do you tell them apart? Here are some questions you must ask yourself before you can make a (more or less) positive identification.

- **Does it twinkle?** If the bright object in the night sky appears to wink and shimmer at you, it is most likely a star. Stars do not actually twinkle (they burn with a bright, steady light), but because they are so far away, they appear to us as mere pinpoints of light. These pinpoints get refracted (or bent) first one way and then another when they pass through the layers of the earth's atmosphere and therefore appear to be shimmering.

■ **Does it shine with a steady light?** If the bright celestial object appears as a tiny disk shining with a steady light, it is most likely a planet or a satellite. Planets don't have any light of their own – they reflect the light of the closest star. The planets we can see from the earth with the naked eye are obviously our neighbours in the solar system, because they are close enough to us, and to the sun, to shine bright enough for us to spot them. Of course the reflected light from planets also has to pass through many layers of the earth's atmosphere to reach us, but because there aren't mere pinpricks of light (because the planets are much closer than the stars), this light is less distorted, making it appear steady rather than shimmering.

■ **Does it rise and set?** Celestial objects are not fixed – they all move (actually, they only appear to move; it is the earth that is moving) in the night sky. But different objects move differently. If the bright spot you are looking at 'rises' in the east and 'sets' in the west, following the path of the sun and moon across the sky, it is either a planet or a satellite. If the object appears to go around the pole star (Polaris) instead, it is most likely a star.

■ **Does it move rather quickly or rather slowly across the 'ecliptic'?** The 'ecliptic' is an east–west band of sky which marks the apparent annual path of the sun across the sky. It is within this band that all the planets and satellites move too. Join the dots between the moon, Venus and Mars on a clear night just after sunset, and you have – ta-da! – the ecliptic. Now look at the celestial bodies in the ecliptic. The shimmering ones are the stars. Among the non-shimmerers. the ones that move pretty quickly – in under an hour, say – from east to west, are likely to be satellites (although our brightest man-made satellite, the International Space Station, does not travel across the ecliptic at all). Those that take a few days to move from east to west are likely to be planets. A steady or blinking light that moves quickly across the sky could also be an aircraft!

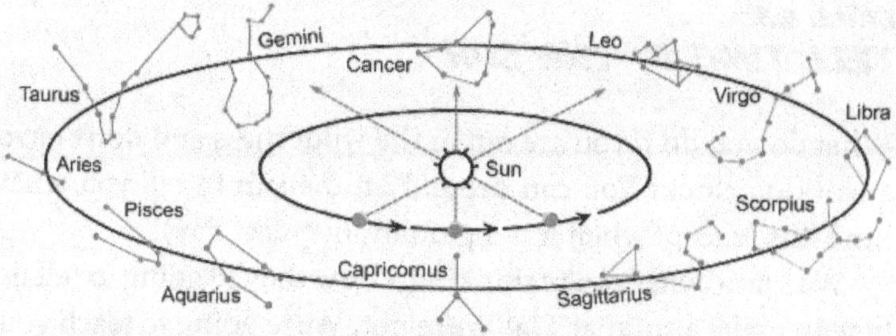

Here's a cool fact about the ecliptic – it passes through all the 13 zodiac constellations each year (only our favourite 12 shown here)!

- **Does it have a colour?** You will have to have exceptionally good eyesight, or a good pair of binoculars or a telescope, to be able to tell the colour of the planets, but if you do, you can tell which planet you are looking at simply by its colouration. Mercury is grey or brownish, and to the lower left of Venus; Venus is pale yellow and very bright (look for it in the east, where the sun rises, an hour before sunrise, when it is most visible – that's why it is often called the Morning Star), Mars appears reddish (as it should, being the 'Red Planet'), Jupiter orange with white bands (it is not for nothing that books colour it that way), and Saturn is a pale gold. Check your star map for your location on Earth and time of year to figure out where to spot each of these naked-eye planets. Stars typically appear white.
- **Does it look like a 'falling star'?** If you see a streak of light shooting across the sky for a bit before disappearing, you are probably looking at a meteor. A meteor is no star – it is a tiny bit of space dust or space rock (called a meteoroid) that has entered the Earth's atmosphere and is burning up due to friction, leaving a trail of light (called a meteor). If the trail disappears, it means the meteoroid has burnt itself out. If it continues to burn until it hits the earth, that means it is a larger than usual bit of space rock; the bit that survives the burning and actually hits the earth is called a meteorite.

SKILL 93
TELL TIME BY THE SUN

What do you do if you are out in the wilderness and don't have a working clock? You can depend on the sun to tell you what time it is (except when it is a gloomy, overcast day)!

We know what you're thinking – now they're going to tell us how to make a sundial. Ha! We're not. We're going to teach you some cooler, and way quicker, time-telling hacks.

Take position: If you are in the Northern hemisphere stand facing the south (if not, face north*). You are now facing the Equator, and above it is the path that the sun follows across the sky each day. If you are facing south, the sun rises to your left (in the east) and sets to your right (in the west).

**If you don't have a compass and don't know where north is, find a tall object that is casting a shadow near where you are (or pick up a fallen branch or stick and place it upright on the ground so you can see its shadow). It is better if the tip of the shadow is pointy and narrow. Mark the tip of the shadow on the ground accurately. Wait approximately 15 minutes. The shadow would have moved a little, in the easterly direction (since the sun moves from east to west, any shadow will move from west to east). Mark the new position of the tip of the shadow. Draw a line joining the two points on the ground. Stand on the line so that Point 1 (or west) is to your left and Point 2 (or east) is to your right. You are now facing due north.*

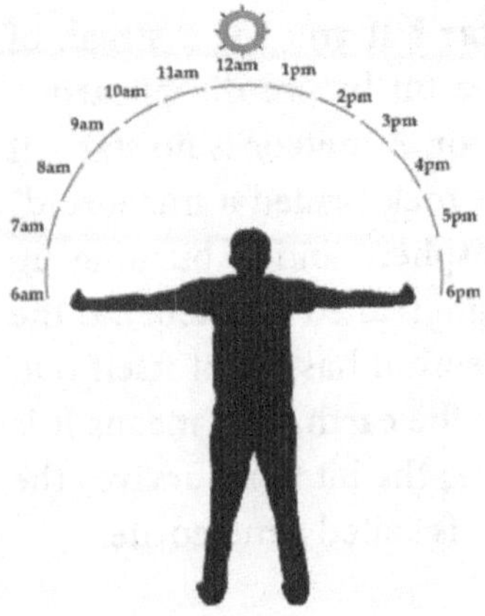

Find the sun: Spot the sun in the sky (without looking directly at it). Is it at its zenith (i.e., directly overhead)? That means the time is close to noon. If it is to the left of zenith, it is still morning; if it is to the right of zenith, it is afternoon.

Divide the sky: Stretch your arms out straight at shoulder level. Your left hand points to the eastern horizon, and your right to the western horizon. Imagine an arc going across the sky connecting the fingers of one hand to the fingers of the other. Divide the sky along the arc into 12 segments to signify the 12 hours from sunrise to sunset. Which segment of the sky is the sun in? Third segment to the right of the zenith? 3 p.m. Second segment to the left of the zenith? 10 a.m.

This works pretty well in southern India through the year, since there isn't much difference in the length of the day whether it is summer or winter. In the north, you might want to think about how long the day is in that season and then divide the sky into as many segments as there are daylight hours.

If you find it difficult to imagine the sky cut up into segments, use your fists to figure out where the sun is. Make a fist at the end of your outstretched left hand. With your feet still facing south, place your right fist on your left, then your left on your right, counting how many fists you need to make on top of each other before your arms are stretched out straight over your head. That's the number of fists you need to reach the zenith. If you needed six fists, count each fist as an hour. If you needed nine fists, say, divide six hours by nine fists to give you two-thirds of an hour, or 40 minutes. Now each fist counts as 40 minutes. Now repeat this fist-upon-fist thing until one fist (at the end of one outstretched arm) lines up with the position of the sun in the sky. Add the number of fists it took you to get there, and you have the time!

The Hands-of-Time Hack: If you're out in the wilderness with a broken watch (or just sea-bathing with your cousins, and all your watches are in your hotel room, and you want to stun them with your coolness), here's how you can tell what time it is (works particularly well in the afternoon, and if you can see the horizon). Stretch your arm out in front of you and bend it at the wrist so that your open palm is facing you (your

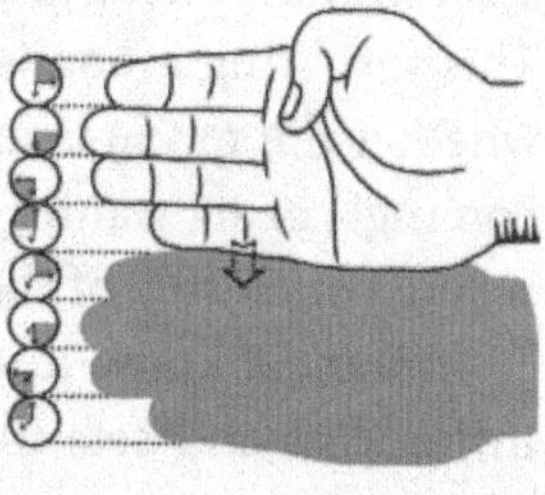

fingers should be parallel to the ground). Place the top edge of your index finger in line with the bottom of the sun to get into starting position. Now stretch your other hand out, bend it at the wrist and place Palm 2 just below the pinky finger of Palm 1. Now move Palm 1 to below Palm 2, and continue doing this until a finger of either hand lines up with the horizon. Count how many palms you needed to get there. Calculate the hours of daylight left by counting each palm between the bottom of the sun and the horizon as an hour, and each finger-width (only in case of the last palm) as 15 minutes. If there are, say, two open palms and two finger-widths between the sun and the horizon, there are about two hours and 30 minutes of daylight left. If you know that it gets dark around 6:45 p.m., you know that the time now is – ta-daaaa! – 4:30 p.m.!

SKILL 94
TELL TIME BY THE MOON

Telling time by the sun is all very well, but how do you tell the time after dark without a clock? You use the moon!

But before you learn how to do that, you need to look at this picture of the phases of the moon and memorize it.

What you see in this picture are the phases of the moon. The moon takes about 29.5 days to complete the cycle from new moon to new moon. In the first half of that period, the left side of the moon is dark, and the lighted part is on the right side and growing until it reaches full moon. This growing moon is called the 'waxing' moon. In the second half of the lunar cycle, the light begins to shrink, fading off from the right side. The darkness grows until the entire moon is engulfed. This shrinking moon is called the 'waning' moon. You can tell whether the moon is in its waxing phase (a full moon night is coming!) or its waning one (a new moon night is coming) by seeing which side of the moon is dark.

You must know, also, that like the sun, the moon also rises in the east and sets in the west. However, unlike the sun in the day, the moon is not visible through all the hours of the night. Only the full moon is seen throughout the night. The other phases are only seen for some hours – the moon rises on time but sets later and later as the moon progresses through its waxing period to the full moon, and sets on time but rises later and later as it progresses through its waning phase to the new moon. Check the moonrise and moonset times for an entire lunar cycle online or in your daily newspaper, starting with the next new moon, to see how it works.

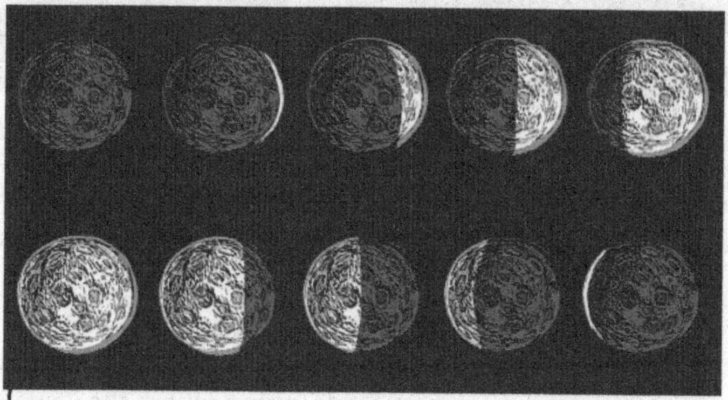

We only ever get to see one half of the moon – the other, which is hidden from us, is called its 'dark side'.

On to the telling of the time now!

Look at the moon. If the moon is full, it will work exactly like the sun – rising in the east as soon as darkness falls and setting in the west just before sunrise. Since the moon will be visible all 12 hours between say, 6 p.m. and 6 a.m., you simply have to follow the exact same technique with the moon as you did with the sun – by dividing the sky, that is – to tell what time of night it is. If it is a new moon night and there is no moon, go back to sleep. There is no way to tell time from the moon when there is no moon. If it is a crescent moon, or a half moon, or a gibbous moon you have spotted, go to the next step.

Cut the moon up into strips. Even if only part of the moon is visible, complete the moon's circle in your head and divide it into twelve (or more, if it's winter and your night is longer; or fewer, if it's summer and your night is shorter) vertical strips. Each strip represents an hour, with the hours of darkness being read from right to left, i.e., the right edge of the right-most strip represents 6 p.m., and the left edge of the left-most strip represents 6 a.m.

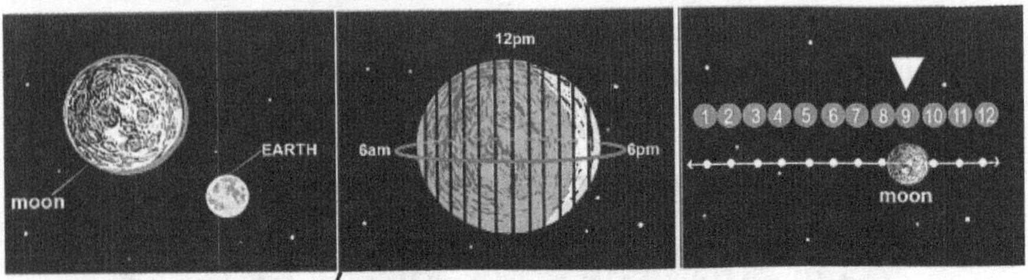

Look! The moon is a clock!

Draw an equator on the moon. Imagine a horizontal line cutting across all these vertical strips. Now read the moon from right to left.

- **If the moon is in its waxing period,** the right side will be lit up and we can predict when the moon will set. Count how many strips the light covers by checking where the 'equator' and the border between light and dark intersect. This will tell you at what time the moon will set. If we take moonrise as 6 p.m. and three strips are lit up, we can tell that moonset will happen around 9 p.m.
- **If the moon is in its waning period**, the right side will be dark and we can predict when the moon will rise the next day. Count the number of dark strips between the right edge of the moon and the light–dark boundary (the equator intersection will help you get a better handle on that). If there are seven dark strips, we will know that the moon will rise around 1 a.m. (6 p.m. + 7 hours = 1 a.m.).

Remember that if it a very small right moon crescent and you go out to try and spot the moon at 8 p.m., you may not see it at all – it might have set already! If it is a small left-moon crescent, you will again not see it at 8 p.m., or even at midnight – it would not have risen yet! So before you conclude that a dark moonless night is a new moon night, double-check online (or with your grandmom's panchang).

Locate the moon in the sky. Like you did with the daytime sky when you were telling time by the sun, divide the night sky into segments from east to west (12 segments for 12 hours, say, for the purposes of this example). There are two things you have to consider now:

- Is the moon in its waxing phase (i.e., you have calculated the moonset time) or its waning phase (i.e., you have its moonrise time)?
- In which segment of the sky is the moon in?
  - Let's say the moon is in its waning phase and it is at its zenith. So does that mean it is midnight now? Not necessarily! It only means that six hours have passed *since the moon rose.* If the moonrise time you have calculated is 9 p.m., then it is six hours since then – i.e., 3 a.m.
  - Let's say the moon is in its waxing phase and it is at its zenith. Let's say the moonset time you've calculated is 2 a.m. If this moon is at its zenith, its moonset time is still six hours away. That means it is now 8 p.m.

Yup, telling time by the moon is a little trickier than telling time by the sun. Start by simply observing the moon each night (when was the last time you really, really looked up at the moon? Be honest, now!) for a couple of lunar cycles, and you'll get to know the moon and her moods.

Maybe you think you will never need to tell time by the moon, and maybe you're right, but that's not the point of this exercise. It's simply part of the slow, gradual and wonderful process of realizing that nature has always had all the answers. Plus, she never runs out of charge, doesn't need extra batteries, and her Wi–Fi network bars are always full*. Seriously, what's not to like?

*Okay, Mum Nature can be unreliable too. An overcast day or night will make it somewhat difficult to tell time by the sun or the moon, but it's still a useful skill to have for the clear-sky days.

THE STARMAN'S CHALLENGES

All the Starman challenges could be combined with the Camper's challenges, especially if you are travelling a little way out of the city and away from light pollution for your camp. It would work particularly well if you had an adult in your group who was a keen amateur astronomer and had a telescope he/she was willing to let you use. Also try contacting an amateur astronomer society in your city. Many of these societies are happy to come over and give talks about astronomy or arrange night-sky viewing expeditions.

#91
THE STARS-AND-CONSTELLATIONS CHALLENGE

#92
THE PLANET-AND-STARS CHALLENGE

Take a trip out of town with your Squad and Squad Leader to observe the night sky. If this is too difficult to organize, visit the planetarium (if your city has one) and take in a couple of shows. Or you can simply wait for a clear night, and go up to someone's terrace with the rest of the Squad with some food and blankets and sleeping bags, lie down flat on your backs, and identify at least eight constellations and at least two planets.

#93
THE TELL-TIME-BY-THE-SUN CHALLENGE

Have a Squad meeting starting around four o clock in the afternoon. Observe the position of the sun in the sky when you start the meeting. Put all watches, phones and any other devices that tell time away inside a dark bag. Continue with your regular Squad activities. When the Squad Leader gives you the signal, go out and look at the position of the sun, and guess what time it is. Come back and look at a clock and see if you were right. Continue with your activities. At another signal, go out once again and guess what the time is now. Once again, check if you were right. If your guess was within 15 minutes of the actual time, you have passed the challenge.

#94
THE TELL-TIME-BY-THE-MOON CHALLENGE

This is an individual challenge. Between one new moon night and the next, observe the moon at least eight times (including on the full moon night and at least twice each in the waning and waxing phases). Guess the time of night from a combination of its position in the sky and its phase (in its waxing phase, you have to catch it soon after it rises or you may miss it entirely; in its waning phase, you will need to wake up early to catch a glimpse of it). Keep a record of your sightings – including the date, the phase (best if you drew a picture of how it looked that day), your guess, and the actual time. Submit your observation record to the Squad Leader to get through this challenge.

WOCOTEEN MERIT BADGE 24

THE SIGNALLER

Scouts have to be clever at passing news secretly from one place to another, or in signalling to each other.
– **Camp Fire Yarn No. 7, *Scouting for Boys***

Human beings have been communicating through signals – hand gestures, facial expressions, growls, cheers, drumbeats, smoke signals, picture codes, flags, light signals, and a million others – forever. Well before formal language developed, we were all exchanging thoughts and information furiously, not only with people we could see but also with those who were far away. Signals served a dual purpose – they were a good way to transmit information, of course, but they were also a great way to do it *secretly*, for each community developed its own mysterious signals that were only understood by its own people.

Today, our understanding of the word 'signal' has narrowed itself down to electronic signals – cellphone signals, television signals, Wi-Fi signals – and that is a bit of a shame, because a *lot* of communication, both between humans – smiles, hugs, emojis, military codes and ciphers – and in nature – the high-pitched alarm calls of the langurs in an Indian jungle ('*Take cover – tiger spotted!*'), the sudden bursting into leaf of bare trees ('*Holi is almost here!*') – still happens through signals. Ergo, the Signaller Badge, to help aspiring WoCoTeens reacquaint themselves with the rich, fertile world of sign language.

In B-P's day, it was mandatory for Scouts to know Semaphore signalling (a visual alphabet where each letter was represented by the position of two hand-held flags) and Morse code (a signalling method where each letter of the alphabet was represented by a series of short sounds [dots] and long sounds [dashes] that could be telegraphed over long distances or transmitted through light signals, or over shorter distances, as Scouts did, using a whistle). It's still fun to learn to send and interpret Semaphore and Morse signals (look them up online), but for the purposes of the 21st-century Signaller Badge, the Squad has included a few more general skills.

SKILL 95
TUNE IN TO SOUND SIGNALS

Those among us who are blessed with the gift of good eyesight come to depend so much on this one sense that we neglect to develop the other senses, which are in fact brilliant receivers for a bunch of other, non-visual signals. Here's how you can develop your listening and echolocation (yeah, that thing that bats do, where they figure out where something is simply through how sound reflects off it) skills.

1. Shut your eyes. To really tune in to the sounds around you, you have to tune out the sights. Also, you're not going to be able to focus if you're not comfortable. So whether you do this exercise at home, in the neighbourhood park, or on top of a hill, find a place where you can sit down comfortably with your back straight. Then close your eyes.

2. Centre yourself. Once you're breathing in a steady rhythm, consciously shut off your thoughts one by one and focus only on the sounds around you. This takes time, so don't even start this process unless you are sure you have at least 20 minutes in hand. Warn the family that you are not to be disturbed during this time.

3. Tag the sounds you hear. Now listen to the sounds around you and try to tag each one. First listen to the closest circle of sounds – the front door closing, your dad's footsteps going past

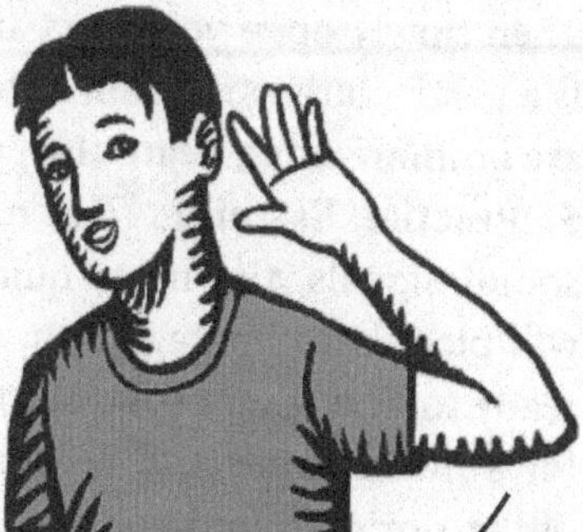

The word 'listen' and the word 'silent' are made up of the same letters – coincidence?

your room, your mom's bangles clacking in the particular way they do when she is brushing her hair. Then expand your hearing to bring in other sounds – the sound of the neighbour's pressure cooker, a dog barking in the street, the muezzin's call from the nearby mosque. Now tune in to the lesser sounds in the background, which your ears haven't paid attention to because the brain doesn't think they are important or has just not trained itself to notice. Listen particularly to the sounds you cannot instantly tag – is that rustle the sound of the wind in the trees or a newspaper blowing along your balcony floor?

If you are doing this outside, in a quiet park or in the country somewhere, there may be several more sounds that you cannot immediately tag (although you will be surprised by how many you can – your brain's sound library is pretty extensive). The sound of insects, bird calls, the soft chirrr of a bicycle's wheels on their way down a slope, the scratchy sound of a squirrel's claws on bark... Don't get obsessed about tagging each sound – simply listen, and learn to appreciate the diversity of all the auditory signals that you miss when you have your eyes open.

4. Locate the sound. From which direction is a particular sound coming? One good way to locate a sound more accurately is to use your thumbs and index fingers to push your ears forward, creating two sound-gathering 'funnels' out of your ears. Then, with your eyes still closed, turn your head slowly from side to side, marking the point at which the sound seems clearest. Then slowly open your eyes and check if you were right. This is a particularly good skill to have in the wild, where creatures are far more often heard than seen.

5. Practise listening. The more you practise tuning in to sound signals, the more quickly and seamlessly your brain will pick them up, tag them, and file them away in its RAM, ready to access at a split-second's notice. Apart from making for a much larger and deeper enjoyment and understanding of the world around you and everything in it, well-developed listening skills could potentially save your life, or help you save someone else's, by alerting you to sounds like a car swerving too fast around a corner (you shout a warning to that woman; you snatch that child out of harm's way) or footsteps getting too close to you for comfort (you swerve around and startle your stalker, causing him to lose his nerve and walk away).

SKILL 96
SIGNAL THROUGH GESTURES

We are all familiar with a vast set of universally–understood informal gestures for Yes (the nod), No (the shake of the head from side to side), Whatevs (the shrug), Super! (a thumbs up), Yuck! (the ugliest face you can pull). But there are also several formal 'languages' of communication that are entirely gesture-based. Learning to signal in – or at least read signals from – a couple of them could open up an entirely new world to you. Here are two to try.

Indian Sign Language (aka Indo-Pakistani Sign Langauge) – There are close to a million deaf people in India, and a stunning 98 per cent of them, according to reports, are illiterate. This is because India has traditionally followed an oralist approach to teaching the deaf.

Instead of teaching through sign language, Indian teachers have always taught deaf children orally, to encourage them to learn to lip-read and imitate with sound. But for this kind of teaching to work, deaf children need hearing aids, which are expensive. Since a large percentage of India's deaf population is poor and cannot afford good hearing aids, they tend to drop out of the school system.

In the recent past, however, there has been talk of making Indian Sign Language (ISL), which a lot of deaf people in South Asia use to communicate, into an official Indian language, just like spoken ones. There has also been a proposal to include ISL as a third-language option for hearing children in CBSE schools, which would be a wonderful way to get more people 'speaking' the language, thus including the deaf in every sphere of social and political life.

ISL has different hand signs for each of the letters of the alphabet, but not all communication is done by spelling out entire words. That would take too long, and would mean having to learn the correct spellings of English words. So while spelling out could be used where proper nouns are involved, ISL also has ingenious ways to sign entire words with one gesture. To sign 'Brother' for instance, the signer would combine the signs for man and for sibling. To sign 'Sister', he would combine the sign for woman with sibling, thus saving himself the trouble of creating completely new signs for brother and sister or having to spell them out. Also, the same hand sign could mean different words – in ISL, the same hand sign is used for Think, Know and Understand – the *position* of the hand determines which of the three it is. If an ISL signer wanted to ask 'Where is the bank?' she would not waste her time using so many words. Instead, she would simply sign – 'Bank where?' Sensible, huh?

In 2001, the Ramakrishna Mission Vivekananda University, in collaboration with Christian Blind Mission International, released the first ISL dictionary. The dictionary, available

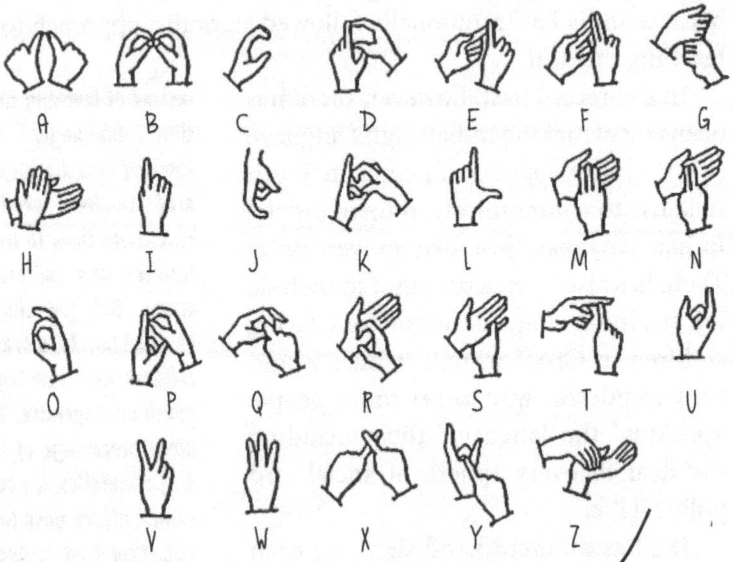

Here's something to help start you off – the alphabet in ISL.

at http://indiansignlanguage.org/dictionary, is a fabulous resource, with videos teaching the ISL alphabet (both single-handed and double-handed versions), and over 2,500 signs collected from 42 different Indian cities (this *is* India, so there are as many different ISL 'dialects' as there are spoken dialects!).

Another great resource is the series of *Learn Indian Sign Language* videos on YouTube presented by Arun C. Rao, in which he talks you through words for food, times of day, days of the week, 25 basic words, and so on. And there are several more out there, making it easy for you to pick up basic ISL pretty quickly!

The Language of the Mudras – Ever been forced to go watch a Bharatanatyam performance because a friend or cousin was performing? Remember falling asleep in the middle because you didn't understand what the heck was going on on stage?

Listen up – the only reason you did that was because you did not know the language of the *mudras*, or hand-gestures, used in Bharatanatyam! If you had, you would have enjoyed the stories that the dancer was narrating so beautifully. Yup, that's what classical Indian dances are about – storytelling! The word 'Natya' does not merely mean dance, it is a multilayered word meaning rhythm, music, emotion, theatre and storytelling all rolled into one.

So get a crash course in *mudra* vocabulary and grammar from someone who knows the dance form well. Ask her (or him)

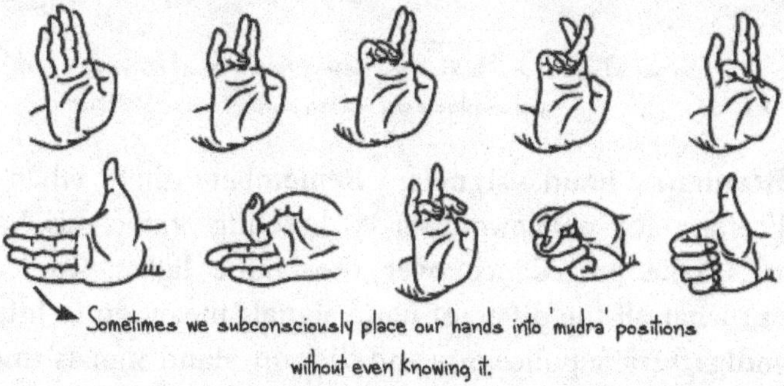

Sometimes we subconsciously place our hands into 'mudra' positions without even knowing it.

to tell you a story – first in words, and then in Bharatanatyam, and let the *mudras* begin to speak to you for the very first time.

SKILL 97
SPEAK THE LANGUAGE OF THE ROADS

Ever thought of road signs, traffic signals, and a policeman's hand signals as the words and phrases of a peculiarly urban visual language? But that's exactly what they are! And that's one language everyone in a city or large town should be able to 'speak' and understand. Here's how you can do it.

Road signs: There are good resources online to educate yourself on all the different kinds of road signs (mandatory signs, cautionary signs, information signs), the meanings of the white and yellow markings on the roads, and the different traffic rules motorists, cyclists and pedestrians are expected to follow. One of them is www.trafficwardens.in. Click on the Road Safety tab to get a wealth of information, nicely classified under different headings.

Can you tell what each of these signs means? Have a Squad discussion and see how many you can identify!

Policeman's hand signals: Remember that when a policeman (or policewoman) is directing traffic, his hand signals take precedence over the traffic lights. To learn about what all the different hand signals mean, go to http://chandigarhtrafficpolice.org/ and click on 'Hand Signals' under the 'Traffic Signs and Markings' tab to access great animations that make the language of hand signals crystal clear.

SKILL 98
LEAVE TRACKING SIGNS FOR OTHERS TO FOLLOW

Remember how clever Hansel sneakily dropped a trail of pebbles when his dad and stepmom took him and Gretel deep into the forest and abandoned them there, and used it to find his way back home the next day? And how the Greek hero Theseus tied a ball of wool to a rock at the entrance to the Minotaur's labyrinth and let it unravel behind him as he went looking for the monster, so that he could find his way out after he had finished the Minotaur off? That's the kind of trail marker we mean when we talk about 'Tracking Signs'.

Hansel's and Theseus' trail markers worked well for them, but the problem with that kind of marker is that it is finite; if the trail had not ended before Hansel ran out of pebbles or Theseus ran out of wool, the technique would have been pretty darn useless. Also, pebbles and wool may not always be ready to hand (as it happened in Hansel's case the second time around). That's why outdoorsmen of every stripe, through the ages, came up with their own, far more sophisticated, tracking signs. They set up these trail markers using materials easily found in the wilderness, not only to help them find their own way back but also to let anyone who was coming up the trail behind them know exactly which way they had gone, and warn them of dangers that lay ahead.

Here is a brief intro to the tracking signs used by B-P's Scouts. You can use these when you go hiking or make your own set of secret signs. Just make sure they aren't so secret that even the people following you don't know what they mean!

This Way – Make an arrow with sticks (or tie long grass into a bundle and bend it in the direction of the trail) to show

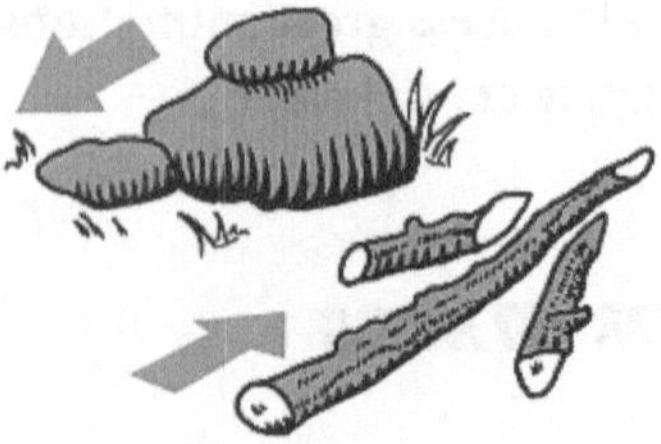

which way you've gone. If you'd rather use stones to make your direction marker, place one small stone on top of a big one to draw attention, and then place a small stone next to it in the direction of travel. Or use your WoCoTeen staff to scratch an arrow into the mud.

No Entry/Danger – A simple 'X' made with sticks or stones, will relay the message loud and clear.

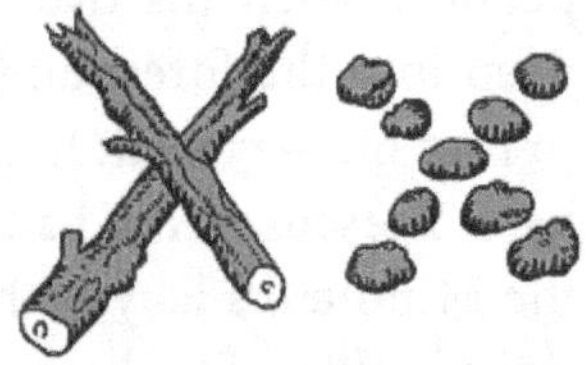

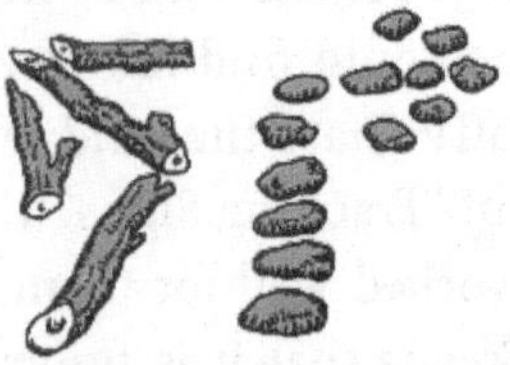

Turn left (or right) – Make a bent arrow in the appropriate direction.

Water ahead – Make at least three rows of inverted 'V' shapes to indicate a water body, and then place an arrow next to it in the direction of the water.

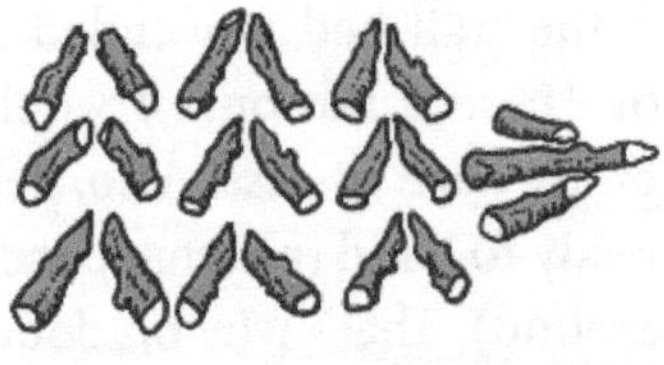

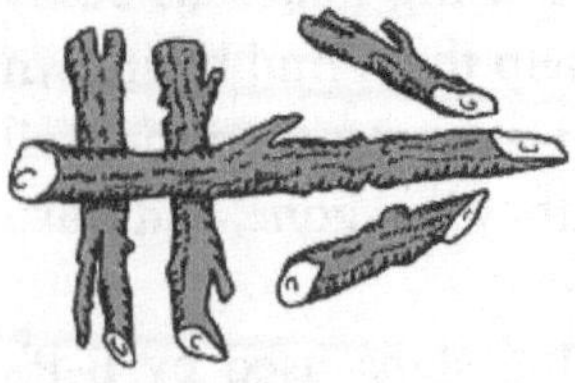

Obstacle ahead – If there is a fence or a wide ditch or some other kind of obstacle ahead, make a sign with two lines crossed by another at 90 degrees. Also place an arrow next to it showing in which direction the obstacle lies.

The group has split – Find a forked branch or twig (or create a fork sign) to show that the group split up at that point, and add arrowheads to show the direction each smaller group

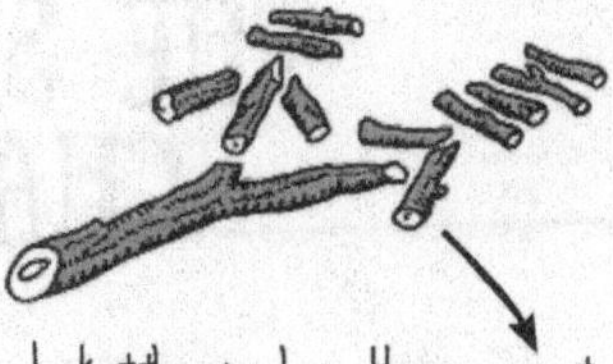

Look at the sign here. How many went down the left fork and how many down the right?

went off in. Add small sticks ahead of each arrowhead (one stick representing one person) to show how many of the group went down each of the paths.

Hidden Message at X paces – Make a square with sticks or stones and add an arrow pointing in the direction of a hidden message. Inside the square, either scratch the number indicating how many paces away the message can be found, or make a cluster of the same number of stones as the number of paces.

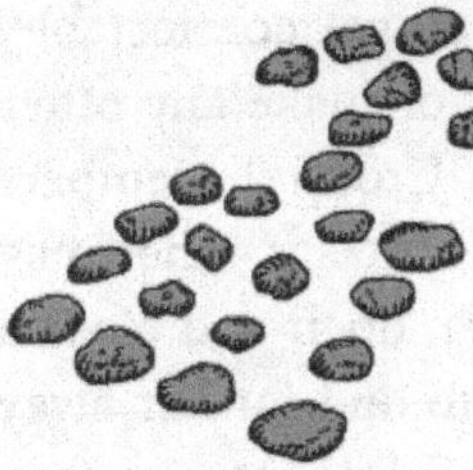

I have gone home – This – a circle with a dot in the middle of it – is one of the most important tracking signs because it indicates that the trail has ended. You can use twigs to form a rough circle and place a stone in the middle to make this sign. Don't forget to leave this one or your followers on the trail will keep searching in vain for the next marker.

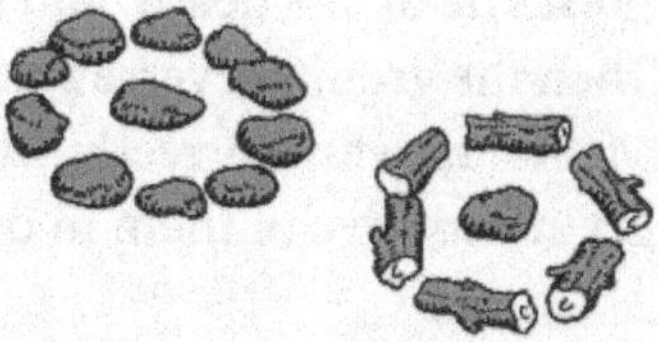

THE SIGNALLER'S CHALLENGES

#95
THE SOUND-SIGNAL CHALLENGE

The Squad is divided into two groups. Members of Group 1 are blindfolded and given 10 minutes to get comfortable, centred and focused. They must not talk or make any other sound (or fall asleep!) during this time. Group 2 members then use 10 different props to make familiar noises – they may ring a bell, strike a match, crumple paper, open and close a door, and so on. They also move closer to and farther away from different members of Group 1 in different ways as they make these noises, click-clacking on high heels, scuffing their feet, stomping. At the end of every minute, one or two new sounds are introduced. After five minutes, the blindfolds are removed, and each member of Group 1 writes down all the noises he or she heard, and the order in which he heard them. Then the groups reverse roles and repeat, with different props. Members who correctly identify at least seven sounds and get at least five of them in order, pass the challenge.

#96
THE GESTURE-CODE CHALLENGE

Dumb Charades is a great way to learn signalling skills, build strong teams and have fun!

The Squad is divided into two teams to play Dumb Charades. The Squad Leader provides simple phrases to be mimed. The team member miming (all team members have to take turns at this) can only use gestures and hand signs from ISL or the Bharatanatyam *mudras* to signal. Spelling out entire words is also allowed using the ISL alphabet. Six phrases are mimed by each team. Teams that get at least four right within the given time pass the challenge.

#97
THE ROAD-SIGNS CHALLENGE

The Squad Leader creates a power point presentation with 10 road signs, appearing one at a time on the screen. Each slide stays on screen for no more than five seconds, to simulate a road sign flashing by as you drive past in a vehicle. At the end, Squad members write down what each sign means, in the order in which the signs appeared on screen. Getting all signs right and at least four signs in order is one way to pass the challenge. The other is to get at least eight signs right AND at least six signs in the right order.

#98
THE TRACKING CHALLENGE

The Squad goes on a picnic to a botanical garden or a large park. Half the Squad remains behind while the other half goes on ahead, leaving trail markers (using *only* things they can find around them) for the ones left behind to follow. On reaching the end of the trail, the team that has gone ahead sends an SMS/Whatsapp message to the Squad Leader. The 'followers' then get on to the trail, with the Squad Leader, who will not participate but observes how good (or terrible) the trail markers are. Once the trail is completed by this group, the other group stays back while the former 'followers' mark the trail. The Squad Leader decides who passes the challenge based on the quality and clarity of the trail markers and the tracking ability of each team. Remember, both teams can pass – this is not a win-lose contest!

SKILL 99
ONE GOOD TURN A DAY

This 'skill' is one of the cornerstones of the Scouting and Guiding movement, so let's have B-P tell you about it in his own words (remember to substitute WoCoTeen for Scout when you read it, though!).

> *It is something to be good, but it is far better to do good.*
>
> *As a Scout, you are obliged to do at least one Good Turn every day.*
>
> *When you get up in the morning, remember that you have to do a Good Turn for someone during the day. Tie a knot in your handkerchief to remind yourself of it.*
>
> *If you should ever find that you had forgotten to do your daily Good Turn, you must do two the next day.*
>
> *A Good Turn need only be a very small one. It is a Good Turn even if it is only putting a coin into a poorbox, or helping an old woman to cross the street, or making room on a seat for someone, or giving water to a thirsty horse, or removing a bit of banana skin off the pavement. But one must be done every day, and it only counts when you do not accept any reward in return.*
>
> **– Camp Fire Yarn No. 2, *Scouting for Boys***

#99
THE GOOD-TURN CHALLENGE

This challenge works on the honour system. No one, not even your Squad Leader, is going to be tracking you and checking if you actually did someone a good turn on every single day between Squad meetings. If you can tell your Squad Leader, hand on heart, at every meeting, that you have kept to the WoCoTeen one-good-turn-a-day code, you 'pass' this challenge – simple! There is no badge to win for this one, but if you are a worthy WoCoTeen, passing this challenge might just be the most satisfying thing of all.

ANSWERS

THE 2-D TO 3-D PUZZLE (PAGE 70)

1)  A cylinder

2)  A cuboid

3)  A cone

4)  A pyramid (four-sided square pyramid)

5) 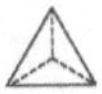 A pyramid – again! (Except this is a three-sided triangular pyramid)

6) 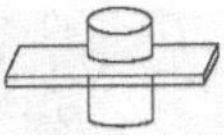 A strange object that looks like this

7) 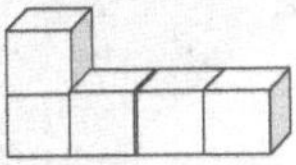 Four cubes placed like so

8) 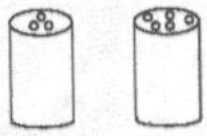 Salt and pepper shakers – ta-da!

THE TRADITIONAL HANDICRAFT 'MATCH-THE-FOLLOWING' (PAGE 68)

Leather shadow puppets (Andhra Pradesh); **Madhubani Paintings** (Bihar); **Dhokra metal art** (Chattisgarh); **Bandhni** (Gujarat); **Walnut wood carving** (Jammu and Kashmir); **Lacquered wooden toys** (Karnataka); **Coir mats** (Kerala); **Black stone pottery** (Manipur); **Juttis** (Punjab); **Marble craft** (Rajasthan); **Bronze sculptures** (Tamil Nadu); **Chikan embroidery** (Uttar Pradesh)

THE TRADITIONAL WEAVES 'MATCH-THE-FOLLOWING' (PAGE 69)

Pochampalli (Andhra Pradesh); **Muga** (Assam); **Tussar** (Bihar); **Patola** (Gujarat); **Jamavar** (Jammu and Kashmir); **Chanderi** (Madhya Pradesh); **Paithani** (Maharashtra); **Sambalpuri** (Odisha); **Kanchipuram** (Tamil Nadu); **Baluchery** (West Bengal)

INDIAN SPICES QUIZ (PAGE 105)

1. Mustard; 2. Cumin; 3. Turmeric; 4. Cinnamon; 5. Clove; 6. Saffron; 7. Asafoetida; 8. Fennel; 9. Cardamom; 10. Peppercorn

The End of the Trail

Take a look at the headstone from B-P's grave in the Wajee Nature Park, Nyeri, Kenya. It is also the tombstone of his (much younger) wife Olave, who was elected World Chief Guide in 1930. Do you see a tracking sign somewhere on it? Can you read the last message the master tracker left for his beloved Scouts? (No? You missed it on pages 11–12!)